ARYA SAMAJ AND INDIAN CIVILIZATION

CULTURE AND CIVILIZATIONS SERIES

ARYA SAMAJ AND INDIAN CIVILIZATION

Editor

Dr. R.K. Pruthi

DISCOVERY PUBLISHING HOUSE
NEW DELHI-110002

First Published – 2004

Reprinted – 2026

ISBN: 978-81-7141-780-3

Arya Samaj and Indian Civilization

Published by:

DISCOVERY PUBLISHING HOUSE

4383/4B, Ansari Road, Darya Ganj
New Delhi-110 002 (India)
Phone: +91-11-23279245; 23253475; 43596065
Mobile: +91 9811179893 / +91 9871656464
E-mail: discoverybooksindia@gmail.com
orderdphbooks@gmail.com
namitwasan9@gmail.com
web: www.discoverypublishinggroup.com

Printed at:
Infinity Imaging Systems
Delhi

PREFACE

The impact of western civilization gave rise to a number of reform movements in India. All these movements contributed to the furthering of Indian renaissance. The Arya Samaj movement influenced political, social, religious and educational aspects of the Indian society.

Objective of this book is to provide to our readers some unique aspects of the movement through writings and other works of the leaders of the movements. This should enable our readers to make their own assessment of the movements on the Indian civilization.

We record our gratefulness to the authorities who have influenced us in attempting to prepare this work.

Librarians and staff members of the institutions and universities deserve special mention for their support.

My publisher and staff both at production and printing stages have rendered all possible help and assistance. I thank them all.

R.K. Pruthi

Contents

Introduction

Just as the impact of Islam gave a fillip to Bhakti systems in India in the middle ages, so has the inroad of western civilization given rise to a number of reform movements in Hinduism in modern times. All these are contributing in different ways to the furthering of Indian renaissance that is going on space. Of these, the Ārya Samāj takes its stand on the bedrock of the Vedas, which, it believes, hold the key to all our socio-religious problems. It challenges the good sense of humanity to subject to a crucial test the time-old wisdom revealed to the *ṛṣis* and see if their life-giving message can be replaced to advantage by the varied materialistic 'isms' of modern days.

Dayananda and the Vedas

Swami Dayananda's interpretation of the Vedas, the 'primeval scripture of humanity,' has given a new orientation to the Hindu faith. Scoffed at and ridiculed in the beginning, the view-point of the Swami has of late been hailed by savants both of the East and the West. Says Sri Aurobindo:

"There is then nothing fantastical in Dayananda's idea that the Veda contains truths of science as well as truths of religion. I will even add my own conviction that the Veda contains other truths of a science which the modern world does not at all possess, and, in that case, Dayananda has rather understated than overstated the depth and range of the Vedic wisdom."[1]

'Immediately the character of the Veda is fixed in the sense Dayananda gave to it, the merely ritual, mythological, polytheistic interpretation of Sāyaṇācārya collapses, and the merely mateological and materialistic European interpretation collapses. We have, instead, a real scripture, one of the world's sacred books and the divine word of a lofty and noble religion.'[2]

The Pavagi, the Veda appears to contain truths of such widely different branches of learning as geology and modern political science. In the opinion of Rele, Vedic gods and figures of biology.

Maurice Philippe writes in his *Teaching of the Vedas:* 'We are justified therefore in concluding that the higher and purer conceptions of the Vedic hymns were the results of primitive revelation.'

Says Edward Carpenter in his *Art of Creation:* 'The same germinal thoughts of the Vedic authors come all the way down history even to Schopenhauer and Whitman, inspiring philosophy after philosophy and religion after religion.'

Dayananda's Attitude Towards Other Religions

Elements of truth are present in every system of divine faith. While prophets in every land have tried to unite humanity, it is the priests that have sown seeds of discord and disunion. Swami Dayananda raised his mighty voice against the confusing babble of the priests. He went so far as to invite a conference of the representatives of all religions on the occasion of the Delhi Durbar in 1877. Keshub Chandra Sen, Sir Syed Ahmad, and Muṇshi Alakhdhari were among those who responded to the invitation. Dayananda's proposal was premature, but his idea that the exponents of various faiths should put their heads together to evolve a formula of united activity was unique in those days, when ideas of jehads and crusades prevailed, and signified the true conception of religion that it was a unifying and not a dividing force. Though the conference led, at that time, to no practical result, yet it paved the way for the later religious parliaments and conferences, in which preachers of different faiths met on a common platform and offered to one another to olive branch of goodwill and peace. To Swami Dayananda, truth, wherever it is found, is of the Veda.

Social Reform and Education

Like every reform movement, the Ārya Samāj set itself first to purge the society, in which it had arisen, of its rampant evils. The Vedas enjoin worship of one formless God. Service of elders, literally 'fathers,' of individual families and of the community at large, is repeatedly insisted on. *Varṇa-vyavasthā*, as taught in the Veda, is the fourfold division of society based on the character of individuals. The Vedic conception of marriage is that of a sacrament that binds a grown-up couple in matrimonial bonds, while the status of woman, recognized in that hoary scripture, is that of a divine helpmate of man in all the spheres, private and civic, of human life. The propaganda of the Ārya Samāj has, in the provinces in which it has had the opportunity of working, extirpated social abuses, which were a perversion of these divine behests. The Ārya Samāj regards untouchability as un-Vedic. It has invested lacs of 'untouchables' with the sacred thread and thus made them honourable members of the Hindu society, enjoying the same social rights as the so-called caste-Hindus. The portals of the Vedic Church have been thrown open even to non-Hindus. Historical researches have proved that Hinduism assumed its non-missionary character in the days of its decadence. All the foreign races and tribes, such as Greeks, Scythians, and Hūṇas, that made India their home in different ages, have been assimilated into the Hindu society. An inscription belonging to the second century B.C., found at Besnagar near Bhilsa, bears testimony to the adoption of the Vāsudeva cult by Heliodorus, a Greek ambassador. Even so late as the middle ages, the Hindu saints, beginning with Rāmānanda and his disciples, allowed the non-Hindus to join the ranks of their orthodox following as members of the same social organisation. This practice has been revived by the Ārya Samāj. The last two reforms, namely, the reclamation of the depressed classes and proselytization of non-Hindus, have cost the Ārya Samāj a number of martyrs, who have preferred death to submission to the arrogant demands of unreasonable superstition and wilful fanaticism.

The uncompromising attitude of the Ārya Samāj against what it regards as 'false gods' and the gauntlet it has thrown in the name of the ancient *ṛṣis* have earned it the epithets 'Church militant' and 'aggressive Hinduism.' The Hindu, at the time of the advent of the Ārya Samāj, was very docile. One might ridicule the gods he worshipped and the faith he had idealized for centuries, yet, in the face of all this vilification, he would not be roused, making one doubt if he was alive with power to feel and act. With the advent of the Ārya Samāj, this attitude of undisturbed indifference was rudely shaken. The Hindu was infused with new faith and dynamism. He began to take pride in his religion and, if need be, was prepared to lay down his life for it. The weapon that the Ārya Samāj has been using, in its campaign against what, in its eyes, in untruth, is that of rational persuasion wedded to unflinching faith. In its self-evoked fight against heavy odds, it has had to offer on the alter of religion the lives of some of its most devoted workers and saints. To the immortal honour of the Church of Dayananda, it has always been the breast of the Ārya Samājist that has been stained with blood, never his hand. The noble example of the founder has been followed faithfully by the devoted adherents of his Church.

The leaders of the Ārya Samāj realized, from the very beginning, the vital importance of education in opening the eyes of the people to their true cultural heritage. In order to propagate knowledge among the people, the Ārya Samāj has spread widely a network of *gurukulas*, colleges, and schools, both for boys and girls, throughout the country as well as in some colonies overseas, where it has been carrying on its beneficent activities. The Gurukula at Kangri, near Hardwar, is the first Indian university to adopt an Indian vernacular, Hindi, as the medium of instruction, right up to the graduate, and even post-graduate, standard. It has resuscitated the Vedic and Sanskritic studies and assimilated to them modern art and science. By the revival of the ancient institution of *brahmacarya* and by giving morality the first place in its scheme, the Ārya Samāj has made it possible to make character the basis of juvenile education. In times of earthquakes, floods, and famine, the work of relief undertaken by the Ārya Samāj has meant a new lease of life for many distressed individual, family, and community. By starting widows' homes and orphanages, it has made provision for the maintenance of the needy, who otherwise, would have been the waifs and strays of humanity. Many of the important reform movements in the Hindu society have found the Ārya Samāj in the vanguard. This position has been won at the cost of continued sacrifices and privations. Being champions of the lowly and the lost, the Āryas have had to face the opposition of the orthodox and the calumny of the unscrupulous. But they clung to their post and won in the end, so that today, emulating the example set by the Ārya Samāj, other societies too have opened institutions for the education of the masses and relief of the distressed. In the matter of social reform, a common outlook is fast developing in the whole Hindu community. All this tremendous work has been accomplished by the Ārya Samāj on the basis of a constitution devised in accordance with the teachings of the Vedas, which in itself is a landmark in the history of the Hindu religion.

The Principles of the Ārya Samāj

The Ārya Samāj was founded on the 10th April, 1875, at Bombay. As is evident from a perusal of the principles formulated then, the original plan of the founder was to establish a central Samāj in every country and append to it a network of subordinate Samājas, which might cover every town and village. In practice, however, this plan did not succeed. The world was not yet ready for concerted activity on such a large scale. In every large town, where Swami Dayananda went, he opened a Samāj, which was constitutionally independent of other Samājas.

With the opening of the Ārya Samāj at Lahore on the 24th June, 1877, the constitution of the Ārya Samāj underwent a formal change. Its *niyamas* or principles were precisely stated. The *upaniyamas* or rules and regulations were re-drafted and incorporated in a separate document. Their importance was recognized to be subordinate to that of the *niyamas*. In the *niyamas*, after stating the two principal items of the creed, namely, belief in God and faith in the Vedas, the universal objects of the Ārya Samāj were set forth in outline. The *niyamas*, formulated by Dayananda himself run as follows:

The first (efficient) cause of all knowledge and all that is known through knowledge is Parameśvara (supreme Lord).

Īśvara (God) is existent, intelligent, and blissful. He is formless, omnipotent, just, merciful unborn, endless, unchangeable, beginningless, unequalled, the support of all, the master of all, omnipresent, immanent, unaging, immortal, fearless, eternal and holy, and maker of all.

Vedas are the scripture of true knowledge. It is the first duty of the Āryas to read them, teach them, recite them, and hear them being read.

One should always be ready to accept truth and give up untruth.

Everything should be done according to the dictates of *dharma*, i.e. after due reflection over right and wrong.

The primary object of this Society is to do good to the whole world, that is, to look to its physical, social, and spiritual welfare.

One's dealings with all should be regulated by love and justice, in accordance with the dictates of *dharma*.

One should promote *vidyā* (knowledge of subject and object) and dispel *avidyā* (illusion).

One should not be content with one's own welfare alone, but should look for one's own welfare in the welfare of all.

One should consider oneself under restriction to follow altruistic rulings of society, while in following rules of individual welfare one should be free.

A candidate, for enlistment as a member of the Ārya Samāj, has to put his signature to these principles.

Swami Dayananda's conception of his Church was that of a democratic body. He did not recognize the intervention of any intermediary between God and His worshippers. Every man or woman who has an Ārya *sabhāsad* (member of the Ārya Samāj) was given the right to vote. While principles were formulated by Dayananda himself, the *upaniyamas* were the result of the collaboration of all *sabhāsads*, of whom Dayananda considered himself one. The founder of a Church placing himself, in the matter of its administration, on the same footing as its ordinary members, and thus upholding the principle of equality, is a phenomenon which is rare in the history of religion.

The danger to the Church of Dayananda does not lie in that the priest or the pontiff will arrogate to himself powers greater than a person can honestly handle, but in that, in the midst of overwhelming odds comprising the laity, his wise counsels may go unheeded and prove to be a solitary cry in the wilderness. The mind of man has been emancipated from the shackles of a privileged priesthood. If the Church of Dayananda is to thrive, it is necessary that every one of its members should assume a part of the rôle of the priest himself.

What Swami Dayananda found impracticable in his own day has, with the passage of time, become practicable. The Ārya Samājas in the different provinces have organised themselves into compact bodies called Pratinidhi Sabhās, to which they return members in proportion to their own numerical strength. The followers of the Ārya Samāj in some of the British overseas colonies have also evolved their own Pratinidhi Sabhās. All these Sabhās, within India as well as overseas send representatives to the International Aryan League or the Sārvadeśika Ārya Pratinidhi Sabhā, which has its headquarters in Delhi. In order to settle questions of creed a Dharma Ārya Sabhā has been established under the auspices of this Sārvadeśika Sabhā.

The inspiration of Dayananda was derived from personal communion with the Divinity. Of this, we find ample glimpses in his autobiographical and devotional writings. He was a dynamic saint and has imparted his dynamism to the entire Ārya Samāj, which serves as a channel for the distribution of his inexhaustible spiritual resources. The Ārya Samāj is Dayananda writ large, and it reflects his versatile personality. It has in it saints, philosophers, organisers, scholars, thinkers, and the laity—all reflecting in their different prisms, in protean ways, the light of the brilliant sun of lofty moral and spiritual ideals that Dayananda embodied. There is no doubt that his personality will leave its impress on humanity, and will influence, in an increasing measure, the religious history of India and the world.

REFERENCES

1. *Dayananda, the Man and His Work*, pp. 18-19.
2. *Ibid.*, p. 16.

Indo-British Civilization

Until the end of eighteenth century physical and linguistic difficulties were sufficient to account for the comparatively small influence which India exercised upon the Western world. We must now consider the last phase of Indian history, during which the whole country has been brought, province by province, State to State, under the control or under the indirect influence of the British Government. Within the last century some millions of educated Indians have learnt English, and the physical barriers preventing easy intercourse with the West have been substantially reduced. It might have been expected that Indian philosophy, literature, and art would have received at last a fuller appreciation in Europe; and that some new form of civilization might have developed from the close contact between England and India. Unfortunately it must be confessed that the last 150 years have proved the most disappointing, and in some ways the most sterile in Indian history. The English, working or domiciled in India, have not provided a good channel for spreading abroad the more valuable elements of Indian culture. Even more surprising is the poverty of the harvest from this hybrid civilization, from Indians working under English influence, or from English inspired by India and the Indian peoples.

The failure must be ascribed chiefly to the conditions of European colonization. Apart from temporary raiders India had usually absorbed and assimilated her Asiatic invaders. These entered from the north, and aimed at conquest and settlement. The Europeans, when they began to come east during the last three centuries, were not impelled by pressure of population, and only to a small extent by imperial ambitions. Neither France, Holland, nor England have ever seriously considered India or the East Indies as *colonies de peuplement*, but only as *colonies d'exploitation*. Portugal, with her visions of mass conversion, began to colonize in India with some object of building up a new Christian civilization. Her government deliberately encouraged the growth of a hybrid Christian population, but her efforts did not pass the experimental stage. The other invaders from temperature climates came originally as traders, and continued as soldiers and administrators, but they never made much attempt to force their religion or civilization upon India. This typically nineteenth-century form of colonization tends to destroy the existing social structure, without encouraging the development of any new culture. There were special circumstances which exaggerated this defect in British India.

During the latter half of the eighteenth century, when the British Government began to accept some responsibility for the territorial commitments of the East India Company, Indian civilization was at its lowest ebb. The break-up of the Mughal Empire left the country at the mercy of adventurers and 'war lords'. Civil war and general disorder caused the complete sub-mergence of all those arts which flourish in times of peace. The English who first went out to Bengal, Madras, and Bombay cannot be seriously blamed for neglecting such Indian culture as still survived. Most of the Company's servants were hardy adventurers, only anxious to 'shake the pagoda tree' and collect what profit they could out of the prevailing anarchy, but from the first there were a few who sought the company of educated Indians, and took an interest in their thought and achievements. Some account of this has been given in the first chapter of this book. It is enough for our purpose to recall that Warren Hastings encouraged Pandits and Maulvies. His motives may have been partly utilitarian, but he helped, in 1781, to found the Calcutta Madrasa for Islamic studies, while another of the Company's servants took a considerable share in launching the Sanskrit College at Benares in 1792. These early administrators were reprehensible from many points of view, but they did not suffer from the self-righteousness and strong Christian prejudices which were so marked amongst Englishmen in India from about 1830 onwards. They found Hindu religious thought and Muslim law in a state of decadence, and certainly did not discourage them. They even tried, without any great enthusiasm, to revive them. There was little literature being produced in any part of India, during the later part of the eighteenth century—the Bengali renaissance was much later—but there was a definite school of orientalists amongst the Englishmen who first went to Bengal. Sir William Jones, Sir Charles Wilkins, and Colebrooke were followed by men like Horace Wilson and James Prinsep. They were all men of great erudition, who 'aimed at a union of Hindu and European learning', and did much to introduce the ancient Sanskrit classics to the Western world. If they failed to find much in contemporary Indian literature or philosophy which interested them, it is at least possible that the reason was because there was very little to find.

The question of English treatment of Indian craftsmanship has, unfortunately, been obscured by later political controversy, but the same general considerations apply. There have always been two distinct types of craftsmen in India—those making commodities needed by villagers, and the far smaller group working for the wealthy and for export. The history of the former, still a large proportion of the Indian population, is hardly relevant, and it was many years before they encountered serious competition from machine-made goods, either imported or made in India. The position of the specialist craftsmen had begun to degenerate before the battle of Plassey. The impetus which the Mughals had given to architecture was exhausted by the time of Aurangzīb, and there was little building during the unsettled period which followed his death. The tradition survived, but only obscurely. The makers of luxury goods suffered equally from the disturbed times which had ruined so many of the princes and landed aristocracy, replacing them by upstarts clinging precariously to place and power. The extension of direct rule over most of India only hastened a process which had already gone for before 1760. The export trade had also begun to decline before that date. Muslins from Dacca, brocades from Ahmadābād, *bandanas* from Murshidābād, shawls from Kashmir, and similar goods intended from a leisured class had been sent to Europe for hundreds of years, but by the eighteenth century 'mercantilist' theories were widely accepted, and a kind of 'economic nationalism' developed which became more intense during the Napoleonic period. The East India Company made a profitable business from the distribution of such goods throughout Europe—their sale in England itself had never been great—but they found themselves blocked by tariffs and prohibitions in nearly every country, including England itself. The Company encouraged the manufacture of such goods in the limited part of India over which it exercised control, and the British Government after 1760 merely maintained the same policy which it had adopted as early as 1720. The Indian 'luxury' export trade was ruined by the development of better craftsmanship in Europe, and by economic theories opposed to the export of bullion, especially for imports which were not strictly utilitarian.

The charge, so frequently made from nationalist platforms, that the British deliberately destroyed a flourishing Indian civilization, will not bear examination.[1] It has obscured the real charge against British rule, which is that after the restoration of peace throughout the peninsula, when the civilized arts might have been expected to flourish once more, and the craftsman return to his hereditary activities, the new rulers failed lamentably to achieve a 'union of Hindu and European learning', or to give any scope to the technical skill and knowledge inherent amongst the people. With the gradual pacification and settlement of all India south of the Sutlej, there developed a new and most unfortunate attitude towards the Indian population amongst the Englishmen who began to come out East as administrators, business man, and soldiers. Former invaders had settled down, brought up their families in India, and either were absorbed by the Hindu system, or, like the Moslems, introduced a new religion which spread sufficiently to give them a real hold in the country. The English did none of these things. From the first the Eurasian and the 'country-bred' were despised. The tone of the administration and of the expatriated community was set by fresh contingents of Englishmen, coming from a land which was itself rapidly changing.

The East India Company in early days patronized both the Hindu and Muslim religions. Offices were open on Sunday but closed on Indian holidays. Troops were paraded in honour of Hindu deities. A coconut was solemnly broken at the beginning of each monsoon, and British officials assisted in the management of Hindu religious trusts. This phase ended early in the nineteenth century. The Company gave up being 'wet nurse to Vishnu', and 'churchwarden to Juggernaut'. The administration became strictly secular, and hence more and more aloof in a country where religion permeates every human activity. In the meantime the evangelical revival in England, the rapid development of industry and science, the social reforms of the thirties, and the breaking up of the English caste system were all reflected in the changed outlook of a new generation of officials. Like Macaulay they came to India, often for only a few years, endowed with a full consciousness of racial superiority. Already in 1817 some of the more broad-minded civilians, like Sir Thomas Munro, were protesting against the new tendency.

'Foreign conquerors have treated the natives with violence, but none has treated them with so much scorn as we; none have stigmatized the whole people as unworthy of trust, as incapable of honesty, and as fit to be employed only where we cannot do without them. It seems not only ungenerous, but impolitic, to debase the character of a people fallen under our dominion.'

The struggle over the employment of Indians in the administration was paralleled by the controversy between 'Anglicists' and 'Orientalists', which was to affect the whole future attitude of the British in India towards indigenous literature, art, and culture. The dispute came to a head over a comparatively small matter, the allocation of a grant of £10,000 a year which the Company had been forced to make to education at the time of the renewal of its charter in 1813. The grant had remained dormant for some years, but in the thirties its disposal brought to a head the differences between two schools of thought in the Indian Government, and in that small section of educated Bengalis who were articulate. It was not a matter of mass education, which few Governments then considered to be their responsibility, but of subsidizing higher education. Behind this minor dispute lay the fundamental question of policy—whether England should try to build upon the existing foundations of Indian language, philosophy, science, and craftsmanship, or whether the Government should start afresh, giving educated Indians a European education, which, according to the 'Filtration Theory' then popular, would gradually percolate down to the rest of the community.

Many factors helped in the defeat of the 'Orientalists'. Bengal was an unlucky field or battle. There were few of those visible signs of Indian skill and energy which abound in many parts of the country. The local Muslims were uneducated, their Maulvis were the decadent hangers-on left over from the collapse of Mughal rule. Hinduism was seen at its worst in Bengal, and a new generation of British officials was at last awakening to some of its less defensible aspects. The younger Englishmen believed firmly that they were dealing with 'a decomposed society', hopelessly corrupt, and they were supported in that idea by a group of reformist Bengalis, of whom Rām Mohan Rāy was the best known. The 'suttee' controversy had important reactions. The unhappy arguments against its abolition, which were used by a leader of the 'Orientalists', Horace Wilson, did much to ruin their cause. Besides the *sahamarana* rite other unfortunate aberrations of Hinduism were coming to light, as the British administration spread and became more settled. Female infanticide was discovered to be prevalent; child marriages, untouchability, and such savage survivals as the *meriah* sacrifices added to the general prejudice. On the positive side the 'Orientalists' were handicapped by the general decadence of Indian civilization. Such religious teaching as had survived was obscurantist, and neglected. Keshab Chandra Sen, writing of his boyhood, describes how:

'the ancient scriptures of the country, the famous records of numerous Hindu sects, had long been discredited. The Vedas and Upnishads were sealed books. All that we knew of the immortal Mahabharata, Ramayana, or the Bhagavad Gita was from execrable translations into popular Bengali, which no respectable young man was supposed to read.'

Vernacular literature was at an equally low ebb. For two centuries there had been no Hindī or Marātha poetry to compare with the work of Tulasī Dās or Tukārām.

The rout of the 'Orientalists' was completed by one of the two Englishmen of literary genius who have spent any time in India. Macaulay entered into the fray with the most superficial knowledge, but with immense gusto. Like Mr. Rudyard Kipling half a century later, he lent his great powers to voicing the prejudices of his less articulate countrymen, marooned in a country for which they had little sympathy.

'The question now before us is simply whether, when it is in our power to teach this language, we shall teach languages in which by universal confession there are no books on any subject which deserve to be compared to our own; whether when we can teach European science, we shall teach systems which by universal confession whenever they differ from those of Europe differ for the worse; and whether when we can patronize sound philosophy and true history, we shall countenance at the public expense medical doctrines which would disgrace an English farrier, astronomy which would move laughter in girls at an English boarding-school, history abounding with kings thirty feet high and reigns 30,000 years long, and geography made up of seas of treacle and seas of butter.'

Macaulay's sonorous Minute on Education served a double purpose. It helped to win an immediate victory for the 'Anglicists,' and its generalizations, coming from a man of such repute, appeased the conscience of those officials who dimly recognized a great field of learning from which they were cut off by linguistic and other obstacles. Nearly everything with which this present book has dealt was included in Macaulay's sweeping condemnation—the Indian epics, Hindu and Buddhist philosophy, the science and craftsmanship which raised and adorned her great buildings, the Ayurvedic system of medicine, and the traditions of a people 'civilized and cultivated; cultivated by all the arts of polished life while we were yet in the woods'. Macaulay in India might with advantage have recalled his Burke.

There were other reasons which account for the success of the 'Anglicists'. For the quarter of a century which preceded the Mutiny, although much of the country was settled, the administration remained chiefly occupied in minor wars, and the pacification of new territory. The Government was continually short of money and obsessed with the idea of building up a prosperous country upon the ruins of the old anarchy. It was typical of these times that Bentinck as Governor-General should have seriously considered the demolition of the Tāj Mahal and the sale of its marble. He 'was only diverted because the test auction of materials from the Agra Place proved unsatisfactory.[2] Indian civilization seemed a subject only fit for the antiquary, and had little interest for the new generation of keen and rather narrow Christians who began to fill the higher places in the administration—men like Charles Grant, Edwardes, Outram, Aitchison, and the Lawrences. They were wildly optimistic, and prepared to apply to all India Macaulay's astounding 'belief that if our plans of education are followed up, there will not be a single idolater among the respectable classes in Bengal thirty years hence. And this will be effected without any effort to proselytise; without the smallest interference in the religious liberty; merely by the natural operation of knowledge and reflection.' There was, of course, some reaction against these extravagances. English became the official language of India in 1835, but by 1855 the need for vernacular educational was fully recognized, especially in the north. Those Indians who had supported the demand for an English education showed little inclination to become Christians, and Debendranath Tagore led a 'counter-reformation.' As the English spread over India they came into contact with more independent and stubborn types than they had met in Bengal, and they found in the north and the Deccan the visible evidence of a comparatively recent Indian administration and civilization. But again India's evil star was in the ascendant. Just as there were signs of a return to a more balanced outlook the Mutiny occurred. Its suppression, and the measures taken to prevent a recurrence, caused a breach between the two races which has never been adequately recognized by English historians. A flood of Englishmen came out to India after 1860 filled with a strong racial antipathy to the inhabitants of the country, and from the resulting bitterness developed Indian Nationalism, which has always been a racial as much as a political movement.

From this time until very recent years the administration remained completely aloof. It was, in Dr. Tagore's phrase, brought from England

and given to the people untouched by hand.' By the eighties British officials had given up any idea of educated Indians becoming Westernized Christians, and of the masses following humbly after them to find the light. The Government's sphere of action was strictly defined. Within certain limits the Indian States were to go their own way, thus leaving two-fifths of the country as a quiet backwater where the 'Old India' could survive as a horrid example to the Indians in British India. Over the remaining three-fifths we would enforce justice along the English model, provide certain utilitarian services, make canals, roads, and bridges, build offices and official residences, and a church or two for the English residents, but not interfere with the social or religious life of Indians. It was a policy which fitted in well with the *laissez-faire* philosophy a Victorian Liberalism, and with the commonly held view that the Mutiny had been caused by excessive Government activity. It killed any prospect of Indo-British civilization. The English community remained a separate caste, with several sub-castes, strictly preserving the usual characteristics of endogamy, commensality, and mutual control by members. The officials had little need, the traders and soldiers had little inclination, to co-operate with Indians in the subjects with which this book is mostly concerned. The Indian Christians, mostly living in the extreme south, were to few in numbers and too little accepted into Anglo-Indian to provide any real contacts with the Indian population. Towards the end of the nineteenth century it was becoming obvious that the English in India had nothing in common with the growing mass of educated Indians, and as a measure of their failure they emphasized, without much justification, their special interest in the illiterate peasantry.

The history of Indian architecture during the last hundred years provides a useful commentary. The English have left a permanent mark upon India by their canals, roads, and railways —honestly and efficiently made. They had, however, little urge to build for the future. Officials, business men, and soldiers were all birds of passage, intending to make their homes in England and seldom spending even their working life in the same Indian 'station.' Soon after the Mutiny they tended to give up the idea that India would become a Christian country, and during much of the century they were uncertain about the future of British rule. Some of the highest officers—Viceroys and Provincial Governors—only stayed five yeas in India.

It was sufficient to put up a bungalow in which to live, some offices in which to work, and, rather grudgingly, a few churches in which the expatriated Englishman could worship his expatriated deity. There were none of the usual motives for erecting fine permanent buildings, except possibly to provide an imposing residence for a Viceroy or Governor. The engineers, to whose department all building was entrusted, were dominated by the same ideas of Indian art as the higher officials who gave them their orders. To them Indian art 'meant no more than a pretty chintz, a rich brocade, or gorgeous carpet, fantastic carving, or curious inlay; and an ancient architecture fascinating to the archaeologist and tourist with its reminiscences of bygone pomp and splendour, but an extinct art useless for the needs and ideals of our prosaic and practical times.'[3] They came out East, with little technical training but some general ideas gathered from Victorian England. These they modified slightly to suit Indian materials and conditions, developing that unpleasing style which is irreverently known as 'dak bungalow Gothic'. The few eccentrics who suggested that India might still contain craftsmen with valuable traditions and a style better suited to the country were completely overwhelmed by official disapproval and scepticism. It was not until the time of Lord Curzon, well into the present century, that the ancient buildings were thought worthy of protection, preservation, or study, and even Curzon's interest in Indian art was almost entirely archaeological. Of the two buildings in which he took a keen personal interest—the Victoria Memorial and the Military Secretariat in Calcutta—the first was entrusted to an English architect, who produced 'an archaeological essay on Kedleston Hall and the Radcliffe Library at Oxford'; the second, part of which was the subject of a prize competition, is a queer production in a 'pseudo-renaissance' style. Lord Curzon's term of office did, however, synchronize with the rise of a new school of artistic criticism in India. The last thirty years has been marked by a far better appreciation of the continuity and achievements of Indian craftsmanship.

The Public Works Department began to function after the Mutiny, at the height of the reaction against everything Indian. The highest officers were not inclined, the subordinates had no opportunity, to encourage indigenous knowledge and skill. Any Indian craftsman who might hope for a post worth more than three pounds a month had to go to Rurki for training. There he imbibed a contempt for Indian architecture, as having merely an archaeological interest, and he acquired a very inadequate knowledge of English architecture at one of its worst periods. Afterwards he would be used to erect offices and public buildings at a salary far smaller than the Mughal emperors had paid their master-masons. Government activities in India cover such a wide field, private building such a limited one, that this policy almost killed the Indian tradition. The hereditary craftsman, however, will continue at his trade until he is forced down to that dead level of Indian living, the standard of the small cultivator. In the Indian States he could still get work. Palaces, such as those built for Indian princes at Benares; temple at Brindaban, Hardwar, and Puri; private merchants' houses at Bikanir and Mewar show that all through the nineteenth century there were Indian builders, without any European training, capable of admirable religious and private architecture, well suited to the climate, to the materials of the country, and to the tastes of educated Indians.

The revival of interest and broader outlook which followed Lord Curzon's term of office were reflected in Mr. Sanderson's Report of 1913.[4] He found 'master masons of Bikanir working at the rate of annas 8 to Rs. 1 daily,' and building a fine row of merchants' houses on traditional lines. At Jodhpur a mosque, at Alwar a railway station, at Jaipur a Hindu temple were being built by men of this type. In each case their work makes one regret the hideous buildings which deface every Indian town where there is a cantonment or a civil station.

A note on modern Indian architecture prefaced to this Report by the Consulting Architect to Government suggests that a saner view on Indian master-builders had at least spread to Simla, but it was too late to prevent the planning of the New Delhi being entrusted to English architects, and the War discouraged any marked change of policy towards indigenous talent.

'It would be a fitting thing if the architectural note we sound in our new Capital were to type the reawakened India of the present and future. In this matter practical and economical considerations seem to me to join hands with those which are artistic and sentimental. We have got our art—why waste it? We have got our craftsmen—why employ them on work for which they have small aptitude—or (which is what would happen) leave our best craftsmen out altogether? There is nothing, as I have already said, in an Indian manner of design that makes it costly, indeed my own experience goes to prove that the costliest manner of building in India is a Renaissance or classical one. Again, why should a Western manner be held to type mostly fittingly the spirit of the Government of India? Why should the style of our Capital be such as to express most strongly those alien characteristics in the administration which every year tend more and more to disappear? And lastly, why sound again a note that is sure to dwindle into decadence as it has done before, rather than one more likely to be worthily sustained by the future generations of indigenous architects for whose advent we might well make it our duty to prepare?

These are admirable sentiments, but old prejudices are strong. The future is still uncertain. The partial triumph of nationalism and the prospect of a Federation with some real measure of provincial autonomy provide grounds for hoping that the Government will now begin to use and organise the Indian craftsmen. It will, however, be difficult to revive in British India an art neglected so long. In the meantime New Delhi has been completed and stands vast, incongruous, and wholly alien to northern India. Its huge range of offices are so unsuited to the climate that they are only used for about half the year. Behind them stands the enormous Viceregal Lodge, which is occupied for two or three months during the cold weather. In front there are miles of bungalows and hostels, a hybrid collection. New Delhi is in many ways a fitting monument to our rule, but it will remain as a *damnosa hereditas* for the new Federation.

An alien Government must build, but has little need to patronize the other craftsmen who cater for a settled aristocracy. These hereditary weavers, silk-workers, and mental-workers suffered even more than the masons. The export trade for fine brocades and other products had vanished altogether. The internal demand was injured by the upset which followed the introduction of British rule and European standards of taste throughout most of the peninsula. The caste craftsmen were not organised to stand the introduction of free competition.

'A great industry in gold-embroidered shoes,' wrote that great authority Sir George Birdwood, 'flourished in Lucknow. They were in demand all over India, for the native kings of Oudh would not allow the shoemakers to use anything but pure gold wire on them. But when we and the kingdom, all such restriction were removed and the bazaars of Oudh were at once flooded with the pinchbeck embroidered shoes of Delhi, and the Lucknow shoemakers were swept away for ever by the besom of free trade.'

Nearly all of these old crafts disappeared before the rush of cheap or showy articles from abroad, displayed before a new type of wealthy Indian. Even the princes were corrupted by their first contact with the West and preferred to spend their money on racehorses rather than on patronizing the hereditary craftsmen of their States. Some of these may still be found in Hyderabad, Gwalior, and other State capitals, producing beautiful work which they cannot sell and eking out their existence on the wages of a coolie.

The neglect of Indian craftsmanship can be partly ascribed to the policy of the Government and to the ignorance or the hubristic outlook of the expatriated Englishman. The sterility of Indian science and art was partly due to these same causes, but also to the hostility which developed between the Indian educated classes and the English community. The latter's habit of disparaging every kind of Indian enterprise is probably a symptom of their own consciousness that their position in India is false, and that the only justification for the kind of government imposed upon India would be a racial superiority which clearly does not exist. Enmity breeds enmity. Whatever may be the origin of the quarrel there is no doubt about its reality and bitterness since the middle of the nineteenth century. On the English side it led to the blind acceptance of such superficial generalizations as those of Macaulay; on the Indian side, especially after the Mutiny, there was a tendency to react against all Western ideas. In religion this led to the 'Back to the Vedas' movement; a return to an orthodox and sometimes obscurantist Hinduism which had its counterpart in many other walks of life.

The history of Indian medicine is typical. There were three indigenous systems—Ayurvedic, *Tibbī*, and *Yunānī*. These undoubtedly contained much that was valuable, including a number of useful drugs, but, as in European pharmacy of the eighteenth century, there was a considerable admixture of superstition. The Ayurvedic systems and practice were further vitiated by restrictions due to the Hindu rules of caste and ceremonial cleanliness. But English medical officers were not going to worry about 'medical doctrines which would disgrace an English farrier', and the indigenous methods were contemptuously rejected without the least consideration of the effect which such a policy would have upon the people or the older practitioners. Instead of a friendly development and modernization of the old systems, which were in some ways suited to the country, the Western and Eastern ideas of medicine became rivals. With the spread of an intense nationalism there was a reaction in favour of Ayurvedic methods, and competition between the two schools of thought became a political issue, which is not yet settled.

The recent history of Indian painting in some ways resembles that of architecture. Those old indigenous craftsmen, the court 'portrait painters,' were sometimes employed by the early 'nabobs', but can now only be found in a few of the Indian States. Very few Englishmen who went to India in the nineteenth century had any interest in painting; the little patronage which they dispensed went to painters in a pseudo-European style. The kind of malaise which settled over educated India seems to have discouraged the development of modern art until the growth of the Calcutta school under Dr. Abinandranath Tagore. Much of their work is wholly admirable, but the Calcutta group has suffered from being too limited in numbers, to dependent on Dr. Tagore, his brother Goganendranath Tagore, and a few pupils like Asit Kumar Haldar and Nanda Lal Bose. Some examples of their work are reproduced in Dr. J.H. Cousins's *Modern Indian Artists*, and E.B. Havell's *Indian Sculpture and Painting*. Both Calcutta and Bombay have Art Schools and it is to be hoped that the great technical ability latent amongst so many Indian races will find better expression in the freer political atmosphere of the future. At present both Indian art and Indian science tend to become 'one-man deep,' relying upon the occasional individual who seems able to transcend the inertia into which the country has sunk.

Literature is the one field of Indo-British culture which has provided a comparatively large harvest, though the average quality is not very good. It is, perhaps, significant that India ceased to be a source of inspiration to English poets about the time when the country came wholly within our jurisdiction. Shakespeare, Dryden, Southey, Campbell, Moore, Shelley, and Wordsworth, were all attracted by the glamour of an unknown India; a land of romantic dynasties, of luxury and exotic beauty, and of mystic religions. To their literary descendants India has become a dull and arid land in which some rather dull and arid compatriots spend their working life. Some mention has already been made of the Sanskrit scholars in the early days of the Company. Their connexion with the Bengali reformers might have led to a literature based on a common culture and tradition, but the interest taken by Western writers did not survive long into the nineteenth century. Schopenhauer's enthusiasm for the *Upanishads,* Goethe's appreciation of Kālidāsa, left no permanent mark on European literature. Emerson's *Brahma,* Lowell's *Mahmood the Image Breaker*, and Whittier's *Brewing of the Soma* continued the tradition in America, but the Western world did not really take kindly to Hindu thought and literature. Buddhism made a greater appeal in the nineteenth century, and has had a more definite effect on European thought. It cannot be said that the work of the early Sanskrit experts, or later that of Max Müller, really roused more than an immediate and superficial interest.

The reactions against Indian ideas can be traced amongst the succeeding generations of Englishmen in India who felt the urge to write. Sir William Jones not only produced some admirable translations—the best-known being of *Hitopadeśa* and *Śakuntala*—but he also wrote the original and very remarkable *Hymns* to various Indian deities. They show a real attempt to understand and appreciate Hindu religious mentality.

> Wrapt in eternal solitary shade,
> Th' impenetrable gloom of light intense,
> Impervious, inaccessible, immense,
> Ere spirits were infus'd or forms display'd,
> BREHM his own Mind survey'd,
> As mortal eyes (thus finite we compare
> With infinite) in smoothest mirrors gaze:
> Swift, at his look, a shape supremely fair
> Leap'd into being with a boundless blaze,
> That fifty suns might daze.

This phase was not fated to last. His successors soon began to adopt that slightly hostile and superior attitude which characterizes the work of Englishmen writing on Indian subjects. John Leyden and Bishop Heber, at the beginning of the nineteenth century, wrote verse of some merit, but they both viewed India as a land of ancient decaying pomp and of dark mysteries. Leyden, like Wellesley, saw and was shocked by the infant sacrifices at Sagur. His verse has an undercurrent of hostility against all Hinduism.

> On sea-girt Sagur's desert isle
> Mantled with thickets dark and dun,
> May never morn nor starlight smile,
> Nor ever beam the summer sun.

From about 1836 this tradition had become firmly established. India was the 'Land of Regrets' in which Englishmen spent years of exile amongst a people half savage, half decadent. This idea runs through Leyden's *Ode to an Indian Gold Coin*, and the works of a number of Anglo-Indian poets, of whom Sir Alfred Lyall is probably the best remembered. His *Meditations of a Hindu Prince* and *Siva* show an attempt to appreciate the Indian point of view, but Lyall was always a stranger in a strange land, looking with contemptuous pity upon a people over whose heads.

> the deities hover and swarm like the wild bees heard in the tree-tops, or the gusts of a gathering storm.

There was no reason to expect any great output of literature from the small community of expatriated officials, soldiers, and business men. Lyall was an exceptionally versatile man, and the 'Services' chiefly produced histories, works on administration, and occasional novels. A few, like Henry Meredith Parker, wrote light verse in the tradition of Mackworth Praed; these were the not unworthy forerunners of Kipling's *Departmental Ditties*. The one considerable Anglo-Indian poet of Victorian times was Sir Edwin Arnold who, after a short time spent in educational work, made a name for himself as a translator of Indian verse, and as the author of *The Light of Asia*. He wrote too easily and quickly to reach the highest rank, but hundreds of thousands in Europe and America have gained some appreciation of Buddhism from him.

> The Scripture of the Saviour of the World,
> Lord Buddha, Prince Siddhartha styled in earth—
> In Earth and Heavens and Hells Incomparable,
> All-Honoured, Wisest, Best, most Pitiful,
> The Teacher of Nirvana and the Law.

Amongst the historians, James Grant Duff and Mountstuart Elphinstone have left two classic works in their *History of the Mahrattas* and *History of India*; both belong to the generation before the Mutiny. William Hunter, G.O. Trevelyan, and the unconventional S.S. Thorburn were administrators who could write of their work and make it into literature. They have had many successors whose books have never been properly appreciated in England. No one can hope to understand the important formative years which followed the Mutiny without reading Trevelyan's *The Competition Wallah;* the great problem of Indian indebtedness without Thorburn's *Mussulmans and Money-lenders in the Punjab* and M.L. Darling's *The Punjab Peasant* and *Rusticus Loquitur*; or Indian education without Arthur Mayhew's work on that subject. A host of works of this kind are a by-product of a great bureaucracy.

Within the Eighth community a new school of writers developed, attempting a wider field than history and administration. After the Mutiny the population of Anglo-India began to increase very rapidly. New types of Englishmen went out East, including journalists and schoolmasters; they brought their wives, and were visited by tourists; within India a domiciled English and Eurasian population was growing in numbers and developing a life of its own. These factors encouraged the production of fiction, partly for the Indian market and partly for those in England who liked to think of India as a country where Englishmen had strange adventures. The Victorian novelists and descriptive writers were really in the direct line from those travellers, like Tavernier and Manucci, who described India under the Mughals. Earlier British settlers in Bengal do not seem to have been much impressed by the hazardous nature of their life, but this aspect appealed forcibly to the generation which conquered central and northern India and later spread over the Punjab and up to the North-west Frontier. The early 'Nabobs' accepted the incidents of their life with the same indifference as they displayed towards 'suttee' or he corruption of the local rulers. Eighteenth century Europe had so much more in common with contemporary India.

Colonel Meadown Taylor made his reputation by *The Confessions of a Thug*, a typical product of this new school. It was written about 1839, towards the end of the campaign against the *phānsīdārs*, of which Sleeman has also left a good account in his *Rambles and Recollections*. Taylor's later works were written after retirement. *Tara, Setta, Tippoo Sultan, and c.*, all contain passages of great vigour and show a real understanding of India, but are rather swamped by the conventional working out of their plots. *Seeta* has a special interest because it marks the transition which took place so rapidly after the Mutiny. Taylor was pre-Mutiny in his outlook, and he idealized a marriage between an Englishman and an Indian which shocked the Anglo-Indian of 1873, when it was published.[5] The British were rapidly developing into a separate caste, strongly reinforced by the new officials, planters, and business men who came crowding out East after 1860. There was a natural tendency for writers to concentrate more upon this colony of their expatriated countrymen, upon what was then called Anglo-Indian society. Rudyard Kipling had, of course, a long line of predecessors as well as imitators. Few of them are of much importance, but any one interested in this subject should consult a recent monograph by Bhupal Singh, *A Survey of Anglo-Indian Fiction*, in which the author pours coals of fire upon our English heads by rescuing from oblivion a large number of forgotten and unreadable books, nearly all of which are grossly offensive to his race.

A few of these are interesting. Mr. Sherwood had peculiar opportunities for knowing the seamy side of pre-Mutiny Anglo-India. Her books are full of little incidental touches recalling that queer society which survived even after the 'clipping Dutchman', Lord William Bentinck, had begun his reforms. Matthew Arnold's brother, W.D.

Arnond, went to India in Government service, and his father stilted novel, *Oakfield*, shows how the new type of Englishman, coming out East in the fifties, revolted against the religious and social life of the times. After the Mutiny, when the old 'Brahmanized' Englishmen had almost disappeared, the new expatriated community began to settle down comfortably to its allotted term of work, as part of a great administrative machine. It could afford to laugh at itself, sentimentalize over its love affairs, carried on under such artificial conditions, and take a mild interest in the native life which flowed round the 'stations', or the flora and fauna in the neighbouring jungle. Iltidus Pritchard's *Chronicles of Budgepore*, Sir Henry Cunningham's *Chronicles of Dustypore*, Philip Robinson's *Nugae Indicae*, and 'Eha's' later *Tribes on my Frontier* are typical of this period. They are still readable for their humour, and interesting for the light they throw upon the bureaucracy during the most static, self-satisfied, and sterile era of British rule, from about 1870 till the end of the century. The greater part of Rudyard Kipling's Indian work is directly in this tradition, though it is illuminated by his own genius and reinforced by his knowledge of Indian customs, animal fables, and jungle-lore. Much of this he probably acquired from his father, Lockwood Kipling, whose *Beast and Man in India* is a wonderful storehouse from which many have drawn inspiration.

Kipling's influence over his generation can hardly be exaggerated. Many Englishmen, especially amongst those directly connected with India, felt that some interpreter was needed for that curious phenomenon, British Rule in India. Kipling supplied the necessary exposition in a manner most flattering to English pride, and in forms—that of fiction and light verse—which were easily assimilated. Coming to India as a young man, he worked for a few years as a journalist in Lahore and Simla. From this rather slender acquaintance with the country his marvellously fertile mind poured out short stories and verse which were of such intrinsic brilliance that they gave a wholly disproportionate value to his interpretation of Indian life. He knew the garrison towns of northern India and the hill stations. His comparatively humble position on a local newspaper gave him as insight into the sub-castes of Anglo-India—the sub-ordinate railway employees and the domiciled European and Eurasian families. Apart from his 'jungle' books, the greater part of his Indian fiction and verse is concerned with these two tiny communities, the officials and military officers, and the subordinate Europeans and Eurasians. Round them surges the immense sea of Indians, but nearly all of this subjected race who appear as individuals are minor characters, mostly domestic servants or women kept by Englishmen. The few educated Indians who come into his pages seem to have been introduced to satisfy the deep-seated prejudices of the English in India. Almost all of them are, in the old school phrase, 'sent up for bad', and Kipling allowed himself the most astounding generalizations about Indian duplicity and mendacity, or the physical cowardice of certain races. Even in the two novels which take a wider scope and deal more directly with Indian life—*Kim* and *The Naulahka*—the Indians are all drawn 'in the flat', as types, the human beings, whereas the Europeans or the country-bred Kim and so indubitably drawn 'in the round'. The one possible exception, the old Lama, is not really an Indian. Not until he had left India for many years could Kipling rid himself of that obsession, driven into the minds of all Englishmen who went East before the War, that a denial of racial superiority was the one deadly sin. *Kim* is a wise and also a comparatively mellow book, but Kipling had to make his young hero assert his superiority as a 'Sahib' over Hurree Chunder Mookerjee, the Bengali, though the latter was his departmental superior.

Kipling can hardly be said to have founded a school, but his attitude towards India is followed by nearly all of the novelists who followed him. Some of these, like Mrs. Steel, Mrs. Perrin. F.E. Penny, and 'Sydney Carlyon Grier', are very capable writers, but they have the same tendency to make heir real characters Europeans while Indians form a shadowy background, types rather than human being. Edmund Chandler's *Siri Ram, Revolutionist* is a very interesting attempt to 'get inside the skin' of an Indian student, but is marred by the contemptuous dislike of the educated Indian which marks the same author's later work *Abdication*. Nor can it be said that English writers have been more successful in dealing with Indian peasants and craftsmen. Leonard Woolf's *Village in the Jungle* stands quite alone in this class, and was written about Ceylon. It may be interesting to compare other European literature in this respect. Couperus, writing of the Dutch East Indies, has something of Kipling's outlook, and a few French writers have dealt successfully with the higher-class Muslims in their Empire. There is, however, a definite group of French novelists, the *grande brousse* school, who have tried to portray the mentality of negroes and of illiterate Muhammadans. There are no English equivalents to René Maran's *Batouala*, Victor Salagen's *Les Immémoriaux*, and Eberhardt's *Dans l'ombre chaude de l'Islam;* or to such negro studies as Marius Lebland's *Ulysse Caffre* and *Zézère,* or Joseph's *Roman vrai d'un noir*.

Of later years E.M. Forster and Edward Thompson have written novels dealing with Anglo-Indian life in which the Indian characters have not been supernumerary actors, dragged on to the stage in various guises to add a little local colour. *A Passage to India* and *An Indian Day* are for this reason outstanding novels amongst the mass of post-Kipling fiction. A few Englishmen, working in India, have also attempted in literature the same Westernized forms of Indian art which are to be found amongst some of the modern Indian painters. By far the most successful are the works of F.W. Bain. *A Digit of the Moon* and *In the Great God's Hair* are admirable examples in a genre which would not bear much analysis, but in themselves stand out amongst the mass to Anglo-Indian literature as would a painting by Gogendra Nath Tagore in an exhibition of Anglo-Indian art. C.A. Kincaid is a less subtle writer, but his *Shri Krishna of Dwarka* and other stories show an appreciation of that mass of Hindu folk-lore and fable which is a sealed book to most Englishmen.

In considering the Indian writers in English a tribute must be paid to the extraordinary brilliance with which certain Indian races overcome linguistic difficulties, Bengalis, Chitpavan and Kasmiri Brahmins, Madrassis, and Parsis have produced a succession of capable journalists and publicists, who have served the nationalist cause by writing clear and trenchant English prose—Tilak, Ghokhale, Arabindo Ghose, Ranade, Sarendra Nath Banerjee, R.C. Dutt, N.C. Kelkar, Pherozshah Mehta, and a host of other writers have shown that Indian English can develop into a powerful weapon of attack. But polemical writing can only with great difficulty reach the level of literature, and very little is likely to survive from the vast mass of political and economic articles and books which have been produced in India during the last half-century. It is unfortunate that the British connexion has not inspired many Indians to try their hands at fiction. Even written from the nationalist standpoint it might have been an effective alternative line of attack. S.M. Mitra, a Bengali writer of considerable versatility, wrote *Hindupore* during the height of the anti-Partition agitation, but it is not a success.

Rabindranath Tagore's novels were written in Bengali and so hardly come within the scope of this chapter, but translations of *The Home and World, The Wreck, and c.*, have provided many Westerners with an insight into Indian life which is unobtainable from biographies, histories, or controversial writing, and add to one's regret that the few Indians who have written fiction should have usually adopted conventional themes and fiction should have usually adopted conventional themes and produced work which is only too clearly derivative. Dhan Gopal Mukerji's *My Brother's Face* is an admirable account, possibly autobiographical, of a Bengali returning to his country after some years' absence. It is perhaps significant that this book, with its remarkable freedom and scope, should have been written by an Indian who has spent so much of his life abroad. Sir Hari Singh Gour is a reformer of courage and originality, but this would hardly appear in *His Only Love*. Sir Joginder Singh has written a capable but not very interesting historical romance, *Nir Jahan;* P.A. Madhaviah's *Thillai Govindan* approaches nearer to being the self revelatory novel which would be so valuable; finally there are two new writers whose work suggests that Indian authors are beginning to see what an enormous field lies open to them in their villages, the complications of their caste system and in the lives of working men and women. K.S. Venkataramani's *Murgan, the Tiller* is excellent, while Mulk Raj Anand's *The Coolie* and *The Untouchable* are probably the most important and promising books ever written in English by an Indian.

The Indian poets who have written in English are a small but very interesting group. Perhaps it is fitting that one should first mention Henry Derozio, a Eurasian or, as he would now be called, an 'Anglo-Indian' poet who lived in Calcutta during the first quarter of the nineteenth century. He died when he was 22, but he managed to make his mark as a teacher, upset conventional Calcutta by his modern ideas, and leave a modest volume of verse—clever, facile writing, but obviously derivative, owing much to Keats and Shelley. He found Greece in the abstract more inspiring than India, but attempted one long poem called the *Fakeer of Jungheera*, which suggests that India might have found, in this lad of mixed parentage, a poet who could ultimately have given us the spirit of the traditional Indian culture fashioned into English verse. During the remainder of the century an occasional Bengali young man or woman would develop the authentic lyric note as a result of a contact with English literature, and in most cases with England itself. The two sisters Toru and Aru Dutt wrote extraordinarily fluent and graceful verse while they were still in their teens, and then died with their great promise unfulfilled. Some of their best work appeared in *A Shaef gleaned in French Fields*, a series of adaptations and translations. This includes those lines by Aru Dutt which first attracted the attention of Edmund Gosse:

Still barred thy doors! The far east glows
The morning wind blows fresh and free.
Should not the hour that wakes the rose
Awaken also thee?
All look for thee, Love, Light, and Song,
Light in the sky deep red above,
Song, in the lark of pinions strong,
And in my heart, true Love.
Apart we miss our nature's goal,
Why strive to cheat our destinies?
Was not my love made for the soul?
Thy beauty for mine eyes?
No longer sleep,
Oh listen now!
I wait and weep,
But where art thou?

Toru Dutt's *Ancient Ballads of Hindustan* seldom reaches such heights, but the longest of her poems, *Savitrai*, suggests that, like Deroziom, she also might have found inspiration in her own country, if she had reached to a more mature age. She and her sister were lost between two worlds. The same also must be said of a later Bengali poet, Manmohan Ghose. Like his brother Arabindo, the great nationalist, he was educated in England, and most of his *Love Songs and Elegies* and *Songs of Love and Death* spring from this early experience, and many from his affection for the English countryside. He returned to India and an academic life. He had that extra portion of sensibility which made him an exile in England, and then doubly an exile in India.

Art thou in the cornfields lonely?
Oh, to be
Where the wide earth ripples green
Like a sea.
There, possessed of verdure only,
Watching dost thou lean?
No not there; for thou wouldst meet
By some stile, some hedgerow fair,
Sweet objects, ah! too Keenly sweet
With the memory of her;
Her, that from their perfume knows
Not a woodbine, not a rose!
No, not there!

From those Indians who are 'English educated', and more especially from those educated in England, there has been a constant succession of minor poets, the excellence of whose work has hardly been appreciated in post-War Europe or America. The trouble is that they are definitely minor poets, admirable in their technique, but without very much to say; living in an age not much interested in a form of art which so many have acquired. Harindranath Chattopadhaya, Ananda Coomaraswamy, Feridoon Kabraji, and many others have written thoroughly competent verse, which in Victorian times might have received a recognition which would have encouraged them to write more. The best of these later poets is undoubtedly Sarojini Naidu. Like so many of her generation she has found politics more enthralling than poetry, but like Manhoman Ghose she has the authentic lyrical note, andw as fortunately persuaded by Sir Edmund Gosse to write of Indian life;

> What longer need hath she of loveliness,
> Whom Death has parted from her lord's caress?
> Of glimmering robes like rainbow-tangled mist,
> Of gleaming glass or jewels on her wrist,
> Blossoms or fillet-pearls to deck her head,
> Or jasmine garlands to adorn her bed?

Possibly English is not a good medium for expressing Indian thought. Certainly no verse in this language has the essential greatness or the permanent importance of Rabindranath Tagore's Bengali poems, or Muhammad Iqbal's extraordinarily interesting Persian mystical poetry.[6]

The future of Indo-British culture is as uncertain as its past has been disappointing. There are no signs that the exaggerated nationalism of the present day is a phase likely to pass quickly away. The next ten years may well see Hindī substituted for English as the lingua franca of India, and modern Europe shows how easily Governments and nationalist movements can set up artificial barriers which more than counterbalance the effects of easier communications. Nothing is gained by ignoring the enmity which exists between educated Indians and educated Englishmen. Much of the world's future depends upon a solution of this futile and unnecessary quarrel. It is hoped that this small book, written by Indian and English hands, may help to remove one cause of that quarrel, which is the Englishman's failure to appreciate the old traditional culture of the people with those destiny that of his own country is so closely intermingled.

—G.T. Garratt

REFERENCES

1. This question, so far as it concerns craftsmen, is discussed at some length in Thompson and Garratt's *Rise and Fulfilment of British Rule in India,* pp. 430-5.

2. E.B. Havell, *Indian Sculpture and Painting*, p. 246.

3. E.B. Havell, *Indian Sculpture and Paintings*, p. 4.

4. Report on Modern Indian Architectrue.

5. Until the beginning of this century the word 'Anglo-Indians' was always used for the English community, resident but not settled in India. It is now officially applied to the Eurasian population—a change which has led to much confusion.

6. Both, of course, have been translated. Unfortunately Dr. Tagore has allowed abbreviated and very banal versions of his poems to appear in English. Muhammad Iqbal's *Secrets of the Self* published by Messrs, Macmillan and Co.

The Life of Dayanand Saraswati

(1824-1883)

An Impressive Personality

Dayanand was born in an orthodox Brahmin family of Kathiawar (Gujarat). He was a physical giant besides being an intellectual one. He was tall, fair, strong built and very handsome.

His Profound Writings

Swami Dayanand was not only an orator in Sanskrit and Hindi and an incessant preacher of Vedic religion but was also a prolific writer. Besides his 'Commentary on the Vedas' and the famous Satyarth Prakash he wrote some twenty-five books during his last fifteen years.

Religious Doctrines

The ten principles of the Aray Samaj, the Satyarth Prakash and the Sanskar Vidhi (ceremonies and rituals) are three main sources, which will give a sufficiently clear picture of the religious teachings of Swami Dayanand, which form the basis of the Arya Samaj.

Founding of Religions

The third essential of an organised religion is supposed to be some founder of the religion. One of the distinguishing features of the Arya Samaj is that it does not believe in any prophet or messiah of God, nor does it accept any redeemer or spiritual intermediary between God and man because it believes in the free destiny of man. The position of Swami Dayanand, therefore, is that of a reviver of the forgotten Vedic religion. In any case, it is a historical fact that he was the founder of the Arya Samaj and, what is more, after his death his religious beliefs and teachings have come to be accepted by the Sarvadeshik Pratinidhi Sabha, the highest authority in the Arya Samaj world.

THE SEEKER OF TRUTH

As originator of the Arya Samaj, Dayananda's place is in the third category, i.e. that of the founders of religions. As we have discussed earlier, the Arya Samaj cannot justifiably be entirely cut off from Hinduism, as is the view of some writers Nevertheless it does have certain individuality also in the sense that it has a set of rules and principles, and the Vedas as its scripture. We might call it a kind of halfway house. Dayanand comes under the category of those who founder insular or world religions.

The great objective, which Dayanand persistently followed, was the quest of truth and Dharma. In his statement of beliefs and disbeliefs—*Swamantavyamantavya*, he quotes two verses from Bhatrihari and Manu on the necessity of pursuing Dharma (which, by the way, is considered to be one of the purusharthas i.e. objects of human existence); and two verses from the Upanishads emphasizing the need of the pursuit of truth. Dharma means following the moral law, and implies such things as one's duties towards various persons one comes into touch with—the duties of father to son, son to father, friend to friend, brother to brother, husband to wife and of the wife to the husband, of the king to his subjects, of the government to the people and of course of mankind to the creator. Then Dharma implies duties cast upon persons by virtue of their profession and standing. For example the duty of a Kshatriya (warrior) is to fight the enemy and not turn his back in war. The proper observance of Dharma implies piety, prayer, worship, and so forth. Thus the Dharma of everyone is according to his individual status and social inter-action. Dayanand believe that one must pursue Dharma assiduously. The Dharma he had in mind was that described in the Vedas. Rule 6 of the rules for Arya Samajists said that in their social relations men should be guided by Dharma. In the advice he gave to them, he said. This is my firm opinion; even if there be many different sectarian beliefs prevalent in India, if only they all acknowledge the Vedas, then all those small rivers will re-unite in the ocean of Vedic wisdom, and the unity of Dharma will come about. From that unity of Dharma will come social and economic reform, arts and crafts and other human endeavours as desired, and man's life will find fulfillment; because by the power of that Dharma all values will become accessible to him, economic values as well as psychological ones, and also the supreme value of 'moksha.' As we have seen, Dayanand believed that the classification of caste is according to a man's deeds. The Veda said that the Brahman is God's mouth, the Kshatriya his arms, the Vaishya his middle and the Shudra his feet, Dayanand gave this a symbolic interpretation. God is not a living being having a mouth, body, hands and feet. What the Veda means is that the Brahmins are heads of the society by reason of their being intellectual and learned, not because of birth. The Kshatriyas protect society by their armed might; the Vaishyas preserve it by earning wealth and the Shudras by manual work. Thus it is occupation, which determines caste, not birth.

Man's living and the ideal mode of conduct are fully described by Dayanand. The usual division of life was adopted by him; the four ashramas, but he was of the view that, for one who had prepared himself for it, sanyasa could be taken straightaway. He deals exhaustively with the duties of parents towards their children, the mode of education, the various natal ceremonies, the wearing of the sacred thread, marriage and family life. An account of these has already been given and repetition would be superfluous. What is notable is the liberal and modern trend of Dayananda's thought in respect of these matters. His attitude is scientific. He quotes the Rig-Veda as saying that all bodies, the sun, moon and the earth revolve in their orbits. The earth in its orbit revolves round the sun. So too is the testimony of the *Yajur Veda*. 'All bodies' it say, are supported in the air and are made to revolve by air and its power of attraction. Dayanand advocated the use of airplanes, ships, and conveyances, which could move swiftly on land. Silver, iron and copper could be used for these. Some verses of the Rig-Veda he points out testify that electric currents were known in those days. Saturn is spoken of as the son of the Sun. Lightning is called Indra, Vraja, and the bolt. The Greek writer, Themistus, speaks of Indians 'fighting at a distance with lighting and thunder'. Alexander the Great speaks of, terrible flashes of flames which Indian soldiers showered upon his armies'. According to Philostratus, Indian soldiers sent 'tempests and thunders down from heaven.' It appears that rockets were being used in India then. Professor Wilson mentions their use. Ctesias, Elian and Philostratus speak of oil manufactured in India, which was used in warfare for destroying walls and battlements of towns. Thus Dayanand brought out the scientific truths contained in the Vedas and cleared a great deal of misconception about these matters.

Ever since the growth of temples and idol worship, priests began to dominate Hindu society. They do to a great extent, even now. Dayanand exposed their nefarious practices and also the various ways, in which the mahants of temples hoodwinked the gullible worshippers, extracting money from them. He prescribed simple ceremonies, which would break their hegemony, and even advocated that if men became well-versed in the shastras they could act as their own priests. We have related how when once he suspected that the description of the human anatomy in a book was wrongly given, he carried out the unpleasant task of cutting open a corpse and verifying for himself.

Truth, however, is very hard to define, particularly when applied to matters, which are beyond the senses. Quite often Dayanand's rationality becomes quizzical, as for example when he says that souls attaining moksha have to necessarily come down to the earth after staying in heaven through the cosmic cycle, because if they didn't God would run out of soul-material! Religion and rationality are more or less opposed. By laying too great a stress on rationality, Dayanand closed the door to one of the ways of approach to God, which has been recognized not only by Hinduism but also by religious, the world over, namely bhakti, or devotion.

Dayanand gave new meaning to old concepts, and in this his guiding principle was truth and Dharma. Devas were men who were wise and learned, not as the word means 'the gods'. Asuras (demons) were those who were ignorant, and pishachas (evil spirits), those who were wicked in their acts. Devapuja (worship of the gods) does not mean paying obeisance to the gods but to the wise and the learned, to one's father and mother and preceptor, to preachers of truth, to a just ruler, to righteous persons, to women who are devoted to their husbands and to men who are devoted to their wives. One can trace in this Dayanand's opposition to a god with form and to image worship.

Dayanand's concept of Dharma is succinctly set forth in his '*Beliefs and Disbeliefs*'. He says, 'I accept as Dharma whatever is in full conformity with impartial justice, truthfulness and the like, that which is not opposed to the teachings of God as embodied in the Vedas. Whatever is not free from partiality and is unjust, partaking of untruth and the like, and opposed to the teachings of God as embodied in the Vedas—that I hold as adharma.' Again he says 'He, who after careful thinking, is ever ready to accept truth and reject falsehood; who counts the happiness of others as he does that of his own self, him I call just'.

Interpreted by Swami Dayanand

Sri Aurobindo said, "*As I regard the figure of this formidable artisan in God's workshop, images crowd on me which are all of battle and work, conquest and triumphant labour. Here, I say to myself, was a very soldier of light, a warrior in God's world, a sculptor of man and institutions, a bold and rugged victor of the difficulties, which matter presents to spirit. And the whole sums itself up to me in a powerful impression of spiritual practicality. The combination of these two words, usually so divorced from each other in our conceptions, seems to me the very definition of Dayanand.*"

Poet laureate Rabindranath Tagore pays his tribute to Dayanand and says, "I offer my homage of veneration to Swami Dayanand, the great pathmaker in northern India, who through bewildering tangles of creed and practices, the dense undergrowth of the degenerate days of our country, cleared a straight path that was meant to lead the Hindus to a simple and rational life of devotion to God and service for man."

The famous Historian Jaiswal believes that, "The rise of Dayanand in the nineteenth century is a phenomena which baffles the historian. But there are such life germs in the civilization of Hindus, which evidently make it indestructible and which are beyond the ken of that empiricist observer called the historian. The present reformed and rejuvenated Hinduism is solely a gift of Dayanand Saraswati. Dayanand had the humanity of the Buddha, but he combined with it the preservative complex of Sankara."

Lala Lajpat Rai, one of the great leaders of the Indian National Congress and also of the Arya Samaj wrote, The Arya Samaj, during his exile from India during the British rule, and it was published in London in 1915. This historical work still remains unsurpassed as the best introduction to the origin, mission and scope of the Arya Samaj. Referring to Dayanand's unique contribution to the rediscovery of Vedas, he observes that, "By declaring that everyone, including women and non-Brahmins had the right to study the Vedas and by rendering them into Hindi, the language of the common people, both of which were considered a sacrilege, Dayananda brought about a revolution which by one masterstroke shattered the shackles, which Hindus had borne for centuries."

Referring to the divine right domination of the Brahmins in Hinduism, Lajpat Rai points out, how Dayanand himself, born into a priestly Brahmin family openly challenged the authority and monopoly of the Brahmin, merely from the right of birth, and held that anyone including a born Shudra (untouchable) can become even a priest and perform yajna and all other Vedic ceremonies by studying Sanskrit and the Vedas from which he was debarred by the Brahmins till then.

Madam Blavatsky, the founder of the Theosophical Society, has rightly said, "*It is perfectly certain that India never saw a more learned Sanskrit scholar, a deeper metaphysician, a more wonderful orator and a more fearless denunciator of any evil than Dayanand, since the time of Shankaracharya.*"

THE SOCIAL REFORMER

(i) Resuscitating Hinduism

It is as a social reformer that Swami Dayanand's place is most prominent, and we owe him a great debt for removing superstition and campaigning against social ills prevailing in Hindu society. Above all he gave an edge to the Hindu religion which had been gradually weakened both by internal dissensions as well as outside attacks.

(ii) Emancipation of Women

His great contribution to posterity, particularly to India, is his reforms. Swami Dayanand did a great deal for improving the lot of women. He gave girls the right to choose their partners, and expressed himself strongly against marriages of minors. He said that women should be given a place equal to that of men, and should be allowed to study the Vedas and to chant the Gayatri mantra [from both of which they had hitherto been excluded]. The Arya Samaj did a great deal in furthering women's education. *The shastras had said that if a girl had her menses in her father's house, her father as well as her brother would go to hell.* It was a ridiculous concept and the Swami phooh-phoohed it. In fostering the ancient practice of niyoga, the Swami showed his broad understanding of the natural sex instinct. Instead of letting it corrupt young widows and women whose husbands had perforce to be away for long, he harnessed it to legitimate sex. It was also a potent instrument for doing away with the stigma attached to women who failed to give birth to a male child. Being recognized by the shastras, niyoga had, he argued, the same sanctity as marriage. Bound by strict conditions it could not be called 'licensed adultery'. Besides, he gave the same advantage, in regard to niyoga, to men as to women. The system was not accepted, because it was an outrageously novel concept, despite the shastric sanction to it. Yet credit must be given to Dayanand for viewing the matter in a wide and startlingly modern light. Under the inspiration of Dayanand many women abandoned the veil and began to attend meetings of the Samaj. This prepared them also for taking part in the national struggle. Many women distinguished themselves in fighting for freedom, and some of them even became revolutionaries. The Swami was for monogamy. He taught women to devote attention to their homes and families and not run after fake fakirs and so-called holy men, who would only cheat and beguile them. Dayanand had no use for horoscopes which he called 'shoka-patras' documents of sorrow' instead of janma-patra (horoscope). He favoured intercaste marriages or at least marriages between different gotras (clan divisions). His belief was that a mixture of different castes led to stronger and healthier children. The couple should be living in distant towns, and marriages ought to be arranged, but of course with both the boy and the girl having said.

(iii) Attitude towards Castes

He gave a new meaning to Caste, making it clear that it was never the intention of the Vedas to divide the people of Aryavarta into classes by birth. It was not birth, which decided a person's status, he said, but his deeds and his worth. Thus caste divisions were not rigid or inexorable. A Brahmin who does not study the Vedas, he said, was not a Brahmin. Veda Vyasa who was the compiler of the Vedas, the Puranas and the Mahabarata was, for example, born of Satyavati, a fisherman's daughter. Dayanand tried to remove the stigma attached to shudras. Many harijans joined the Arya Samaj. He once ate the food brought to him by a shudra. When a Brahmin objected, he explained that food could be polluted only if it was brought with dishonest money, or was dirty.

- **Apostle of Modernism**

Dayanand was strikingly modern in his approach, particularly the scientific one.

(a) *Hindi, the National Language:* Sanskrit, which had been considered to be useless and obsolete by many modern reformers who imbibed the British Culture, was his medium of instruction. Though himself a Gujarati, long back he realized that Hindi could be the only unifying force among the speakers of so many regional languages. He advocated a three-language formula according to which everyone ought to be taught Hindi and English in addition to his regional language.

(b) *Marriage and other Ceremonies:* Hindus believed that when Venus was in the Sun's zodiac, marriages could not take place. Dayanand debunked this belief. Arya Samaj marriages take place at all times. The marriage ceremony (as indeed many others in Hindu society) was greatly simplified by him.

(c) *Industries and Swadeshi:* Dayanand favoured industrialization and scientific progress. He was in favour of Indians going abroad without restraint, and gathering knowledge about trade, industry and science. He even made inquiries in Germany if he could send a batch of Arya Samajists to study there. He wanted education to be compulsory. All students were to be treated alike in his Gurukuls (seminars) whether of rich or poor families, coming from the aristocracy, or commoners.

- **Cow Protection**

Dayanand opposed the slaughter of cows on economic grounds. The cow provided milk and cow-dung could be used as fuel and fertilizer. He campaigned for the protection of cows and achieved a great deal of success. According to the Vedas the cow is called Aghanya i.e., never to be killed. His movement won the sympathy of all Hindus, which was again for the Arya Samaj.

TORCH BEARER: SWAMI DAYANAND SARASWATIs

"*Lord Accept the fruits of our labour, grant us New Life, and raise among us Rishis who may enrich us with Wisdom's wealth"—Veda*

What is the greatest asset of a nation? Its pioneers and Prophets. One of them was Swami Dayanand. He is the character of a man of whom any nation and any age may be proud. Think of his passion for truth. He is not afraid of being inconsistent. Consistency, says Emerson, is the hobgoblin of little minds. Truth as he sees it, is what Dayanand worships. He leaves Saivaism for Vedantism and again Vedantism for Saivaism and Saivism for Vedism as seen in the light of Sankhya-Yoga. He is not afraid of changes; he must follow the light where it leads. An admirer says to him— "Sir: give me guru mantras." He says:— "Have I not given you the Guru mantra already? This is my guru mantra:— Believe what you regard as true and give up untruth." Can there be a nobler Religion than Reverence for Truth? Princes have no terror for this truth-teller. "Don't speak against image-worship, and the Maharaja or Kashmir will be pleased," says a high official to Dayanand. He answers with an apt quotation from Bhartrihari:

The wise do not swerve from the path of rectitude. They care neither for praise nor blame, neither for riches nor poverty; they care not if they die in a day or after the lapse of a millennium.

A high official tells him: "What you preach is good except your remarks against image-worship. Drop this part of your preaching and everyone will follow you." Dayanand says: "I cannot give up Truth." "The purpose of my life," he says in his Autobiography, "is the pursuit of truth in thought, speech and deeds. "For the sake of truth he wanders over mountains and plains for 15 years and more, visiting sadhus and sanyasins, and at the age of 36 years he becomes a pupil sitting at the feet of Swami Virajanand and serving his guru in strict accordance with the noble ancient law of the brahmachari order.

Some find fault with him for being hard upon Hindu orthodoxy. They forget it was his passion for truth that made him hard. "All creators are hard, must be hard." Said Neitzsche. He hammered hard against Hindu society to shape it a new for the service of the nation. He hammered hard to make Hinduism strong for the service of Humanity. And he was not half as hard on others as on himself.

Some find fault with him for having parted company with Madame Blavatsky, Col. Olcott and others of the Theosophical Society. Dayanand had profound belief in a "Personal" God. Worship of the infinite, as Sat-Chit-And of the Eternal as the Self-Conscious Spirit was part of Dayanand's being. His philosophical outlook, too, was different. He could not, for instance, endorse Madame Blavatsky's view of Re-incarnation— a view which we find expressed in her Isis Unveiled in the following words:

"We will, now present a few fragments of this mysterious doctrine of reincarnation, that is the appearance of the same individual, or rather of his astral monad, twice in the same planet is not a rule in Nature, it is an exception. If reason has so far developed as to become active and discriminative there is no reincarnation on this earth; for the three parts of the triune man have been united and he is capable of running the race. But when the new being has not passed beyond the condition of monad, or where, as in the idiot, the trinity has not been completed, the immortal spark which illuminates it, has to reincarnate on the earthplane as it was frustrated in its first attempt."

He desired unity whole-heartedly. "I detest," he said, "the religious warfare of sects; for they give vent to their angry passions and crude notions in the form of religion." "Extirpation of evils," said Dayanand, was "a purpose" of his life. And he would not purchase external unity by coming to terms with what to him seemed wrong. His view of unity was not pragmatic.

Even at the height of his fame, he gives himself no supernatural airs. He founds no gaddi. He refuses to make known his real name and birthplace lest after death one of his relatives be set up as his successor. He declines to be the dictator of his Samaj. He wants it to be truly democratic. He accepts no title except the simple one of "Upadeshak" i.e. "Preacher." Some of his admirers, after consulting several other members of the Arya Samaj, approach him with a request to accept the title of "Director" or "Dictator" of the Samaj. Dayanand laughs at the proposal and says: "Your suggestions smell of Guruism. I am out to break it. I do not wish to start a new sect by becoming a Guru myself". I recall the words of Confucius who was content to call himself" a transmitter and not a maker, believing in and loving the Ancients". They purpose to give Dayanand the designation: "Param Sahayak," "The supreme Helper." Dayanand laughs and asks: "Is not the Master of the Universe the Supreme Helper?" Then he says to them: "You may enlist me as an ordinary member. I am one of you."

He claims no infallibility for his views. He repeatedly asks his comrades to seek and follow truth. In his Autobiography he does not suppress truth; he confesses his faults. He relates the story of how he ran away from home to escape marriage, and how after sometime his father caught him and rebuked him for having disgraced the family. Dayanand confesses that frightened by the sight of his infuriated father he said what was *not* true: "Father: I myself desired to return home." He did *not* desire it: he ran away again and concealed himself behind the shady branches of a big tree to escape being caught again and given away in marriage when his inner resolve was to remain a life-long brahmachari, "Unfortunately", he writes in this Autobiography referring to his stay in a temple, I acquired a bad habit here. I used to drink *bhang* and sometimes I lay senseless under its effects. "Dayanand loves truth and will not suppress it. He is smoking *hookah* one day. "Look here," he says to Lala Jiwan Das who is present, "I have wished to give up smoking; I am sorry I have not yet given it up; I give it up from this moment." He never smoked again.

Dayanand trained himself in a school of hardness. In simplicity was his grandeur; in tapasya, was his strength; he became a fakir for the service of his race. Therefore has his work been blessed, and his name endures. As I have read incident after incident of his life, beautiful in brahmacharya, radiant in sacrifice. I have recalled to myself the words of Laotze, the Sage of China. "Heaven endures and earth is lasting; and why can heaven and earth endure and be lasting? Because they do not live for themselves. On that account can they endure? Therefore the True Man puts his person behind and his person comes to the front. He surrenders his person, and his person is preserved, it is not because he seeks not his own? For that reason he accomplishes his own."

TORCH BEARER

God raised this man to hold high a Torch at a time when India's millions wandered in the night. Dayanand is one of the torchbearers who have appeared, from time to time, to lead India out of darkness into the light. Dayanand's Torch was Vedic wisdom.

A German critic of Dayanand rightly says:—

"Dayanand Saraswati was a man of large views. He was a dreamer of splendid dreams. He has a vision of India purged of her superstitions, filled with the fruits of science, worshipping One God. Fitted for self-rule and honored as the primeval source of the world's science and religion. All will admit that the vision of Regenerated India seen by the prophet and founder of Arya Samaj is a splendid and inspiring one."

This splendid vision makes him, indeed, a seer, a rishi—a descendant of those Great ones who inspired and enriched the life of Aryavarta. "Teaching what is learnt from the Vedas is the work of Rishis. And whoever of those Ancient Masters does the service of teaching the Wisdom to other is a Rishi himself."

CALL OF THE DAWN

The Veda! A little over 1000 hymns having more than 10,000 mantras! And the Upanishads, too, are tiny scriptures. But how rich in wisdom! How strong in vision! How sublime in aspiration!

"May the living God purify the head! May the Holy God purify the eyes! May the Blessed God purify the throat! May the All Wise God purify the feet! May the Eternal God purify the brain! May the All pervading God purify all places!"

Mantra after mantra and sukta after sukta sound such notes of longing and aspiration, the purest ever breathed out by man. And again and again rises before these rishis the vision of God as the "All-Father," the "All-Life," the "All-Joy". "Maker and Lord of all regions," the "Supreme Being," the "Spiritual Light," that "dispels the darkness of sin." And again and again is the thought thrown out: "Peace to all heavenly bodies, to space and water and earth and air! Peace to animals and plants! Peace to all and every thing! And may this peace be ours also!"

In these hymns of our Aryan ancestors we hear voices which, we profoundly believe, have a value for the modern world. There is an Ancient that is not old, -an Ancient that dies not but like Nature renews its strength everyday. Ushas (Dawn) is, in a Vedic hymn, said to be the mother of the Gods. The Aryan rishi who lived in the Dawn of history sent us a message, which I believe to be for the salvation of the nations. And we must listen to the call of the Dawn if, indeed, we would know how to re-construct civilization. Anatole France rightly said: "Let us not lightly cast aside anything that belongs to the past; for only with the past can we rare the fabric of the future."

The scientific spirit and rational organisation of the modern age are very valuable. We cannot do without them. But the danger of these days is in their obsession with one side of life. Hence the spirit of negation and material accumulations and violence. Hence the agony of individuals and nations. It is the Spirit, the Atma, the intuition of the Eternal we have stupefied. It is the vision of Unity and Purity we have trampled upon "As the body is purified by water, so is the mind purified by truth, and the soul by tapasya—sang the Aryan rishi. It is the message of Knowledge, Unity and Tapasya the Aryan sages have left for us. There is but one life, oneself in all. And is it not true that ignorance divides but knowledge unifies? Knowledge is synthesis. Knowledge seeks unity: so we read in the old books. The message of the great Unity, of the community and kinship of all things in nature, of all nations in Humanity, of all creatures in Cosmic-Life; this is the message of an Elder-Race, the Aryan people who lived closer to the World Soul than we do in this civilization of 'bhoga' and confusion. This message this wisdom of the rishis is the call of the Dawn. And is responding to it is the hope of the awakening of those creative forces, which we need at once to build Swaraj and to help India to inaugurate a new Renaissance, a Greater Renaissance, a Re-birth of Civilization.

THE NATIONALIST

Swami Dayanand used the word 'Swaraj' for the first time. "It is a religious duty," he said, "to get rid of Europeans and all the evils that attend them. He attributed India's slavery to "idleness, negligence and internal dissensions." However good others may do, he believed "Self government is the best government." He was of the view that once people accepted the Vedic religion, which would thereby remove the prevailing sectarianism and mutual animosity, freedom would come of itself. He was in favour of democratic institutions and a people's assembly (Sabha).

THE EDUCATIONIST

Swami Dayanand believed knowledge to be of primary importance. He wanted India's young men and women to know about their ancient culture. He believed that the aim of education was not to provide jobs but to develop moral character and an ideal code of conduct. That was why he counted parents and gurus as the best teachers. He wanted education to be compulsory and universal, not excluding girls. Education could not, thus, be divorced from religion. Education did not mean mere book learning. Moral development as well as the maintenance of a good strong body was of far greater importance. Dayanand sponsored the Gurukuls in which the Vedic system of education would be adopted. Ancient Indian philosophy and literature would be taught in these. The ancient Hindu system of Brahmacharya would be revived in them.

History of Arya Samaj

Dharma means 'duty', 'virtue' or 'moral law'. According to Hindu belief there are three worldly pursuits, namely artha (possessions), kama (delights) and dharma (virtue). These are the trivarge. Beyond these is moksha or liberation. These four are known as purusharthas (literally 'what is sought by men'). Dayanand's belief was that the Vedas, and the Vedas alone, were worthy of pursuit as a means of obtaining moksha. The insistence on the Vedas did not quite impress his Calcutta audiences. Nor were the prominent reformers he met there much taken up by it. For one thing they did not favour Sanskrit and they were too westernized to accept it. Besides, they were more interested in social reforms than in religions. Christianity had taken a firmer hold there than elsewhere. The Calcutta reformers were breakers of old dogmas but they had little to offer in their place. The *Dharmatattva* observed that the Swami was still firmly embedded in the Vedas and his way was that of dharma but not 'the way of love and devotion.' That could only mean that bhakti, of which the greatest advocates were the vaishnavas, was higher than just the moral law. That was just the kind of doctrine, which Dayanand had been crusading against. Calcutta, which was in a way the home of Bengal vaishnavism, could not shake off the vaishnava fervour. So when Dayanand decided to turn to Bombay in pursuance of a long-standing invitation he had to visit the city, he began almost a new chapter of his life. The invitation had come from two prominent Bombay businessmen namely Jaikishendas Jivanrama and Dharmsi, the brother of Seth Lakmidas Khimji.

Before Dayanand's arrival, Karsondas Mulji had been carrying on a movement against the abuses of the maharajas of the Vallabhacharya sect. During the course of this he started a paper, the *Satya Prakash* (1855) and wrote an article in it entitled 'The primitive Religion of the Hindus and The Present Heterodox Opinions', the maharajas sued him for libel because of certain observations made in the article. Karsondas won the case. During the hearing, the question as to the fact whether the old Hindu doctrine had been perverted by innovators, arose a number of times. After the case ended, Karsondas pursued the matter further and brought out a pamphlet in Gujarati entitled *Veda Dharma*. In this he favoured calling the Hindu religion by the name 'Arya Dharma.' He also spoke in glowing terms about the Vedas saying that the nucleus of a pure religion was to be found in them. After Karsondas's death Lakhmidas Khimji and Mulji Thakarshi continued his work. A Veda Sabha was set up at Bombay. Lakhmidas Khimji's brother was impressed when he heard Dayanand speaking on the Vedas in Benares. Another man of the same brotherhood, Sevaklal Karsondas, rendered the account of the Benares debate into Gujarati and published it in the *Arya Mitra* before Dayanand's arrival in Bombay on 20 October, 1874. He wanted to spend eighteen months in this area, and stayed about ten months, in Bombay city. He visited western India during this period particularly the towns of Ahmedabad, Poona and Baroda.

THE GERM OF ARYA SAMAJ

The idea of an organisation had long been brewing in the Swami's mind. He had tried to form a society at Arrah in 1872 and at Benares in 1874. But these had not borne fruit. His visit to Bombay renewed the desire to form his organisation. He had already completed his *Satyarthaprakash* which would soon be available to people interested. He had written the *Sandhay* and two books on rituals, and was planning a series of documents carrying a commentary on the Vedas. Thus there was enough material to propagate his doctrines. Jordens suggests that the first mention of an organisation was made by Swami Purnanda in a pamphlet he published on behalf of Dayanand on 16 November in reply to twenty-four questions raised presumably by some Vallabhacharyas. But that had nothing to do with the Arya Samaj. Some persons who were impressed by Dayanand's exposition of the Vedas were eager to form an association. However, their efforts were overshadowed by people who were caste-minded. It was thereafter at Ahmedabad in December that Dayanand was invited by the Prarthana Samaj there to speak at their annual function. In his speech he suggested that an Arya Samaj could resusciate Hinduism by rescuing it from superstition which had caused it to degenerate. Thus it is clear that Dayanand's initial idea in constituting the Arya Samaj was not to form any body opposed to Hinduism, but only to remove the defects which he believed had crept into it. It was thus that the basis of the future Arya Samaj came about.

THE FORMING OF ARYA SAMAJ

It was against this background that Dayanand's first Arya Samaj was formed when the Swami visited Rajkot, the land of his birth, in January 1875. This however, was a kind of transformation of the existing Prarthana Samaj. It consisted of only thirty people and the Swami drew up rules for the new body. The Swami's views on certain subjects, like niyoga and early marriages, did not find favour with them, however, and Dayanand, flexible as ever, agreed not to press them. This first Arya Samaj did not last long, and was dissolved within six months due to political developments in Kathiawar leading to the dethronement of the Gaekwad by the British government. Another attempt to form an organisation made a few days after, also came to naught because the idea of the superiority of the Vedas was not acceptable to most people. When the Swami returned to Bombay on 17 February, 1875 yet another attempt was made. Rajakrishna Maharaj suggested that the Vedantic concept of the identity of atman and Brahman might be the prop for the new Samaj. But Dayanand, who did not quite share this vedantic belief would not have it.

Despite these attempts proving abortive, a general consensus was growing in favour of such as organisation which gave precedence to the Vedas. Rules were framed for such a body by Panachand Anandaji Parekh, and Dayanand went through them. On 10 April, 1875 the Arya Samaj of Bombay was inaugurated formally. Twenty-eight rules were adopted to begin with. A committee was elected from the one hundred founding members. Having had the experience of the Brahma Samaj and realizing its inherent weakness. Dayanand firmly refused to head the newly formed Samaj, and he was enrolled as an ordinary member. The Bombay Arya Samaj was the only one which lasted, and efforts to open its branches in Poona, Broach and other places proved futile.

THE PEOPLE IN THE SAMAJ

The main supporters of the Arya Samaj were the Gujarati businessmen, the shetias as they were called, and the intelligentsia, particularly Maratha brahmins. As time passed the trading classes joined the Samaj in large numbers, particularly the Vanias. Individuals of note who supported Dayanand were few. Among them was Mulji Thakarshi, a Kathiawar millower. He had been to England, and had waged a crusade against the Vallabhacharya maharajahs. He also favoured social reform and widow-remarriage. Lakhmidas Khimji, leader of the Bhatias who was engaged in the same activities as Mulji, was a member of the Bombay Arya Samaj. Mathuradas Lowji, a rich man of the Bhatia community gave large donations for the bringing out of the *Vedabhashya*. He offered a prize of Rs. 500 to anyone who could defeat the swami in debate. Chhabildas Lallubhai, who was active in municipal affairs, gave his support to Dayanand. The renowed leader M.G. Ranade got fifteen of Swami's lectures published. Although Ranade was not in complete agreement was Dayanand, he saw in the Swami a great leader and reformer, and gave him his support. He also delivered talks at the meetings of the Samaj. Another admirer of Dayanand was Mahatma Jyotirao Phule. One of the staunch supporters of the Swami was Gopalrao Hari Deshmukh. He was a famed writer who was associated with the Peshwa, and after getting an English education, had become a sessions judge in Ahmedabad. Deshmukh was against the tyranny of brahmin priests and exposed their evil ways in a series of articles he wrote for the *Prabhakar*. He was also the co-founder of *Indu Prakash*, a weekly. Though he was not favour of widow-remarriage, in practice he was bold enough to fight tradition and agreed to undergo penance for having attended such a marriage. Gopalrao became a foundation member of the Ahmedabad Arya Samaj and later president of Bombay Arya Samaj. Gopalrao was very close to Dayanand. He supported the Swami's cow-protection movement and was one of the trustees of Dayanand's will. When the Swami died, he brought out a long biographical article in his paper, Lokahitavadi.

Most of the supporters of the Arya Samaj came from the middle and lower classes, was formed its hard core. The business class formed the majority, but the brahmins too had a large membership, around forty per cent. Quite a few were drawn from the lower services such as clerks and there were a fair number of students. Members were not from the highly educated classes, and barely a fourth were maticulates. Of the students, one, namely Shyamji Krishnavarama, became a revolutionary in the freedom struggle. A detailed analysis of the various classes and strata of society forming the Bombay Arya Samaj has been made by Jordens. This shows that the business class were in the majority. Quite a number of them were supporters of the reform movement started in Bombay by Karsondas Mulji.

Organisation

The main crux of the twenty-eight rules adopted by the Bombay Samaj was that the members were to believe in God who was one, infinite and perfect. He could not be conceived of or worshipped as an idol. The theory of avataras was discredited. The Vedas were to be accepted as authoritative and followed as far as was possible. Each province was to have one main branch of the Samaj and it would have sub-branches in different places. The main branch would run a library containing Vedic literature, bring out a weekly and look after Vedic schools. The basic requirements were good character and interest in the peoples' welfare. The shows never really took shape, not in Bombay at least. Another interesting function of the committees which were formed by the Arya Samajists was the propagation of the principles of the Samaj. It was doubtless that the Christian missionaries and the Brahma Samaj which were the inspiration for this move. It was quite natural for the Arya Samaj to have preachers. Almost every new sect or religion has them, the exception being Hinduism, in which there were priests but no preachers and in which truth was to be established by open discussion and debate.

Members of the Samaj were required to work for it in so far as their domestic duties allowed. They were expected to contribute to the Samaj regularly one per cent of their earnings. They could give donations if they so desired. The funds collected went to run the Samaj, the weekly, and the Vedic schools. The Samaj was doubtlessly broadbased, and apart from belief in the Vedas, no binding principles were incorporated in it. According to one vie that is supported by Jordens and others—the Arya Samaj, was only a kind of reformed Hinduism. Jordens says, 'He (Dayanand) wanted to bring together all Hindus who agreed on a couple of very broad issues: a dedication to religious and social reform, and a conviction that this reformation had to come through a revival of Vedic religion. Bahadurmal's view is that the Arya Samaj is only a reformed version of Hinduism and that Dayanand never intended to lay the foundation of a new religion. The other view is that the Aryas were quite removed from Hindus. Perhaps the truth lies somewhere midway. The main factors in which Dayanand differed from Hinduism were only a few. Hinduism is a term which implies a variety of beliefs. A Hindu may believe in one Absolute, called Brahman. That is the advaita view of Shankara. Or he may believed in idol worship—which Dayanand abhorred. He may go every day to a temple to make his obeisance, or may not. He may wear the sacred thread or discard it. As in every religion, there are two aspects—religious philosophy and rituals. As far as the ritual aspects of Hinduism, it varies from north to south and east to west. So too does the philosophical aspect. We have already noted that there are four important points common to Hindus, whatever their philosophical beliefs and ritualistic practices. To repeat, these are—belief in the cosmic cycle (the yugas), belief in the presence of suffering in the world (called mrityuloka), belief in rebirth and a future life, belief in dharma as the moral law and in moksha (libration) as the goal of all human endeavour. The Arya Samaj believes in rebirth. The presence of suffering is implied by the theory of Karma, in which Dayanand believed. The Arya Samaj also believes in a future life, in dharma as well as in moksha. In the *Satyarathaprakasha* Dayanand defines mukti or moksha as getting rid of sorrow and acquiring happiness and being one with Brahman. Further he says: 'Mukti is achieved by obedience to God's commands; being free of immortality, bad company, evil thoughts and tendecies; fostering truthfulness, benevolence, knowledge, and justice which is impartial; practising dharma; singing God's praises, prayer, and fasting i.e. the practice of yoga; acquiring knowledge and transmitting it to others, and by pursuing dharma advancing wisdom; doing that which is noblest and impartiality and equity in all that one does—all these confer mukti on a person and does what is contrary to it leads to bondage.'

This is not much different from the Hindu belief. About the broadbasedness of the Arya Samaj, Jordens remarks that the Arya Samaj's most striking characteristic were the 'the paucity of its requirements in matters of faith the religious and social duty and the instance on decentralized autonomy...The aim of the Samaj, as expressed in rules 1-17, was kept very broad: the uplift of the whole society in both its spiritual and material aspects'. 'So too, it might be said is the case with Hinduism. One authority, a writer, who is by no means charitable to Hinduism, says 'When we think of Hindu religion we find it difficult, if not impossible to define it or even adequately describe it...It may broadly be described as a way of life and nothing more.' Belief in incarnations (avataras) and image worship, while being popular with Hindus of most schools, are not essential features of Hinduism. So when Dayanand was condemning these two, he was not necessarily breaking away from Hinduism. He disagreed mostly with the ritualistic practices of Hinduism which had been brought in by those who wished to exploit that religion for their own gain. The eclecticism and catholicity of Hinduism has caused many persons to fall into error about it, so that they have demurred even at calling it a religion. We will revert to this subject when we discuss Dayanand's philosophy.

Dayanand had studied the Brahma Samaj closely, and therefore his primary endeavour was to keep the Arya Samaj free of the defects which had led to the fall of Keshab's organisation. So he did not force any readymade doctrine on the members of his Samaj. He did not want it to become just another sect with a leader, which would cease to exist when the leader was no more. In this respect he was much like the Buddha, except that while Buddha evolved a philosophy of his own. Dayanand made the Vedas his oars and sailed on the waters of Hinduism. That was why while the Arya Samaj remained largely confined to India, Buddhism crossed the seas and became a world religion.

THE SPREAD OF ARYA SAMAJ

Dayanand's triumph in Punjab resulted in the spread of the Samaj all over the adjoining areas. People became more responsive to his ideas. Whereas previously he was taken to be an ordinary sannyasi, now he was a man of stature, a reformer as well as a sage, making out specific programmes of his visits, travelling only to prominent places and that too on invitation, accomplished by a retinue of helpers, assistants, scribes and carrying with him a sort of mini-library. He left Punjab in July 1878, and at that time he had only a little over five years of life left to him. These he spent in the United Provinces and Rajasthan, and just about six months in Bombay. He had a premonition about his approaching end and told Colonel Olcott that he (the Swami) would not live to see 1884. Despite the fact that the strain was telling on him, we worked even harder. These years witnessed:

1. The widening of the Arya Samaj and an abnormal increase in the number of its branches.
2. The spreading out of the arya Samaj towards Hinduism.
3. Efforts to extend the Arya Samaj in the land of the princes, and
4. The hectic pace of Dayanand's writings, lectures and debates. We will go on to dwell upon these points.

The Arya Samaj Spreads

(i) Dwindling Health

Dayanand's signal success in Punjab was followed by the opening of many branches of the Samaj in the plains of the United Provinces. Over sixteen branches were established here. The Swami had a sturdy frame and a healthy constitution. But the hard work now began to tell on him. During his visit to the Kumbh at Haridwar in February-April 1879 he had an attack of dysentry. He partially recovered at Dehradun, but was still weak. His condition became worse at Aligarh and he was forced to rest for five weeks at Chalesar. In early July he caught an infection of the bowels and had attacks of high fever. By now enmity had taken its toll.

As we have related the Swami's outspoken criticism of various faiths set many people against him. There were, consequently, many efforts to do away with him, particularly by poisoning. While at Badaun, he sadly remarked 'My health has been ruined [because of repeated attempts to poison him]'. He said he could have lived a hundred years, but now there was not hope of this. Nevertheless be never slackened his pace even for a moment. During his stay at the Haridwar Kumbh he met people from nine to eleven. From one to five he gave discourses, followed by talks and discussions. From seven to nine he gave special preaching to those close to him. At Agra, on a visit of about three and a half months, he gave thirty two lectures on various subjects such as God, the Vedas, cow slaughter and so forth. A branch of the Arya Samaj was established there. He followed up by twenty-six lectures at Ajmer in May-June 1881. This led to the establishment of a branch of the Samaj there too.

(ii) Debates

The debates (shastrarthas) continued unabated. However, having learnt the chaotic outcome of many of them. Dayanand's attitude changed. He insisted that rules be drawn up and that the debates were properly held with a regular chairman, scribes and so forth, and that the subject matter was pinpointed. Regular proceedings should be kept, he insisted, and the time for the debates should be prescribed. These factors, however, did not succeed in making the debates any better organised. Quite a number—as many as ten—fell through because of there being unnecessary correspondence. There were debates with the missionaries at Ajmer and Bareilly. The former, with Reverent Grey and Dr. Husband, did not materialize because of disagreement on the method of conducting the debate. The missionaries suggested written arguments while Dayanand wanted to exchange views verbally. The Bareilly debate was with Reverend J.J. Scott, the subjects being rebirth, divine reincarnation and forgiveness of sins. The discussions were inconclusive but it was a lively debate.

The debates also took place in the native states which, as we shall relate in another chapter, the Swami visited. Often the rajahs and princes were themselves keen for them. The Rao Bahadur of Masuda initiated a debate between Dayanand and Dr. Schoolbred from Mewar and another between the Swami and Jain sadhus. The former took the form of written exchanges. The Jain scholar, Sadhu Siddhakaran discussed the question of ahimsa and the practice of Jain monks wearing a cloth over their mouths to keep off insects. Dayanand disagreed with this practice. Some questions were exchanged and answered. But the Jain sadhu did not want to continue, and the debate ended abruptly. Another organised debate was held in September 1882 at Udaipur between Dayanand and a local judge, Maulvi Abdul Rahman. The discussion was about the Vedas. The Maulvi was no match for the Swami, and soon conceded the debate to him.

(iii) Pamphlets and Controversies

As we have seen, quite often written questions and answers figured in the debates. The arguments on both sides were recorded by scribes and exchanged. Thus the debate proceeded, and at times the procedure became so complicated that the debate had to be abandoned out of sheer despair of completing it. This method of question and answers, much like legal plaints and rejoinders, soon became popular whenever there was a conflict of ideas or exchange of views. Sometimes the controversies took an acrimonious turn and resulted in hard feelings. The pandits of Farukhabad sent a list of twenty-five questions to Dayanand. He replied through the local Arya Samaj journal *Bharatsudashapravartak*. The subjects covered sannyasa, free will, creation, freedom, emancipation, astrology, rites such as marriage and offerings to the ancestors, suicide and so forth. Another controversy arose between Rajah Shivaprasada and Dayanand over the Vedas and their distinction from the Brahmanas. The Swami answered the rajah's questions in a pamphet titled *Bhramacchedan* ('the destruction of error'). After the rajah's rejoinder to this Dayanand brought out a rebuttal in his *Anubhramocchedan*. Unfortunately in the latter part of the controversy, there appeared a great deal of bitterness and sarcasm which befitted neither of these two worthy opponents.

We have already mentioned a debate with a Jain Sadhu. Soon the Swami became involved in an unseemly controversy with Thakurdas, which lasted almost two years and created a great deal of bitterness. Unfortunately Dayanand was not content with stating his own views and propounding his theories. Rebuttal of various schools does form the method of approach in Indian religion and philosophy. In *Satyarathaprakasha* too, Dayanand's practice was to postulate an imaginary questioner and proceed to answer his 'question'. But it was the roughness of his approach that was sometimes resented by his opponents. It had none of the finesse of the Sanskrit aphorisms. When he criticized other faiths his outspokenness often hurt. Thakurdas objected to the Jain faith being lumped together with the Charvakas, who were more or less hedonists.

There were several stages in the philosophy of the Charvakas. In the first stage it was known as barhaspatya. It called in question all kinds of knowledge-evidence, perception and inference. It denied the authority of the Vedas. In the second stage it assumed a positive attitude and evolved the philosophy known as lokayata. The third stage was one of unadulterated hedonism whose aim was 'eat, drink and be merry, for tomorrow you may die.' In its fourth state it assumed the nature of nastika-veda. It was then that is assumed an atheistic character and ranged itself against the Vedic rites. In this it joined hands with Jainism and Buddhism. Nevertheless it was only in this single aspect that it could be considered akin to Jainism. This Dayanand's linking Jainism to the Charvaka philosophy was only in the nature of a half-truth. Both Buddhism and Jainism were much more broadbased. They could compare with Hinduism, but certainly not with the hedonistic Charvaka philosophy.

Thakurdas's indignation was, therefore understandable when in the first edition of the *Satyathaprakasha* he found the three philosophies—the Buddhist, the Jain, and the Charvakas mentioned together. Besides, Dayanand almost equated the three. In *Satyarthaprakasha* he wrote: 'The Charvakas...Buddhists and Jains believed the world to be created; that matter combines with the gunas (qualities) and creates all that exists; that there is no creator of the world. But while the Jains and Buddhists believe in the other world and in the atman, the Charvakas do not. For the rest, barring a few things, these three religions and identical in their beliefs.' Thakurdas also objected to Dayanand's claim that certain verses, quoted as being from the Jain scriptures in Dayanand's book, were actually from these. They were not to be found in any Jain scripture. Thakurdas said, and if Dayanand could prove they were so, he would apologize to the Swami and withdraw from the debate. It was a reasonable stand. But from there on the high tenor of the debate was abandoned and it sunk lower and lower.

The secretary of the Meerut Arya Samaj kept writing offensive letters to Thakurdas, but not answering the point raised by him. Finally, Dayanand closed the issue by writing two letters in which he said that the Charvaka philosophy was also the system of Brihaspati who was called Lokayata and who was a follower of the Jain sect. But still the link between the Charvaka system and the Jain sect remained to be proved. Thakurdas took the support of the Jain Rajah Shivaprasad and kept sending challenges to Dayanand for a debate, which was not taken up. Ultimately he intimated through his lawyer that if anyone could prove that the verses were opposed to Jainism he would exclude them from the second edition of the *Satyarthaprakasha*. There the matter rested. The controversy led to the Swami making a close study of the Jain faith. We find signs of this in *Satyarthaprakasha*.

Dayanand's method underwent a change during this period in as much as he tried to develop the Arya Samaj where it had taken root, instead of seeking fresh fields. An exception was his effort to spread the Samaj in the native states. Though he continued to give lectures, he depended more and more in writing books and letters.

Organisation and Rituals of Arya Samaj

Apart from these metaphysical doctrines, the religious practices and rituals of the Arya Samaj are also few and very simple. Swami Dayanand has himself laid down the procedure of their performance in his book Sanskar Vidhi.

The important occasions in man's life, such as birth, initiation for learning or education, marriage and death are celebrated in a simple way without any regard for inauspicious days or other astrological superstitions.

There is a belief in prayer and mediation for spiritual peace only, but there are no temples or idols or any prescribed sacred place of worship. The morning and evening prayers called sandhya can be briefly recited at any place within ten minutes. The shrines and certain rivers and mountains may have historical and other importance, but their is nothing divine about them. Even the cow is not a sacred animal. Dayanand advocated its protection because of its usefulness.

The Arya Samajists do not believe in fast or vigil for religious merit. They do not worship the fire as is commonly misunderstood. The haven or yajna is performed in order to recite Vedic mantras. This is done mostly on special occasions when the relevant hymns and mantras are recited and these recitations and generally explained in the language of the people.

A religions to be a living force must also provide some practical guidelines to its followers besides prescribing doctrines and tenets. The Arya Samajists do this in a simple and practical manner. It demands are neither too many nor too heavy. However, those who want to achieve higher spiritual merit and satisfaction, can do so by yogic meditation in which Swami Dayanand himself had achieved high proficiency. He however, denounced the exhibition or show of yogic feats or miracles, which are the tricks of the trade of most of the present day Godmen in India.

The Creed—Arya Samaj

The beliefs of the founder, Dayanand Saraswati, which now form the theology of the Arya Samaj, are given at the end of the Satyarth Prakash under the title "Swa Mantavya Amantavya", i.e. "my beliefs and disbeliefs."

We have already described Dayanand's conception of God and the acceptance of the Veda as the revealed book of God (Principles, 1, 2 and 3). He has explained them in chapters VII and I of the Satyarth Prakash as well as in "Swa-Mantavya Amantavya". The following are some of his other religious tenets, which constitute the distinguishing features of the Arya Samaj from other facts:—

Eternals

There are three eternals, that is without any beginning or end (anadi and anant). There are God, the Soul and the Matter. There are the root cause of the universe.

Thus, according to Dayanand matter or the prakriti and the soul have their independent existence, coequal with God and therefore, God is not the 'creator' either of the material world or of the souls of man.

The creation or srishti means the organised conjunction of separate substances into various forms. Thus God is supposed to be only the shaper or arranger of things already in existence.

The Creation

In chapter VIII of the Satyarthprakash, Swami Dayanand explains his theory of the creation of the universe and the principle of causation and says that God is only the nimitya karan, i.e., agental cause while prakriti or matter is the material cause or upadan karan and the tools or means used is the sadharan karan or the auxiliary cause. For example, the potter is the agental cause or nimitya karan; while the earth with which the pot is made is the upaḍan karan or the material cause, and the wheel on which the pot is made is the auxiliary cause or sadharan karan.

Salvation or emancipation is the release from all sorts or pain and immersion in the all pervading God and his universe.

Dayanand, therefore does not believe in the transformation of soul into God, which is the usual meaning of salvation according to Vedanta. According to him the soul is the eternal and immortal and enjoys bliss by way of emancipation.

"I understand by the terms Deva, a man of learning, by Asur, the uneducated and ignorant, by Rakshasha—the sinner, and by Pishacha—the unclean," says Dayanand.

This refutes the commonplace belief in gods as some superhuman beings. It also rejects the conceptions about the existence of demons, spirits, or devils so commonly found amongst the Hindus, and some other religion.

Teertha (sacred place) is that which helps in crossing the ocean of misery. (Literally, teertha is derived from tira or to swim and hence this interpretation.) Dayanand further says that, "Teertha consists of all good actions, such as truthfulness, learning, good company, the practice, of Yoga, diligence, education, etc. I do not look upon any waters or places of pilgrimage as Teerthas."

This is a revolutionary concept which refutes the common Hindu belief that a dip in the sacred water of the Ganga or visits to the so-called sacred places such as Kashi and Pushkar are means of salvation. According to Dayanand, moral life and not rituals or superstitions can bring about salvation.

He says, "Dev Puja according to my belief, is the reverence shows to men of learning and to mother, father, precepter, guests, just ruler, virtuous people, a wife loyal to her husband, and a husband true to his wife. Anything contrary to this is worship of antigods. The person of the above said qualities is worthy of homage (idols of reverence) but other insentient idols of stones etc. are entirely unworthy of worship."

Swami Dayanand was the most uncompromising crusader against idol worship in any form or shape and considered it the cause of not only individual and social degradation but even of the downfall of the country. His strong opposition to idol worship is voiced in detail in chapter XI of the *Satyarthprakash*.

"Aray means the excellent man. Dasyu means a wicked man. I take these words in this sense only." The Swami Dayanand does not use the word "Arya" either in the religious sense or in the racial sense, as is commonly believed.

"Soul is free in its actions, but dependent on the law of God in facing the consequences of the actions. Similarly, God is free in doing only what is right.

"Swarg (Heaven) is the enjoyment of special kind of happiness and the acquisition of material which is conducive to such happiness.

"Narak (Hell) is the special kind of pain or the presence of that which produces that pain."

People of other religions, and particularly, Hindu believe that heaven and hell and particular places of enjoyment or of punishment for the soul. Dayanand denounces this superstition and says that these are only the conditions of the soul.

Arya Samaj in its True Perspective

The foundation of the Arya Samaj by Maharishi Dayanand Saraswati on 6 April, 1875 at Bombay was commemorated with great enthusiasm during its centenary celebrations held in 1975 all over India and at many places abroad. The colourful processions and mammoth meetings held on that occasion proved that the Samaj continues to be a popular and effective organisation in India. Glowing tributes were paid by the President, the Prime Minister, and other eminent persons to the great services rendered by the Arya Samaj in the sphere of national and political awakening, social and religious reforms, the spread of education and the emancipation of women and the downtrodden depressed classes, and its role in attempting to free the people from the shackles of caste, purdah and priesthood.

However, this record, glorious as it is not and should not be an excuse to make us complacent. It is necessary to evaluate the past achievements in order to formulate its future programme which may ensure yet another glorious century of greater service and success.

Before we venture to think of the future it is essential to understand and delineate the actual position of the Arya Samaj because of the many, misconceptions and misinterpretations about its historical background, real mission and scope. Unless this is done its future work is likely to be either hampered or misdirected.

There is no doubt that the Arya Samaj began as a revolutionary movement of all-round reformation and reawakening in the peculiar circumstances of the nineteenth century India. The advent of Swami Dayanand has been rightly described as a baffling historical phenomenon in the unlikely conditions of those days. But it was not and was never meant to be merely a reform movement, otherwise it should have come to an end like all other movements when its immediate object was realised. There was no need to have branches in India and abroad and thousands of institutions on a permanent basis.

Did the Arya Samaj complete its mission? There are people both inside and outside the Arya Samaj who have already begun to say that it has achieved its objective of paving the way for reforms in Hindu Society. Modern Hinduism is a proud achievement of the teachings and sacrifices of Swami Dayanand and the relentless efforts of the leaders of the Arya Samaj. They point out that the constitution of free India enshrines in its Directive Principles as well as in the Fundamental Rights almost everything preached and advocated by the Arya Samaj. Untouchability has been made unlawful, caste distinctions have no legal recognition, women have been granted equal status, child marriages, purdah, dowry are all on their way out. Swadeshi and Swarajya, the twin dreams of Swami Dayanand have been realised. *It was he who, although himself of Gurjarati, first declared that Hindi should be our national language.* All this is true and very satisfying; but if we remember the real aim of the foundation of the Arya Samaj and the scope of its mission, we would not fail to realise that its aim and mission were of far more abiding nature. The reform of Hindu society and freedom of India were only its immediate objectives. Perhaps a revitalised Hindu society was a necessary base for its onward march. Similarly, a politically enslaved India could not claim to preach a universal religion to the world.

A World Religion

It is significant that form its very inception the horizons of the Arya Samaj included the entire world. The ten principles are so broad-based and universal that they could easily become the basis of a world religion. The sixth principle says that, "The chief object of the Arya Samaj is to do good to the entire world, and to bring about physical, spiritual, and social progress of entire humanity." The ninth and tenth principles contain and ingredients both of socialism and democracy. They insist that the individual good can only be achieved through the good and welfare of all. Similarly, every individual has been reminded that while he is free in his personal affairs, he is bound to act according to the general will of the society in all other matters. Neither in these principles nor in any of his books is there any reference to the emancipation of Hindus only. In fact the word seems to have been deliberately avoided. Everywhere, the word "Arya" has been used and that too not in the popular sense of any race or colour, but in its original Sanskrit sense of a good, honest and a brave human being irrespective of caste, creed or nationality.

The aims and by-laws of the Paropkarini Sabha, founded by Swami Dayanand, speak of 'desh deshantar' and dweep dweepantar" i.e. all the countries and islands and habitations of the universe as the sphere of its work. Conversion of the whole world to Arya Samaj was the lofty ideal which Dayanand put before his followers. The Arya Samaj today is an international organisation with its branches and temples in India and abroad. It has over one thousand educational institutions for boys and girls and other institutions of religious and charitable nature.

It is a misconception to consider the Arya Samaj either as a reformed sect of Hinduism or only as a movement or timely organisation. At one time it was even dubbed as merely a political or even a seditious society. According to Ramsay Macdonald, former Prime Minister of England, the British Government looked upon the Arya Samaj as a secret political movement. It is well known how Sir Valentine Chirol in his book '*The Indian Unrest*' alleged that the violent and revolutionary activities against British rule were the direct results of the preaching of Swami Dayanand and the activities of Arya Samaj leaders like Lala Lajpat Rai and Bhai Parmanand and others. Sir Valentine, after a visit to India every in the nineteenth century, wrote in *The London Times*. "The whole drift of Dayanand's teachings is far less to reform Hinduism than to rouse it into active resistance to the alien influences, which threatened in his opinion, to denationalise it." This may be and is certainly true so far as the fact goes that before the foundation, ten years later in 1885 of the Indian National Congress, the Arya Samaj founded in 1875 was the only organisation which stood for nationalism and took pride in our ancient culture and civilization. Dayanand's teachings were bound to inspire national and political awakening. But, he intended the Arya Samaj to play a more abiding and permanent role in human affairs.

As he explained, during the hectic period of his wanderings and preaching throughout India and also in the vast literature left by him, Dayanand's mission, as well as that of the Arya Samaj founded by him, was to re-establish the universal religion of the Vedas.

The history of world religions show that every existing religion is either a revival in modified form or an improvement on some earlier old religion and therefore, even if Swami Dayanand did not claim to be the founder of any new religion, the Arya Samaj as it has grown or developed after his death, is undoubtedly a distinct religion in the same sense in which Islam and Christianity are. A comparative study of Vedism, Buddhism, Zaurastrianism, Judaism, Christianity and Islam proves that every founder of a new religion was only a reformer of some old religion and Dayanand was undoubtedly one who aimed not only at reforming but replacing the Hindu religion with the ancient Vedic religion.

Arya Samaj as an Organised Religion

The Oxford Advanced Dictionary defines religion as a "belief in the existence of a supernatural ruling power, the creator and controller of the Universe who has given to man a spiritual nature which continues to exist after the death of the body."

As explained later in this work, the very first two principles of the Arya Samaj fulfil this essential condition of a religion. The first principle declares that God is the source of all true knowledge and the second affirms the faith of the Arya Samaj in God and defines in detail its monotheism. Belief in God is only the general though indispensable requirement of a religion. An organised religion must have some separate scripture or book of God. The third principle of Arya Samaj fulfils this condition. It declares the Vedas to be such books.

Thirdly, there must be some founder or discover of a religion. Maharshi Dayanand occupies this position in special sense. Anyone wishing to join the Arya Samaj has to declare in writing that he believes in the teachings of Dayanand besides accepting the ten principles. In the words of Lala Lajpat Rai, the beliefs of Swami Dayanand from the creed of Arya Samaj. Lastly, the Arya Samaj is a separate organisation with its definite and written constitution. Thus, it fulfils all the essential conditions of a separate religion more than any other accepted or established religion of the world.

There is, therefore, no question of the Arya Samaj being a sect or part of Hinduism or any other religion. This misconception requires to be removed at the outset because it is as widespread as it is baseless.

This popular confusion is the result of the use of the word "Hindu" in a loose sense. It is also incorrect to confuse the terms "Hindu", "Hinduism" and "Hindu Religion", because one can be a Hindu without being a follower of Hinduism or the Hindu religion. Scholars agree that Hindu is a geographical term and originally referred to all inhabitants of Hindustan, irrespective of their religion. There cannot be any religion based on geography. We have no "Americanism", "Germanism" or "Japanism" as the religion of the people of these countries. Similarly, there is no Hinduism as the religion of all the Hindus living in Hinduism. It is significant that till recently the Americans used to call everyone from India a Hindu. Even Sir Syed Ahmed, the founder of Aligarh Muslim University, claimed to be a Hindu because he considered all those who lived in Hinduism as Hindus.

Many competent foreign observers and a large number of our own, have often credited the Arya Samaj with reforming and consolidating Hinduism. Some have even called it militant and reformed or modern Hinduism. Sir Herbert Risley had warned that, "The flame of patriotic enthusiasm will not readily arise from the cold grey ashes of philosophic compromise of Hindu religion. Before Hinduism can inspire an active sentiment of nationality, it will have to undergo a good deal of stiffening and consolidation." He further says, "The Arya Samaj seems to be striking out a path which may lead in this direction, but the tangled jungle of Hinduism bristles with obstacles and the way is long." In this context the following observations of Mr. Blunt are also significant. He says, "Orthodox Hinduism is too apt to lead to irreligious dogma. A religion which gives rituals in place of a creed and unintelligible mantras in place of religious instructions, is bound to have such a result. And a thoughtful man will often be driven to other creeds. Amidst all the religious, such a man has the choice of four. Brahmo Samaj is nothing but a limp eclecticism. It has discarded the Vedas and put nothing in their place. It has adopted a belief here and a doctrine there, and when doubt arises, leaves the individual to decide for himself. Such a religion has little vitality. Christianity and Islam are utterly irreconcilable with Hinduism in any shape or form but Arya Samaj is different."

Lala Lajpat Rai quotes Mr. Blunt to say that "An element of the strength in the Arya Samaj is its freedom from the formlessness and indefiniteness of Hindu polytheism on one side and the weakness of the Brahmo Samaj on the other. The Arya Samaj alone has provided a manly and straightforward creed." While it is correct and also a matter of great satisfaction for the Arya Samaj that its religious teachings and doctrines have been acclaimed and considered to be the basis of new and modern Hinduism yet we have to be careful in the assessment of these tributes and avoid confusing the reality with more wishful thinking, however well meant.

The Rational Basis of Arya Samaj

Reason and Religion

Religion is generally considered to be incompatible with reason and science. This is because of the many superstitious beliefs that dominate most religions and because every religion has some dogmas which are untenable in the light of modern knowledge. As scientific knowledge grows, the mysteries of nature cease to be inscrutable and supernatural and therefore, they no longer inspire awe and fear of the unknown, and the superstitions based on the fear of the unknown no longer hold good. The people begin to lose faith in these superstitions and consequently in the religious beliefs and dogmas based on them. Efforts are therefore made either to give symbolic and rational meaning to them or they are discarded by new reforms of these old religious.

One may therefore say that as knowledge proceeds, religion recedes and in the future or for some, even in the present, there will be no place or need for religion in the accepted sense of the word. It is, however, strange that comparatively newer religious like Islam and Christianity and Pauranic Hinduism have more superstitions than the simpler and older religions, such as that of the Vedic Aryas. This may be due to the occasional or periodic deterioration in the social, political and moral conditions in different countries. There seems to be a kind of cycle of enlightenment in human knowledge. There is a greater crises of faith, or scepticism and disbelief in those religions, old or new, which have a greater share of superstitious beliefs. Belief in astrology has thus become the most vulnerable aspect of Hinduism. Ordinary natural phenomena like eclipses still cause irrational panic amongst even the educated Hindus.

The modern concept of religion is based on the spiritual needs of man. In any case, it is safer to leave the mysteries of nature to the scientists and confine religion to spiritual problems related to God and the soul. These problems are and would probably always remain beyond to domain of physical science.

Belief in God or some supernatural being is essential for every religion. With growing scientific knowledge, the need for any super-human being is no doubt greatly diminished. The location of God and his throne, as well as the existence of Heaven and Hell, somewhere above or below, have lost credibility. Similarly, many functions e.g. cures attributed to God, have been taken over by doctors. Sins against God have either ceased to inspire fear or have been transferred under the jurisdiction of the estate as crimes.

All this did not, however, exclude the necessarily for the existence of God. It only made him the constitutional head of the universe. Belief in God is probably ingrained in human nature or perhaps has some intrinsic affinity with the soul and therefore, man cannot help believing in so such ultimate power or shelter, if only for his psychological and spiritual satisfaction. Even some lifelong and confirmed atheists have in their last days succumbed to this weakness as some would call it. The belief in a personal or physical God can be easily replaced by a superhuman or supernatural power, with as few functions as would be compatible with the position, and the need for God and also with the freedom of the soul. Perhaps, religion as an institution and God as its basis can survive forever or at least for a longer period life the constitutional king, if their powers and functions are limited.

The third area of challenge to religion today is the secular or non-religious aspect of our individual and social life. Whatever may have been the reason and justification for old religions to claim every aspect of life under their domain today, a religion can survive only if it restricts itself to the affairs of God and soul and leaves the rest to the social, political and other relevant human institutions. In other words, there must be complete separation, though not conflict or confrontation, between religion on the one hand and our social and political obligations towards fellow human beings on the other. That is the real meaning of secularism or separation between the state and the church.

A common civil code would take care of marriage, divorce, succession and other personal relations, which were part of religion before and are so even now in many polities. A state based on democratic socialism should look after every other human need except for the strictly spiritual ones, which cannot be and need not be regulated by the state. The concept of morality also has become secular today. This, is our opinion, is the only way in which we can respect all religions whether we consider them all true or none of them as true. This will avoid conflict amongst their followers themselves as well as with the state or the stability, the respectability, popularity and even durability of religions.

The Claims of the Arya Samaj

Let us examine the claim of the Arya Samaj that it comes nearest to fulfilling all the requirements of a rational religion and see if Dayanand was justified in exhorting his followers to convert the whole world to this universal religion *Kranvanto vishwam Aryam*. If we examine the constitution, organisation and the religious tenets of the Arya Samaj, we would find that an effort has been made to reconcile a definite creed with a rational and progressive outlook on life. This is a happy though difficult combination. Without a creed or some distinguishing and clear beliefs, it would have ceased to be a an organised religion. At the same time, without the freedom to "accept the truth and discard the untruth" as envisaged in the fourth principle of the Arya Samaj, it would have ceased to be rational and progressive. The Arya Samaj claims that it gives us a philosophy of life for this world as well as for the hereafter.

The teachings of Swami Dayanand have come to form the religion of the Arya Samaj. Some of its salient and distinguishing features are:

The ten principles of the Arya Samaj have been widely acclaimed for their universal appeal and practical unity. In fact the founder had declared them to be the only articles of faith and no other condition was laid down for joining the Arya Samaj except a declaration of belief in them. The first two principles deal with the belief in and the concept of God and the third refers to the Vedas as the book of all true knowledge. These three principles fulfil the requirements of an organised religion. The remaining emphasise the broader scope and universal appeal of the Arya Samaj movement. They are such as would be readily accepted by persons of any religion and nationality irrespective of their caste, race or creed.

The fourth principle is perhaps the most extraordinary injunction which any religion could dare give to its followers. It plays: "We should be ever ready to accept the truth and to discard the untruth." Dayanand wanted to liberate man from the clutches of all superstitions. He therefore declared: "I believe in a religion based on universal and all-embracing principles, which has always been accepted as true by mankind...which is above the hostility of all human creeds whatsoever. My sole aim is to believe in truth and help others to believe in truth."

The fifth principle emphasises that mere acceptance of truth is not enough. All our actions should also be in accordance with what we consider to be the truth, called Dharma or religious duty.

The sixth principle refers to the universal mission of the Arya Samaj. It says, "To do good to the whole world is the chief aim of this Samaj." This has been further expanded when the conception of doing good is explained in concrete terms as the all round welfare both of the individual and society. The good of the individual includes both his physical and spiritual well being. In other words, "this worldly as well as the other worldly happiness." And in the end we are reminded that the individual good is part of social progress. It is significant that this sixth principle has been described as such because the actual application of the remaining principles is intended to be achieved through this principle. The Arya Samaj tries to fulfil this aim through widespread social welfare and philanthropic activities carried out by it all these years, and which have earned for it the reputation of a great reform movement of the nineteenth century India.

The seventh principle propounds a code of individual conduct and social justice. It says, "Love and affection should be the basis of all our behaviour and dealings with other, but at the same time everyone must be given just treatment which he deserves." What can be a better reconciliation between the principle of justice and equality?

The eighth principle ordains that "The dissemination of knowledge and removal of ignorance is the duty of the Samaj and its followers." The network of over a thousand D.A.V. and other Arya Samaj schools and colleges for boys and girls without discrimination of caste or sect as well as specialised institutions like the Gurukuls, stand out as the living examples of this principle.

The ninth principle has been rightly described as the basic ideal of modern socialism. Swami Dayanand was the first modern exponent of socialism in our country. As a timely antidote to the purely individualistic and other worldly Hindu view of life, this was an inspiring call and a reminder that personal or individual good can not be realised without social good. "One should not remain contented with his own progress but should consider the progress of all as his own". This principle, therefore, contains the best solution suggested by any political thinker of alleged conflict between the individual and the society.

The tenth principle contains the secret of the successful working of modern democracy. Many a foreign and even Indian observer, wondered how Swami Dayanand could think of, and, what is more, advocate, such a concept of democracy so long before the western educate Indians and their English oriented leaders could think of adopting it. This principle reminds us that, "While we are free in individual matters, we cannot claim personal liberty in matters concerning the welfare of the society as a whole." Swami Dayanand has thus anticipated in this principle and the ninth one, those concepts of socialism and democracy, which are now the basic features of the Indian constitution. It may be pointed out that the Arya Samaj was itself organised by its founder on strictly democratic lines. In fact, it was the first democratic organisation of modern India.

Genuine Monotheism

The Arya Samaj does not accept any mediator between God and man. It actually rejects the very idea as a deviation from true belief in one, and only one God. According to Dayanand, monotheism in the real sense is inconsistent with the authority and necessity of any prophet, redeemer or guru. The exclusive and most exalted position of God is thus the distinguishing feature of the monotheism, which the Arya Samaj believes in the preaches.

An other distinctive features of the monotheism of the Arya Samaj is that, it does not believe in any physical or personal God. And therefore, there is no question of his residing in heaven or taking birth as an avatar or incarnation. The first principle says that "God is the primary and original source of all true knowledge" and the second principle describes "all the essential characteristics of its conception of God." God is incorporeal and therefore, there is no question of his being a person or having any physical existence or identity. That is why. He is "all pervading" and "free from birth, death, fear, disease or decay."

One may say that if there is a God, He can be only one who has all the characteristics given in this second principle, otherwise, there would be many inconsistencies and contradictions about Him. For example, if he is born. He cannot be immortal. Similarly, if He has a body or an abode in Heaven. He cannot possibly be everywhere or all powerful. If He is just and merciful. He cannot do or undo anything as he likes nor can He be flattered by our prayers or angered by our indifference to Him. In other words, Dayanand has tried to so rationalise the conception of God that while it satisfies the need or urge of man for God, it also makes it possible for him to continue to believe in his existence in spite of the growing advance in science and human knowledge. God is not a person whose existence we can deny or refuse to accept but it is a power, which even those who do not believe in Him can accept as the law of nature.

The Vedas are also not the name of any books as such, but they represent all true knowledge. In fact the word "Veda" means "to know" or knowledge" and therefore any scientific truth or advance in human knowledge would only mean the revelation of the secret of Nature as a result of man's wisdom inspired by God who is therefore rightly called the primary source of all true knowledge.

Search for Truth

It is significant that the fourth principle which follows the first three concerning God and the Vedas enjoins upon everyone. "To accept what has been established as truth." In fact, truth was the burning mission of Dayanand's life and by insisting on the truth as revealed by god, he has given a rational basis for his monotheism as well as for the need for the knowledge enshrined in the Vedas.

Few and Simple Rituals

Apart from these metaphysical doctrines, the religious practices and rituals of the Arya Samaj are also few and very simple. Swami Dayanand has himself laid down the procedure of their performance in his book *Sanskar Vidhi*. The important occasions in man's life, such as birth, initiation for learning or education, marriage and death and celebrated in a simple way without any regard for inauspicious days or other astrological superstitions. There is a belief in prayer and meditation for spiritual peace only, but there are no temples or idols or any prescribed sacred place of worship.

The morning and evening prayers called *Sandhay* can be briefly recited at any place within ten minutes. The shrines and certain rivers and mountains may have historical and other importance, but there is nothing divine about them. Even the cow is not a sacred animal. Dayanand advocated its protection because of its usefulness. The Arya Samajists do not believe in fast or vigil for religious merit. They do not worship the fire as is commonly misunderstood. The haven or *yajna* is performed in order to recite Vedic mantras. This is done mostly on special occasions when the relevant hymns and mantras are recited and these recitations are generally explained in the language of the people. A religion, to be a living force must also provide some practical guidelines to its followers besides prescribing doctrines and tenets. The Arya Samajists do this in a simple and practical manner. Its demands are neither too many nor too heavy. However, those who want to achieve higher spiritual merit and satisfaction, can do so by yogic meditation in which Swami Dayanand himself had achieved high proficiency. He, however, denounced the exhibition or show of yogic feats or miracles which are the tricks of the trade of most of the present day godmen in India.

We may sum up the religious principles and practices of the Arya Samaj in the words of some impartial observers. Sir Herbert Risley say, "The Arya Samaj has tried to clear the tangled jungle of Hinduism by providing a definite creed, resting upon scriptures of great antiquity and high reputation. Its teachings are bold and masculine." Mr. Blunt, in his Census report on India for 1911, says, "The Arya Samaj alone has provided a manly and straight forward creed. Amongst all the religions, such as man has the choice, the Arya Samaj offers a bold and straightforward monotheism. It bides its followers to discard all those superstitions, which he most specially dislikes. It based the order and its whole teachings on the Vedas, which he reverences deeply. Though he probably reverences nothing else, it gives him a creed that he can believe, ceremonies that he can himself carry out and a hope of salvation if his deeds are good."

Role of Arya Samaj

A reorganised Arya Samaj completely free from the vagaries of current Indian politics can, and should, not only work for the fulfilment of its universal religious mission but also play a significant role, in keeping with its glorious past, in building a new generation through the network of its educational institutions, and contribute towards the uplifting of the present deteriorating tone of our public life.

In *Rashtriya Charitra Aur Aikta* (National Character and Unity), I have ventured to give a broader meaning to "Character" by emphasising the difference between individual and personal behaviour and a social code of conduct. The post-independence politics of our country, especially of the last decade, should convince impartial observers that it is the failure to lay the foundation of a common national character, worthy of our newly acquired freedom and a corresponding code of public conduct worthy of the newly imposed responsibilities, which is primarily responsible for most of our present ills and the sorry state of our public affairs today.

No doubt, our traditional morality was individualistic, but it was based on definite spiritual and liberal religious considerations, all of which are more appropriately expressed through the unique concept of dharma or duty. In our anxiety to surpass the western concept of a "non-religious" secular state we adopted an "all religious" secularism. We even went to the extent of divorcing our entire educational system from any commonly accepted moral standards. No wonder the post-independence generation is not only indifferent to these values but is antagonistic to them in practice. Most of our younger politicians, administrators and public leaders represent this generation of the people whose individual and social behaviour is not guided by any recognised moral values. They are guided by selfish considerations only. This has resulted in the failure of almost all our present democratic institutions. They may be a transitory phase but, it does not make it less distressing. The all round deterioration in our public and political life has greatly affected even our social institutions and religious organisations, particularly the Arya Samaj, because it is also based on the same democratic pattern.

The post-independence period of the corrupting influence of politics seems to have also destroyed most of the gains of our social reform movements, as well as the traditional moral values. We should remember that man is the measure of everything and no form of government or social system can succeed if the basic human factor is not equal to the task. No wonder, therefore, our ideals are distorted and moral have been perverted on account of the political ex[illegible]

The population explosion has no doubt been one of the contributing factors. Most of our material and moral problems may be traced to the alarming rate with which our population is multiplying. The land of thirty-three crores of the legendary gods is now a simmering slum of about 70 crores of semi-fed and semi-clad illiterate people. The one striking impression which every visitor to this ancient land of milk and honey gets, is one of crowds, and crowds everywhere in the streets, in the schools, in the trains and of course in the slums. How can any political moral or even human value survive the resultant cut-throat competition for everything in this cruel struggle for sheer existence.

Nehru was supposed to be agnostic. He tried to keep the secular distance religion and politics. His successors are on the other hand making cynical use of religion, for political gain. Their real or pretended religiosity does not have even the saving grace of ignorance of credulousness. In fact it is openly admitted that their systematically published visits to pilgrim places, temples, mosques, gurus, saints, graves and tombs and their patronage of the astrologers, *tantrics* and other charlatans, was not actuated by any religious belief in them. It is merely a democratic gimmick. In fact it is admitted that they do all this only to demonstrate their solidarity and illiterate masses. It is however conveniently forgotten that this populist approach can do and is doing incalculable harm to our proclaimed objectives of making the country a progressive modern nation. These vote catching devices encourages and even promote all kinds of superstitions practices and irrational and even anti-social beliefs which not only distort our secular ideal but take the country several centuries back into the pagan or dark medieval ages from which the leaders of our renaissance tried to take it out.

There have been all kinds of plans for economic development but we never thought of laying the foundation of the basic human element by providing for a rational basis of common character without which no plans can succeed. We have made so much fuss about changing and improving our system of education but what have we achieved so far? We have only been tinkering with its external and formal structure without touching the real problem. The number of years, the number of subjects, and the frequency of examinations or at best, the medium of education have bothered us more than the real question of the national aim of education, so that it could meet the needs and requirements of the free India of our dreams. During the last 35 years we have not succeeded in producing even one generation through our schools, colleges and universities which could represent the new social order which we have been wanting to usher in, all these years. What we needed was young men and women with traits and qualities befitting the new nation and a new generation which could have replaced the old generations which were contaminated by centuries of foreign domination. It seems we laid misplaced emphasis on eschewing only religion from politics in the name of secularism but defeated the very objective by introducing politics not only in religion but in everything else, including education and morality, with disastrous consequences which are apparent. Political freedom was thought to be the panacea for all our ills but our politicians have only succeeded in destroying even some of our old virtues which we have been able to preserve in spite of long political slavery. It is a pity that only the darker side of our individual and social life has come to the surface as a result of the abuse of the political freedom and the democratic form of government, which we adopted with so much fanfare. It seems that the political freedom has removed the many constraints which kept our individual and social weaknesses suppressed so long. We have removed the old moral, religious and social checks also in the name of individual freedom. The illiterate and poverty-stricken masses on whose votes our democracy is based and our leaders thrive, hardly understand the ideology or programme of political parties. They are mostly concerned with the satisfaction of their material needs and problems of daily life and are even now guided by their traditional feudal mentality of worshipping their heroes or gods and goddesses. The only difference is that they now have political heroes and gods to follow blindly. They are too fatalistic to question and much less resent the failure of their new heroes whatever may be their faults. That is why there is no end to the capacity or ability of our people to suffer in silence. They still believe that their sufferings are the result of their own past deeds (*karma*) or the curse of gods.

S. Mulgaonkar, ex-editor of the *Indian Express*, has summed up the situation in India today as consisting of "The abyssmal poverty of the masses, the myriad of social injustices, the corruption of the ruling classes and the administration, the overbearing bureaucracy, the lawless police services, the rampant unemployment, the rising crime waves, the pressure of inflation and the shortages of essential commodities...One may indeed marvel at the extent of the Indian people's patience and suffering...An awesome responsibility rests on Mrs. Gandhi in this matter. A change of direction is imperative. The elements in that change are obvious enough. Electoral reform can brook no delay. The independence of the judiciary must be made secure against the shifting political wind. Safeguards must be created to immunize the administration from the vagaries of capricious rulers. Education at all levels must be rescued from its lost sense of purpose and direction."

The maxim that "the people get the government which they deserve", is thus fully exemplified in modern India. The party system which is supposed to be indispensable in democracy has been completely perverted in our country. While the party in power does everything to see that no opposition party thrives, or functions, the party in opposition feels that its very existence or justification depends in seeing that the government is not allowed to function. When the ruling party happens to be in opposition, it follows in the footsteps of the opposition; strikes or *dharmas*, unruly processions and protests, destruction of national property and loss of innocent lives have become features of our public life. There is no respect for law or any fear of punishment for its violation. We have seen former Chief Ministers and even Chief Judges leading agitations and courting arrest shouting anti-government slogans and asking their followers to defy the law. It is this Chief Minister who when returned to power again brazenly harangues the people to abide by the law and not to take recourse to agitation. It is taken for granted that in our present system of government it is not the merit or justice of a demand but the political sanction and strength behind it and mostly the nuisance value of the claimants, which are deciding factors in conceding them. The result is that demonstrations, boycotts and fasts have become the most popular means of getting some of the absurd, unjust and even harmful demands accepted. It is believed that creating chaos, confusion, deadlock and even resorting to political blackmail, is much more effective than the normal constitutional methods for redressing genuine or imaginary grievances. It seems our politics has gone berserk. Gandhiji laid so much emphasis on the means while our politicians have their eyes only on the ends, howsoever selfish. For them ends are more important than means which may be as unfair and foul as can be imagined. Self is considered above the party and party above the country. All the virtues are assumed in one's political followers, while every political opponent is considered to be a devil incarnate, however good, honest and sincere he may be. There are instances where proved crimes, frauds, and other misfeasances have been condoned and even pending cases on proved facts have been withdrawn with the change of the political party in power. On the other hand innocent political opponents have been persecuted and even punished for crimes which they never committed. All these facts show how dehumanised our politics has become.

The cultural revolution ushered in by Dayanand was brought to its political fruition by Gandhiji but the heady wine of newly acquired freedom so intoxicated the power hungry politicians that their in-fighting soon killed Gandhism itself, after the battle of freedom was won, as the "Yadavi" had killed Krishna after the Pandavas won the battle of Mahabharat. May be the Arya Samaj is destined to retrive the situation by reviving the true democracy of Dayanand's conception.

As we have seen earlier Dayanand did not believe only in the political democracy of free elections based on "one man one vote" irrespective of the quality of those elected or those who elect. He laid particular emphasis on the moral and intellectual calibre of our representatives. The Arya Samaj was perhaps the first and the only organisation in modern India to have a written constitution based on the democratic principles of free elections. But it is significant that Dayanand laid down some additional moral qualifications besides formal enrolment and payment of subscription. It was necessary to complete at least one year of probation period of good conduct or *sadachar*, which included not only some education but even conjugal fidelity of both the husband and wife and expressly excluded falsehood, hypocrisy and bribery—all of which were considered *durachar* or misconduct. The constitution also exempts persons of special qualifications such as learning, selfless public spirit and integrity from other conditions applicable to ordinary members. Obviously Dayanand would not have approved of what goes on in the name of democracy in our country today. He would not have accepted only the majority of numbers but would have insisted upon its quality also. He conception of majority was akin more to Rousseau's real will rather than the will of all. He recognised the importance of minority and even of the individual of democracy.

The Significance of the Arya Samaj

The Vedic Church

The Vedas are the origin of Light and the source of Truth. The Vedic Church is undoubtedly a Universal Church. It preaches that the Veda was revealed in the beginning of creation for all races. It contains germs of all sciences—physical, mental and psychical. But it cannot be denied that the glorious period of the supreme achievements of the Vedic Church was the bright period of Indian history. When India was the centre of Vedic propaganda and missionaries were sent from it to different parts of the world, it was also the seat of a world-wide empire; and Indian kings exercised direct sovereignty over Afghanistan, Baluchistan, Tibet, etc., and Indian colonists colonized Egypt, Rome, Greece, Peru and Mexico. When, therefore, the Arya Samaj sings the glory of ancient India—the land of expositors of Revealed Learning, the sacred soil where Vedic institutions flourished and put forth their choicest fruits, the holy country where Vedic Philosophy and Vedic Metaphysics attain their highest development, the sanctified clime where lived examples who embodied in their conduct the loftiest conceptions of Vedic ethical teachings—the health forces of nationalism receive an impetus, and the young nationalist who had persistently dinned into his ear the mournful formula that Indian History recorded the lamentable tale of continuous and uninterrupted humiliation, degradation, foreign subjection, external exploitation, etc., feels that his dormant national pride is aroused and his aspirations stimulated. It is also true that the nationalism which seeks the shelter of the Vedic Church is a great agent of unification of Indian races and is least productive of racial animosity or sectarian bigotry. The Arya Samaj takes us back to a Buddhism, Christianity and Mahomedanism. Rama and Sita, Krishna and Arjuna, are national heroes and heroines of whose magnificent deeds and righteous activities all Indians—without distinction of caste, creed or race—might well feel proud. The Upanishads and the Darshanas are in a peculiar manner the common heritage of all Indians in whose veins flow the blood of Kapila, Jaimini, Vyasa and Patanjali, no matter to what religion they belong now. If Sanskrit is wonderfully perfect in its structure and capable of infinite development, the credit is due to the remote ancestors of all Indians who lived and taught ages before religious squabbles, which have now split up the children of India into warring sects, were even dreamt of. So patriotism, which is the handmade of Vedicism, is lofty, inspiring, vitalizing, unifying, transquillising, soothing, bracing and exhilarating. Instead of fomenting discord, it promotes love and fosters harmony. Instead of teaching Indians to hate their foreign rulers, it trends to unite the rulers and ruled in a fraternal embrace, because it inculcates the valuable historical truth that classical culture directly and modern European culture indirectly were derived from Indian sources and therefore Europeans, being the descendants of the disciples of our forbears, are our brothers in spirit—their traditions and arts having a common origin with ours. The Vedic Church supports Indian nationalism, not only by inspiring nationalists with pride in the past and hope in the future, but also by creating reverence in the minds of non-Indian Aryas for India—the birth place, nursery and seat of development of the system of thought which alone has given them solace of mind. If devout Buddhists all over the world regard Kapilvastu with feelings of profound reverence, if the mention of the very word Palestine touches untapped springs in the Christian heart, India and especially the peninsula of Gujarat, where Dayanand was born, will become a place of pilgrimage for Aryas all over the world. Though, as we have shown above, Vedicism fosters healthy patriotism, which statesmanship like that of Morley and Minto recognizes as a force to be encouraged and enlisted on the side of law, order, evolution, orderly development and evolutionary political progress on democratic lines...there is yet another fruitful cause of misunderstanding. The Vedic Dharma, like all great religious movements that have left their mark in the world, is not only a creed, but a complete system of thought, a complete code for the guidance of humanity in all relations of life and all departments of human activity, a polity as well as a science of living—in short, a way of looking at things, a point of view. The Vedas teach us all about the ideals of individual and social conduct, of social governance and political philosophy. But they also teach us that the supreme rule of progress is righteousness. It is righteousness that exalteth nations. Righteous activity is the keystone to the arch of social polity and political authority. No nation can be regarded fit for the exercise of collective responsibility unless the individual units composing, it have learnt to be righteous in their conduct and dealings. 'Dharma is the supreme governing authority in the world the Veda declares in unequivocal terms.[1]

—Mahatma Munshi Ram And Professor Ram Deva

REFERENCE

1. One of the Authors of this article Mahatma Gandhi Ram was later known as Swami Shraddhanand—an acclaimed leader of the Arya Samaj.

Politics and Arya Samaj

Dayanand was not only a social and religious reformer, he was also the harbinger of national and political awakening. As we have seen the Arya Samaj was founded in 1875, a decade before the Indian National Congress. Dayanand had already prepared the ground long before and had declared that a good government is no substitute for self-government. The British probably had a better understanding of this aspect of Dayanand's contribution. In the words of Lala Lajpat Rai. "The foreign rulers of India have never been quite happy about the Arya Samaj. They always disliked its independent attitude and its propaganda of self-confidence, self-help, and self-reliance. The national side of its activity aroused their antagonism. The progress it made, the impressive hold which it acquired on the minds of the people, the popularity which it won in spite of its heterodoxy and its iconoclasm among the Hindus, the influence which it possessed, the immense 'go' which characterized it in all its doings, the national spirit which it aroused and developed among the Hindus, they ready self-sacrifice of its members, the independence of their tone and the rapidity with which the movement was diffused throughout India, and last, but not least, the spirit of criticism which it generated, gained for it the suspicion of the ruling bureaucracy. This suspicion more than once brought the wrath of the authorities on its members which took the shape of deportations, prosecutions, dismissals, etc."

We have seen how several contemporary English observers, both official and non-official, considered the Arya Samaj a seditious body. It was even alleged that Dayanand was more interested in resisting the foreign influences, which he considered to have denationalised the Hindus, rather than in reforming Hinduism. When the Arya Samaj became suspect in the eyes of the alien rulers, many people were dismissed from civil and military services on the sole ground that they were members of the Arya Samaj. While many weaklings deserted the organisation in the hour of its crisis, most of its leaders, who were not in politics, showed the courage of conviction and declared.

The Arya Samaj makes no secret of its mission to make men better, morally, intellectually, spiritually and socially. The Aryas cannot but recognize that they have special ties, religious, social and national, with all those who accept the Vedas as their scriptures, and as such it is their duty to do everything which will contribute to their social efficiency and make them worthy descendants of worthy forebearers (however remote). It is its mission to unfasten the chains of intellectual, moral, religious and social bondage. The Arya Samaj is for everything good in human nature, and if loving one's country and one's people is good, the Samaj stands for it and is not ashamed of it. The Arya Samaj stands for progress on solid foundations and is, therefore, engaged in building up the character of its people. Whatever the Samaj does, it does openly our schools are open, out meetings are open, our services are open, and we challenging anyone to give one single proof of the Arya Samaj having ever encouraged secrecy. In fact the complaint sometimes is that it is too outspoken and too open. It discourages sycophancy and double dealing of all kinds. Well, if all this leads to a desire for political freedom, it has no reason to say 'No' to it.

This open expression of patriotic feelings at a time when the mere utterance of *Bande Matram* (Hali Mother India) landed people in jail, involved a risk which the post-independence generation may not be able to appreciate, much less understand.

National, not Political

This critical phase in the history of the Arya Samaj should leave no room for any doubt about its national character and patriotism and that too long before the advent of any organised political parties or associations. The Arya Samaj has however, always maintained that it is a religious, social and cultural organisation and therefore it is necessary to explain its relation with politics in order to understand its true position. As noted earlier, it is national in the context of India but it is not a political organisation in the accepted sense, though it is not always possible to draw sharp lines of demarcation in human affairs. However, its world mission precludes its being a purely parochial body. During the British period nationalism became synonymous with politics and therefore even the National Congress had to swear its loyalty to the British rule, before making even modest prayers and petitions for constitutional reforms in the administration of the country. Lokmanya Tilak and Lala Lajpat Rai were supposed to be extremists because they wanted to change the loyalist character of the Indian National Congress. They were even accused of terrorist activities, involving violence and murder. It was, however, clear that they never advocated such methods, and wanted only to assert their political demands through more self-respecting and effective means It was Mahatma Gandhi, who later on made the Congress a mass political movement in the real sense. In bringing out this transition from a moderate to a radical approach, the Arya Samaj movement played a significant role as admitted by Dr. Rajendra Prasad, the first President of independent India. In fact, this radicalism in politics was similar to the approach of the Arya Samaj in the field of social and religious reform. The Congress under Mahatma Gandhi not only accepted Swarajya or full independence, which was first advocated by Dayanand, as the goal of the Congress movement, they also took over most of the social reforms initiated by the Arya Samaj as part of the national movement. This should be considered a major contribution of Dayanand. As has been noted elsewhere in this book, political radicalists like Tilak opposed even moderate social reforms in the name of nationalism which, according to them, meant defending everything of "our own", whether good or bad. On the other hand those like Gokhale and Ranade, who supported the social reforms, were considered to be pro-British moderates in politics, because they believed that political reforms must be preceded by social reforms. On the other hand the Arya Samaj took a courageous and unprecedented stand and advocated not only full political freedom but also far-reaching changes in the social and religious beliefs and practices of the people, many of which were responsible not only for their downfall but of the country as well. This stand was fully vindicated subsequently when the Congress adopted the removal of untouchability, the emancipation of women and other reforms as an important plank of its platform.

Obviously this combination of political and social change made the call of Gandhiji to join his movement all the more irresistible for the followers of the Arya Samaj, and as Gandhiji has admitted, a large number of them became his active supporters. In fact Gandhiji only took over the political leadership of the social and cultural renaissance ushered in by Dayanand. Unfortunately, the Congress lost its true character after independence, when it became a political party only. It is well known how Mahatma Gandhi apprehended and anticipated this undesirable change in its role and therefore had advised it to wind up as a political body and concentrate all its energy on constructive work. The great scramble for political power and patronage in the Congress organisation was responsible for the deplorable deterioration in the moral values for which Gandhiji stood. Other political parties also followed the bad example set by the Congress. We can imagine the fate of a religious organisation like the Arya Samaj when it too began to indulge in power politics in its own organisation.

Another damaging consequence of the inroads of power politics in the Arya Samaj movement, was the weakening of its reforming mission. Politicians have of necessity to play a populist role and cannot afford to displease the people by pointing out and much less criticising their deep-rooted prejudices and social or religious evils, as the reformers do. The Arya Samaj is primarily a religious and social reform movement and as such it is a non-political organisation. Its members are however free to join any political party, provided it is not opposed to the aims and objectives of the Samaj, Political activities, who are also active in the Arya Samaj, have however succeeded in the softening of its reformist role. In fact some observers believe that this political influence has made the Arya Samaj almost ineffective.

This may be a transitory phase but all the same it is no less distressing. The period covered by Lala Lajpat Rai's classic book on the Arya Samaj, published in 1915 marks the rise of Arya Samaj. Its subsequent history from 1920, when the Congress became popular under Gandhiji's leadership, may be considered to be the beginning of the decline of this once most powerful movement of national regeneration. This political resurgence of the pre-independence days sapped the strength and influence of the Arya Samaj, but that was in good cause and was a worthy sacrifice of which it may feel proud. But its failure to escape the corrosive influence of the all devouring Hinduism was unfortunate because it threatened its very identity.

Hindu-Muslim Politics

During the Congress movement its leaders like Lala Lajpat Rai and Swami Shradhanand, who rose to national eminence in the freedom struggle, were permanently lost to the Arya Samaj. Hundreds of thousands of its followers, who participated in this political upheaval, kept only nominal ties with the parent body which was the original source of their inspiration.

Then came the call from the Hindus. Mahatma Gandhi's over-emphasis on the cooperation of the Muslims in the freedom struggle and the failure of his Khilafat movement, gave rise to new communal tensions. Hindu leaders, including many in the Congress, began to feel that in his anxiety to placate the Muslims, Gandhiji was prone to yield to their unreasonable and even anti-communal demands. Most of these demands were at the cost of the Hindu. Thus a new era of communal politics began to replace the secular and national politics of the earlier period. It was alleged that under Mahatma Gandhi's influence the Congress failed to keep up its original secular stand and joined the race for weaning the Muslims from the British rulers and in the bargain itself assumed a communal stance. Mohammad Ali Jinnah actually called Mahatma Gandhi only a Hindu leader and the Congress merely a Hindu organisation with some Muslim showboys. The Hindu Mahasabha on the other hand dubbed Gandhiji as pro-Muslim and Congress as anti-Hindu. The resultant reaction to the alleged pro-Muslim policy of both the Congress and the British.

According to many Hindu Sangathan leaders, including Savarkar who was one of the early sufferers in the cause of the country's freedom, this was nothing but political blackmail by the Muslims who became willing pawns in the imperialist game of Divide and Rule. It was argued that the Hindus not only formed the backbone of the country, being in the majority, but also bore the actual brunt of the freedom struggle. It was therefore unfair to them and also inconsistent with wider national interest, to ignore their rightful claims in order to win the doubtful support of Muslim League and other communal bodies. The contention of these leaders was that even if the Hindu Sabha under a proven patriot like Savarkar was communal, its communalism was not anti-national even if it was considered anti-Muslim, while Muslim communalism was not only anti-Hindu but anti-national as well, because of their extra-territorial loyalties based on religion.

Subsequent events proved that the Hindu-Muslim unity formula of Mahatma Gandhi, could neither solve the communal problem, nor build a common national state. In fact, the country was actually divided on the basis of Hindu-Muslim religious differences. Perhaps the greatest bloodshed and loss of property in the history of modern India was the direct result of this division and the creation of Pakistan. It is ironical that while the secular Congress continued to recognise the communal and religious differences of the people even in political life, the so-called communal Hindu leaders advocated purely secular citizenship with equal rights for every Indian irrespective of his caste, creed or religion. The only snag in this reasoning was that the Hindus, being in majority, would always be in a dominant position. But it was argued that in democracy you cannot deprive the majority of its legitimate rights. The only rational approach was to safeguard the religious interests of the minorities, but there can and should be no political minority in a secular state.

However, this development affected the Arya Samaj a second time, as it could not ignore Gandhiji's call to join the freedom struggle in view of Swami Dayanand's strong views on self-government, so also its leaders could not refuse to come to the rescue of the Hindus in the hour of their need. Several prominent leaders of the Arya Samaj, including Bhai Parmanand who like Savarkar was sentenced to life imprisonment by the British, went to the extent of declaring that the Hindu Sangathan was their new religion. Thus the Hindu Sangathan movement depleted the energy and vitality of the Arya Samaj still further. The prospects of political power and prestige after independence proved more attractive than the doubtful gains of loyalty to the Arya Samaj. Those who did not or could not remain in the Congress joined the Hindu parties such as the Jan Sangh and the RSS. Even many of these who rejoined the Arya Samaj or remained in it, did so to exploit it for their political ambitions. In fact, they have done and are still doing, greater harm to it than those who left it. Some of them bend backwards to prove their secularism by disowning some of the basic principles and policies of the Arya Samaj or by even denigrating Swami Dayanand's religious teachings. The protagonists of Hinduism, on the other hand, have been trying to gradually infiltrate into places of authority and control in the Arya Samaj so as to absorb it back into the Hindu religion or at least to make it a reformed sect of Hinduism.

It is thus obvious that these political activists, both inside and outside the Arya Samaj, are a great source of danger to its future, which can be averted only by keeping it strictly aloof from power politics on the one hand and by insisting on its separate religious identity from Hinduism on the other. It was Lala Lajpat Rai who had long ago foreseen this dilemma. He had observed, "in the increasing friendliness with orthodox

Hinduism lies the strength of the Arya Samaj, but therein also lurks the danger of a lowering of the standard of reform. We should not like the Arya Samaj to the lost in the vast sea of Hinduism."

The developments during the 65 years since Lala Lajpat Rai gave this warning have left no choice. The Arya Samaj may or may not be in a position to defend the Hindus, but it is certainly facing its own eclipse. The Hindus today are better organised and have other and more effective means to defend themselves, and therefore the Arya Samaj should first think of preserving its own identity and existence. I would however, like to make it clear that it is not any lack of enthusiasm or love for the Hindus that makes me emphasise this need for the separate identity of the Arya Samaj. On the contrary, I feel that it is in the larger interest of the Hindus themselves that the Arya Samaj is not merged or lost in it, so that it may replace it by the simpler, rational and progressive religion of the Vedas as interpreted by Dayanand.

Political Outlook of Aryasamajists

[On 4th November 1927, it was probably for the first time that the Presidential address of Mahatma Hansraj at the Aryan Conference at Delhi, gave expression to the political views of the Arya Samajists. Here are some relevant extracts.

The conference, among others, was attended by national figures like Pt. Madan Mohan Malaviya, Shri Jamnalal Bajaj, L. Lajpat Rai and Shri Ganesh Shankar Vidyarthi.]

Swami Dayananda Saraswati believed that the Vedas are the fountain source of all the truth prevailing in any religion. He felt that there could be an end to all the communal strikes if he could convince people of the futility of most of their concepts and notions. Thus inspired, Swami Dayananda commended the right and condemned the wrong. He did not enunciate anything new to create a sensation. Every reformer when starts on his mission, judges everything on its merits and commends or condemns it accordingly.

Swami Dayananda wanted to bring reform among all the races and religions and thus to bring all of them together under one banner—the Vedic Dharma...

Yet those who wish to crush the Rishi's voice understand that this way they stand in the way of the progress of this world. If the reactionaries to Buddha, Sankara, Christ, Mohammad and Luther had succeeded in their attempts, this world would have been much backward to-day.

Those who want to suppress the Rishi's voice must remember that the English people will not give up their policy of religious tolerance. It has become a part of their conduct.

The reformers see the evils around them with such an anguish that they can't but use strong words to denounce term. The victims of these evils are thus agitated. But, in fact, the reformers' dislike is only towards the evils they see and untruth they observe. They do not, in the least mean to injure the religious sentiments of the followers of any religion.

The truth enunciated by Swamiji was meant for the entire humanity. He opened the doors of Vedic Dharma for all those who accepted this truth. It is true that for some time the Hindus had shut all the doors around them. It was not easy to open them all at once. Still, Arya Samaj has succeeded to open them gradually. It has successfully brought outsiders into its fold. Naturally, the non-Hindus are unhappy about it. They could never imagine this possibility. They believed that they could convert the followers of the Vedic Dharma into their own religion and there will come a day when not a single Hindu would be found in the whole of India. Arya Samaj has dashed all their hopes. Any one can easily understand Arya Samaj. I think this has led to the present scathing criticism of Arya Samaj by the Mohammadens. But in my opinion Mohammadens are exhibiting only their weakness by raising their voice against 'Purification' (*Shuddhi*); for centuries together, their activities of *tabligh* (Religious conversion) of the Hindus have gone unchallenged. Now Hinduism or Arya Samaj has opened its doors, for that the Mohammadens should not feel agitated. It is gratifying that all wise Muslims accept the right of the Hindus to bring people back to their fold. It is sometimes said that the Hindus are going against law in doing that. Fortunately, however, not a single instance can be quoted to illustrate or prove that the law has been broken. Contrary to it, the excesses of so many Muslims are clearly seen every day.

Some Muslims were so agitated at our unprecedented success in the efforts of 'Purification' (*Shuddhi*) that they brought tyranny on the Hindus. Some of them have fatally attacked the people, busy in this work.

These bloody events scare some Hindus. But ladies and Gentlemen, nothing can scare me or disappoint me even in this old age. When I see these things, a fire awakes in my heart—a fire of love for my religion. I am sure that the blood of the martyrs will bring good-day for the religion, for such appears to be the Lord's law. The history of various religions bears testimony to it.

It is not a touch-test the Hindus who are being struck like this? Is it not a matter of pride that in spite of this all, we have not taken law into our own hands. It is here that we see toleration in action. The reason is clear. Hindus do not consider such violent means to be a weapon for their preaching.

Not this alone, elsewhere also the Hindus have given an example of tolerance. History bears not a single comparison of the scandalous literature now published against the Hindus by certain Christians and Muslims. More than three hundred books and pamphlets have been published by the Muslims alone against Arya Samaj. Swami Dayananda has been abused in all possible manner. But Arya Samaj is proud that it neither took law in its own hands nor did it ask the government to ban this literature. It is true that certain Aryasamajists did not ignore them and wrote pamphlets in reply to these arguments, I, however, do not approve of this spirit of vengeance.

The religious teachers, irrespective of our difference of opinion, must always be respected for they made efforts to bring understanding among the people. By abusing them we close the doors of truth for their followers. These books do not fulfil the very cause for which they are written.

There is a new obstacle in the way of Hindu-Muslim unity. Muslims now want that no music be played before the mosques. It is a new demand but very strange. It is unfortunate that because of this demand, the religious processions of the Hindus have been banned. This demand is a great curb on the normal activities of the citizens which no freedom-loving person would ever tolerate. There have been mosques in India for centuries. Music has been played before them. Even in the reign of the Mohammadens, there were no restrictions on the playing of bands. Moreover, so many mosques are situated in the crowded localities of the cities—full of noise and din. Till the other day, the Muslims never objected to the band as a disturbance in their '*Namaz*'. It is a highly scandalous demand. I shall be failing in my duty if I no not say that at so many places, the local governments have not only been careless in the matter but they have been partial against the Hindus. It is the duty of the government to safeguard the interest of the peace-loving citizens. When their normal rights are being affected: it is the oppressive element that should be put to task, rather than it should have its way. In my opinion, the solution of the problem is that the Muslims should abide by the local customs.

Arya Samaj, founded to preach the Vedic Dharma in the world, considers its first duty to eradicate every evil from the present Vedic Dharma. This will strengthen its hand in its work of social reform. The founder of the Arya Samaj put forward a programme before us, which I will name as National Reconstruction Scheme. According to this scheme, we have to work on 3 fronts:

1. To plug all the holes which make the Hindus go out of their folds.
2. To make the people conscious of the fact that they should make them strong—specially physically.
3. To unite these people.

...second, but equally important, task for the national reconstruction is to improve the lost of the individual members. For this every Hindu should be physically built. It is the duty of the rich to start the *Akharas* (the wrestling centres) in order to keep their poor brethren strong. We should also find employment for the unemployed Hindus, so that they may not only earn their livelihood, but also keep themselves in proper physique. Our health has declined very much because of the evil of child-marriage. We have become very weak for want of *Brahmacharya* (chastity). Consequently not only is our birth-rate sharply declining but also we are becoming easy victims of any disease. It is, therefore, essential to stop the child-marriage forthwith. In order to build our health, we should be careful about our diet and instead of wasting a major part of our income on the performance of various customary ceremonies, we should spend in on our food.

In order to be strong and make life happier, we must have an active faith in God.

Third thing is to unite these people. The weak threads, nicely collected together, make a strong rope which can hold the ship against the storm. A disciplined and trained group of a thousand soldiers can defeat an army of thousands of untrained soldiers.

Led by Mahmood or Shahbuddin Gauri, a small country like Afghanistan defeated a number of Rajput kings with their divided groups of soldiers. A small nation though, England has yet united itself in a way that no country can stand against her. There was a time when Japan was so weak as to submit itself to the conditions of the four American ships. When, however, the Japanese succeeded in uniting themselves, they became powerful enough to defeat Russia and win respect from all quarters. These are the miracles of unity. The third thing is to unite the Hindus.

The Hindus have never recognised the value of unity. It must be understood that unity cannot be brought about merely by speeches on this subject. What we need is constant training by our parents and teachers from the very day of our birth to the day when we enter the threshold of domestic life, as to make discipline a part of our nature. This will bring cordiality in our social life.

The greatest drawback with us is that we don't know how to work as a team. As a *Rigveda* says, our salvation lies in our ability to sit together, discuss together and understand each other. The life of a nation exists in its collective force. When this unity diminishes, honesty evaporates and self-respect and culture suffer a setback. The Vedas declare that we should live like the parts of a single body; but we have wrongly interpreted it as supporting the endless divisions of Brahmanas, Kshatriyas, Vaishyas and Sudras, thus giving the Hindu Nation such a form, which has made it a laughing stock for the whole world.

Swami Dayananda attached primary importance to collective living in Arya Samaj and acting on this principle he developed this institution on democratic lines...

—Mahatma Hansraj

Arya Samaj and Education

Amongst the many valuable contributions of the Arya Samaj to our national life, its educational work is perhaps the most popular and extensive and can easily claim for itself to be the pioneer in the field of national education.

Soon after the death of Dayanand, his followers took up this work in all seriousness and it developed into a country-wide movement. The establishment of the first gurukul at Kangri was another great effort to revive the ancient system of gurukul education.

Inspired by Swami Shradhanand, who later became a prominent leader of the Indian National Congress, the Gurukuls did maintain their radical national character. They were completely independent of government control. The educational institutions of the Arya Samaj on the whole were considered to be the centres of anti-British seditious activities as was alleged by several British officials and Christian missionaries. Sir Valentine Chirol was the first to accuse Swami Dayanand and Arya Samaj leaders of anti-British activities in a series of articles in the *Pioneer*, which was then a loyalist Anglo-Indian paper.

However, it was the politically moderate wing of the Arya Samaj represented by the D.A.V. College movement which made a greater impact on the educated middle class, which was in the forefront of the Indian Renaissance in the nineteenth century.

History of English Education

The history of modern education in India is an interesting story of how and why English education was first introduced in our country. It was a subject of great and prolonged controversy not only between the Indians and the foreign rulers but also between the two groups of English men called the Orientalists and the Anglicists. The former were for status quo, that is, the use of Sanskrit by the Hindus and Persian or Arabic by the Muslims in their respective pathshalas and madrasas.

The proposal to convert the Oriental College at Agra into an Anglo-Indian College was vehemently opposed by the Orientalists because they were not in favour of introducing English literature and science excluding Sanskrit and Persian as suggested by the Anglicists. Another interesting fact was that Raja Ram Mohan Roy, as the sole spokesman for India, strongly supported the Anglicist point of view. He sincerely believed that the study of the English language and literature would open the doors of modern knowledge and liberal thoughts to our backward people. There were two other factors in support of the so-called English school. The East India Company wanted English speaking Indians as clerks in their offices so that the cost of recruiting Englishmen from England could be reduced. On the other hand, a number of Indians also welcomed it as a new opportunity for employment. Later on, when the rule of the East India Company was replaced by the British Parliament, several other administrative, political, cultural and even religious motives reinforced this Anglicist point of view which, no doubt, proved a mixed blessing or a blessing in disguise.

On the basis of Lord Macaulay's famous Minute, the then Governor-General Lord Bentinck ruled in favour of the English school, and thus the controversy was finally resolved to the great resentment of the Orientalists. Bentinck's biographer writes: Of all the acts associated with the administration of Lord William Bentinck there was none more important or of greater consequence than the new education policy inaugurated in 1834, which was based on the establishment of English as the official language of the country. This policy was an innovation, and was regarded by some of the most experienced men in India as full of danger. The East India Company respected the language as well as the religion and customs of the people, and the Orientalist school predicted innumerable evils and misfortunes from any attempt to interfere with it. To introduce English into the schools and to make it the vehicle of knowledge was represented as destructive to national learning.

It is not necessary to discuss here the danger or evils predicted by those who opposed this decision, but it is relevant for our present purpose to refer to the real motives and intentions of some of the strong supporters of this far reaching change in the education system.

The Brown Englishmen

It is believed that Lord Macaulay and more specially the Christian missionary lobby who favoured English education were motivated by the desire to alienate the English educated people from their ancient culture. It is alleged that the real intention of Lord Macaulay, who himself was the father of this new policy, was "To raise a class of persons, English in everything except in colour and blood." It was even claimed by him that no Hindu who has received an English education even remains sincerely attached to his religion. Some continue to profess it as a matter of policy, but many become atheists and some embrace Christianity. It is my firm belief that if our plans of education are followed up, there will not be a single idolater among the respectable classes in Bengal 30 years hence.

Even Macaulay made fun of the entire Sanskrit and Arabic literature when he said "A single shelf of good European library is worth the whole native literature of India and Arabic." Although he confessed, "I have no knowledge of either Sanskrit or Arabic," yet he condemned oriental literature and religion and asked, "Are we to teach false history, false astronomy, false medicine because we find them in company with false religion?" The East India Company also had no "nobler objective than to manufacture clerks to serve the needs of the British Company."

Christianising India

Another eminent educational leader of the period Dr. Alexander Duff who had influenced the introduction of English education in India said, "While we rejoice that true literature and science are to be substituted in place of what is demonstrably false, we cannot but lament that no provision has been made for substituting the only true religion-Christianity—in place of the false religion which our literature and science will inevitably demolish."

In the words of Sir Valentine Chirol, "Duff had made up his mind, that the supremacy of the English language over the vernaculars must be established as a preliminary to the Christianisation of India." Chirol further says, "The remarkable success which he had achieved not only as a teacher but as a Missionary, amongst the highest classes of Calcutta society no doubt led him to hope that, even without any active cooperation from Government the spread of English education would in itself involve the spread of both Christian ethics and Christian doctrine." Chirol further observes that the number of students in the mission schools was four times that in government schools.

Conversion and not Education

According to Syed Nurulla, "Education was never the main object of the missionaries. They aimed at conversion and were obliged to take up education work in order to meet the needs of the converted population and more specially to train up Indian assistants for their proselytising activities." Referring to Duff, Nurulla says "Duff was not satisfied with the conversions only of orphans or the members of lowest caste, described as 'Rice Christians' and therefore he wanted to liquidate Hinduism by converting Brahmins and other higher castes through the Missionary educational institutions and hoped that by this method mass conversions to Christianity would automatically follow.

Why was Arya Samaj Opposed?

In view of these revealing plans and motives of the early sponsors of the new education the apprehensions of the founders of the D.A.V. institutions were genuine and real. However in the process of meeting this challenge the Arya Samaj and its educational institutions came to be looked upon with suspicion both by the British Government as well as by the missionaries. In the words of an American contemporary visitor Myron Phelps, "It is believed that misrepresentations have been made to the Government both by Mohamedans and by Christian Missionaries. The latter particularly, having ready access to those in authority, are credited with a great deal of responsibility for the false impression. I have myself known of Christian Missionary statements being quoted as authority by a Government official against both the Gurukul and the Arya Samaj, which statements I am satisfied were outrageous slanders. As we have noted, the very fact that these institutions were established and administered by the Arya Samaj without any assistance of the government and were aimed at inculcating a spirit of self-help and patriotism, was more than sufficient in those days, to consider them as "the hotbeds of seditious activities."

D.A.V. Movement in India

[Lala Lajpat Rai in his historic book The Arya Samaj, *1915, writes: "The Eighth of the Ten Principles of the Arya Samaj points out to the Arya that he should endeavour 'to diffuse knowledge and dispel ignorance.' The Samaj as a body, and its members in their individual capacities, have accordingly been engaged in educational work of considerable importance. In the Punjab and the United Provinces, its work, its extent and volume is second to no other agency, except Government. Christian Missions maintain a large society of schools, but no single mission can claim to have as many schools for boys and girls as the Arya Samaj".*

Sri Darbari Lal is an experienced educationist, and with him as the Secretary of the Punjab D.A.V. College Trust and Managing Committee, the D.A.V. institutions are now flourishing all over the country. Outside the Punjab, there are a large number of D.A.V. Schools, which are controlled by independent Aryan trusts, not under the control of the Punjab Committee.]

Maharishi Svami Dayananda Sarasvati breathed his last on 30th October, 1883 lamented and mourned by the nation, he had so mightily striven to serve and rebuild. After his demise, followers gathered at Lahore and decided to raise a befitting memorial to perpetuate his memory.

Among the ten principles, which the Maharishi laid down for the guidance of humanity, the eradication of ignorance and illiteracy through the spread of education with the harmonious blend of Eastern Philosophy and the Western Science, was the key-stone. It was for the fulfilment of this great and noble task that the Dayananda Anglo-Vedic College Trust and Management Society was founded in 1885, which was by no means a small event in the history of Indian Renaissance in the 19th century.

The idea of establishing a High School and a College, at Lahore as mooted by Society, would have remained a dream, had not one bright young graduate of the Punjab University, Shri Hans Raj, offered to serve the Society without remuneration.

A large number of workers zealous and strongly attached to the cause was attracted towards this great soul and pioneer of the D.A.V. movement. The D.A.V. High School, Lahore, soon grew into a full-fledged D.A.V. College with Lala Hans Raj as its first Principal.

Within the span of a few years, a network of institutions sprang up to meet the demands of the changing society. After fulfiling his pledge of 25 years of honorary service, Lala Hans Raj voluntarily relinquished his office to undertake the task of religious and social uplift in the country, which, as he thought, was no less demanding.

In earlier years, the D.A.V. Society was greatly helped by Lala Lajpat Rai who later on appeared on the national scene as an illustrious patriot. His tremendous achievements in this field are a standing inspiration. He proved to be a source of great strength to Mahatma Hans Raj.

Very soon after its establishment, the D.A.V. College Trust and Management Society started expanding, with Lahore as the nucleus of its activities. Besides the usual schools and colleges, with their Science and Arts classes, it established an Ayurvedic College, and Industrial Training School, a Technical Institute, the Dayanand Brahm Maha Vidyalaya for training preachers in Vedic principles and philosophy, a College for Women, a Department of Indological Research and Publications and a Teachers' Training School. It may thus be clear that the Dayanand Anglo-Vedic Movement was a bold attempt at the creation of a new synthesis of values, taking the best elements of Eastern and Western cultures.

The demand for schools and colleges in other towns of the Punjab grew space and slowly a net-work of D.A.V. Schools, High and Middle sprang up in almost all the important towns of the undivided Punjab, Baluchistan and the D.W.F.P.

By 1947, the D.A.V. Movement had spread all over India. In respect of the educational institutions, maintained and administered by it, the D.A.V. College Managing Committee held a premier position, with 9 Arts and Science Colleges, 7 Professional and Technical Institutions, and 45 directly-managed and affiliated schools, besides a Charitable Dispensary and orphanage. A big complex of D.A.V. Institutions had been set up at Sholapur, having an Arts College, a Science College, a College of Commerce and a Law College. The total annual income of the D.A.V. College Managing Committee that year was Rs. 10,15,000/- against a recurring expenditure of Rs. 9,59,000/-. It will be worthwhile to point out that the income of the Society was mainly derived from fees charged at very nominal rates and donations collected. The British Government was offering substantial amounts of grants. But the Society repulsed the same for it did not want any strings to be attached to its functioning.

The partition of the country in 1947, with its holocaust, dealt a crippling blow to the D.A.V. Organisation, which had most of its institutions in Lahore and the erstwhile West Pakistan. The society suffered incalculable losses in men and material. Property worth over two crores of rupees was left behind. Over six dozen institutions, big and small were uprooted.

The size of our institutions left behind can very well be imagined by the extent of the accommodation we had at the hostel campus of the D.A.V. College, Lahore. Under the supervision of late Principal Mehar Chand, this hostel served as an official transit camp for the evacuation of the Hindus and the Sikhs of West Pakistan. Sometimes, as many as 25,000 refugees were being received and set everyday out of this camp. This great seat of learning and the last citadel of the Hindus and the Sikhs, rendered a great service during the dark days of partition. The end of this great institution was no less glorious than its beginning.

The D.A.V. College Managing Committee reeling under heavy losses and with its affairs in utter disarray, moved to Jullunder where it found itself completely out of its moorings. Hundreds of its employees were uprooted from their hearths and homes and were clamoring for relief and re-employment. This was not the only problem it had to face. The challenging task of catering to the educational needs of the thousands of displaced students confronted the custodians of this great Organisation.

The members of the D.A.V. College Managing Committee not least unnerved by the magnitude of the problem, stated afresh with grim determination and renewed vigour. All the available resources were mobilised for the rehabilitation and reconstruction of the uprooted institutions from Pakistan.

A Rehabilitation fund was floated and public donations were invited. The late Dr. Mehar Chand Mahajan, Former Chief Justice of India with his lieutenants and close associates, tried to meet the challenge in a big way. This herculean task was started and completed slowly but steadily. The role played by Dr. Mehar Chand Mahajan in placing the D.A.V. College Managing Committee again on a sound footing and shifting the headquarters from Jullunder to the capital of the country shall always be remembered with pride and gratitude. The name of this great luminary will be written in letters of gold in the history of the D.A.V. Movement.

The post-partition period has been a period not only of resettlement but also of planned growth and expansion. During the last three decades, the D.A.V. Institutions have not only been established in almost all important towns of the Punjab and Haryana where some sort of foothold already existed but the field of our activities has also extended far beyond these states.

We have also a number of institutions in the backward area of Orissa and Bihar. Recently we have extended our activities to North-East India and have se up recently at Agartala and Tripura State where we are engaged in the uplift of the tribal people and the weaker sections of the society. It is hoped that in years to come our unit at Agartala will develop into a big centre from where we could spread to all the States of North-East India.

The number of institutions run or managed by the society has been progressing steadily. In 1947 it stood at 60, in 1951 it rose to 82 and in 1967 to 110. Today the number has surpassed all previous levels and stand at 196 with 33 Degree Colleges, 15 Professional and Technical Institutions and 148 schools and other institutions, such as Craft Centre, Vocational Institute, Adult Education Centre and Creche/Bal Bhavan.

The Society is today a leading educational organisation in the country in the private sector. The institutions run by it are known for their patriotism, selfless service, efficiency, discipline and high standards of attainment in the academic and cultural fields ever since their inception. In the words of Mahatma Gandhi, the Arya Samaj Educational Institutions have done more than any other organisation to revive Sanskrit learning and the Vedic Culture. The Society has a proud record of dedicated service to the nation spread over almost a century. It has made tremendous contributions to the cause of education and has played a splendid role in the reconstruction of the country.

Lakh of students have passed out of the portals of the D.A.V. Institutions established by this society.

Public School

Recently there has been a great demand in our country for the public schools. It appears that the State owned schools or Govt. aided schools are not able to cater to the needs of the middle class society so far as the school education is concerned. Also, it has been noticed that more and more Christian missions are starting this type of schools, where a large number of poor Christian students are being educated at the cost of non-Christians. We in the meantime have acquired a fairly good success with our newly started public schools during the lest ten or fifteen years.

During this period we could start only three/four public schools and recently the Managing Committee has taken upon itself the responsibility of establishing a number of Public Schools in the name of "D.A.V. Public School" at various places in India and in order to implement the decision of the Managing Committee the following D.A.V. Public Schools Advisory Committee has been appointed with Shri M.N. Kapur as Chairman and Shri Darbari Lal who had been working as Administrative Officer for the last about 15 years, as Organising Secretary. The Other members of the Advisory Committee are: Shri Din Dayal, Km. V. Anand, Principal T.R. Gupta, Principal Mrs. S. Taneja, Principal Kanwal Sud, and Principal B.B. Gakhar.

It is gratifying to note that during this short span of three four years, ten Public Schools in Delhi have been set up and at Chandigarh, Panchkula and Surajpur, three more Public Schools have been established. We are also contemplating to start such Schools at Ambala, Amritsar, Panipat, Ghaziabad, Gurgaon, Jaipur and Meerut for which applications for the purchase of suitable plots of land have since been submitted. Under the able stewardship of our President, Shri Veda Vyasa, who is very keen to start such Public Schools for the benefit of the Society and during the next four or five years when we are going to celebrate the Centenary of the D.A.V. Movement in 1985-86 as many as 200 such schools will be started.

The Coal India Limited Calcutta, Central Coal field Limited Ranchi, have invited us to open D.A.V. Public Schools in the coalfield areas with the financial and other facilities to be provided by these Companies. An agreement to this effect has already been executed with these Companies. Principal N.D. Grover, Dayanand College, Hissar, has been appointed Organising Director for a period of five years in the first instance. Thus we are on the threshold of another resolution in the field of School education.

Further the A.C.C. Managing Committee have also invited us to open a complex of such schools at Surajpur and other places where their factories exist. The entire expenditure on land and buildings required for the schools will be provided by them. Thus the beginning of this century saw us starting the large number of schools in India in order to bring literacy to the lower middle and poorer classes of the country and the closing years of the century is going to see us catering to the needs of upper middle and middle classes who are keen on more meaningful education. Thus pursuant to this programme as many as 20 new Public Schools have already been opened this year.

Rural Development Project

Arya Samaj and the D.A.V. Institutions have always been in the forefront of social service activities of all descriptions. Establishment of Rural Development Centres is, at present, the most useful project for comprehensive social service in India. Its vital importance in our national economy is demonstrated by the fact that most of 20-Point Programme recently announced by the Prime Minister is related to Rural Development. It has, therefore, been decided that a vigorous programme of Rural Development Centres be taken in hand by the D.A.Vs.

During the next four years, at least 50 per cent of D.A.V. institutions should have a Rural Development Centre associated with them. We have over 200 Institutions at present and during the above-mentioned period of four years, the number is bound to the almost doubled, in view of the rapid expansion of our educational enterprises. The D.A.Vs. shall be celebrating their Centenary in June, 1986. It is expected that the D.A.V. Rural Development Project should have attained full maturity by then.

—Darbari Lal

The D.A.V. Institutions: Their Past and Future

The position of the Arya Samaj vis-a-vis the Hindu religion has assumed a new important bearing on its educational work, which has been an integral part of its aims and objects. As a religious organisation it has the same right as other religious minorities to impart religious instruction in the schools and to run educational institutions for this purpose. Under Article 25 of the Constitution every citizen is free to profess, practice and propagate his religion. Therefore, any group of individuals are also free to form an association or institution on the basis of their religion. This is further guaranteed under Article 19 (a), (b) and (c).

Educational Network

Article 30 (1) of the Constitution, however, gives certain special rights to minorities based on religion and language to establish and administer educational institutions of their choice. As a well known, the Arya Samaj has got a network of educational institutions numbering about a thousand all over India, mostly in the north, and in several places abroad. These D.A.V. schools and colleges for boys and girls, Sanskrit Vidyalayas, and Gurukuls including the Gurukul University at Haridwar have been functioning for about a century. The next largest number of non-government educational institutions belong to the Christian missionary societies. There are some denominational institutions of the Sikhs, the Jains and the Buddhists also. During the last few years the state governments, the universities and even the Boards of Secondary Education have been trying to interfere into the day to day working of the non-government educational institutions. Their internal administration is also sought to be controlled and led by the state on the plea that they receive financial assistance from the state.

What is still more surprising is that this increasing interference is resorted to in the name of "better organisation and development of education". It is however well known that many of these institutions are already doing better than similar state institutions. The real object of this control seems to be more political than academic and therefore it is all the more undesirable and objectionable.

The government have laid down conditions that unless these institutions submit to their direct or indirect control they may not be given financial aid or even academic recognition. The Christian missionary educational institutions were the first to protest against this tendency to interfere in the internal administration. A number of writ applications were filed in the Courts from time to time under Article 30 (1) against these restrictions. The High Courts and even the Supreme Court have consistently held that these restrictions on the educational institutions run by the religious or linguistic minorities are ultra-virus and contrary to the fundamental rights guaranteed under Article 30 (1).

National Objective

The D.A.V. and other educational institutions of the Arya Samaj have a glorious record of almost a century old national services. Its contribution not only in the field of education but also in almost every sphere of national activity is well known.

Unlike the mushroom growth of many communal, caste and even private personal institutions which have cropped up after independence under political patronage, the D.A.V. institutions were established with some mission and were built as a result of considerable sacrifice by devoted patriots, like Lala Lajpat Rai and Svami Shradhanand. The famous Dayanand Anglo-Vedic College at Lahore was founded soon after the death of Svami Dayanand in 1884. This College became the focal point of the D.A.V. movement throughout the country.

The aims of this movement of national education would be clear from the following excerpts from the account of its foundation:

The VIIIth principle of the Arya Samaj enjoins on its followers to diffuse knowledge and dispel ignorance.

The Samaj as a body and its members have accordingly been engaged in educational work of considerable importance.

The aim of this educational effort was described in these words: "To secure the best advantage of education it is necessary to make it national in tone and character." Referring to the rush of foreign ideas and introduction of English education and deploring its consequences on our society the report said. "This results…is the inevitable consequence of the one sided policy of education imparted through a foreign agency." To remedy this situation it was decided "To make provision for the efficient study of national language and literature and carefully to initiate the youthful mind into the habits and modes of life consistent with national spirit and character." Mahatma Hansraj whose sacrifice for the cause of D.A.V. movement is well known therefore decided to dedicated his life to "the call of duty to religion and mother land." About the policy of management of the D.A.V. institutions "it was laid down in the rules that the management should be in the hands of the elected representatives of such Arya Samajes as contributed to its funds, with the addition of few Hindus representing the professional classes."

It may not be easy to realise today, how courageous and risky it was in those days of the British rule to even think of a national language and initiate "the youthful minds with national spirit and character" and to come forward to answer "the call of duty to religion and motherland." The Arya Samaj through the D.A.V. institutions accepted this challenge and suffered for it as the history of the Arya Samaj would show. It may be remembered that the Arya Samaj sponsored this national cause ten years before the Indian National Congress came into existence. At its inception the Congress was an organisation loyal to the British rule and thanked "province for the blessings of the western education and the British rule in India." It became a national movement under Lala Lajpat Rai and Tilak and later on under Mahatma Gandhi.

Special Features of the D.A.V. Movement

The aims and objects of this new venture in the field of education are best explained by one of its founders—Lala Lajpat Rai presiding over the foundation day in London in 1914 he observed.

…It was provided in the rules that the management should be in the hands of elected representatives of such Arya Samajists as contributed to its funds, with the addition of a few Hindus representing the professions and the classes; and that rule has been acted upon without exception. No non-Hindu has been associated with the management of the College.

The second principle, nowhere recorded but generally accepted, was that the teaching should be exclusively done by Indians, and there has been no exception on this point... The results have been excellent. Our students have often headed the lists of ordinary passes, as well as honours passes, in Sanskrit and Mathematics. They have several times headed the list of English, Political Economy, History, Philosophy, Chemistry, Persian and other subjects. A considerable number of Government and University scholarships, granted on the results of University examinations, have every year been won by our students, and also medals and prizes. In the M.A. class we coach only in Sanskrit. All this has been achieved by the labours of Indian teachers unaided by any foreign agency.

The third principle (which is also an unwritten law) imposes on the managers the moral obligation not to seek monetary assistance from the Government. This principle has been acted upon, unless a petty grant of a few thousand rupees made by the University be considered an exception.

The fourth principle was to aim at giving free education. The paucity of funds, and University regulations have prevented us from giving effect to this; but still our fees have generally been 50 per cent less than those of government schools and colleges.

About the object for these principles he says:

They were not adopted in any spirit of hostility or antagonism to the British, or the Government, or any other community. The object was primarily to try an experiment in purely indigenous enterprise; secondly, to develop a spirit of self-help and self-reliance in a community in which those qualities had, by lapse of time and lack of opportunity, degenerated. Everyone who knows the Punjab, knows how well we have succeeded in this direction; probably no other province in India has developed private enterprise in education to the same extent and with the same success as we have in the Punjab. This spirit of self-help, called exclusiveness by our critics, has cost us dear, because on that account we have always been under the shadow of official mistrust. No bureaucracy loves people who can do big things without their help and guidance; much less a foreign bureaucracy. They wish to keep the strings of all public activities in their own hands, or in the hands of those who can be use as tools. We set a different standard, and so were disliked. Yet, on the whole, the attitude of the Department and the University towards us has not been unfair. They have generally given us credit for our work, and praised our public spirit, but they have never been at ease with us. Once or twice when we sought their help to acquire land for a building site and play grounds, they would not oblige. Lately they have compulsorily requisitioned a piece of land, which we had secured with great trouble and after protracted litigation, and refused to give us in lieu one of the Government plot lying under our own walls. But this is only 'en passant'. The general attitude of the Department and the University has been fair, though both have often been influenced in framing new regulations by the fact that our School and College were formidable rivals to the Government and aided institutions of similar nature.[1]

Freedom and Initiative

Even now it is generally admitted that most of the non-government educational institutions have proved better in many respects than the state managed ones, primarily because they enjoy a certain amount of freedom and initiative which may not be possible in government schools under the rigid government rules and regulations. Moreover, these institutions are run by persons who are by and large devoted to a cause and are actuated by a spirit of service. Therefore, they take personal interest and identify themselves with these institutions in a way which cannot be expected from government servants. The principals and teachers in government institutions are liable to be transferred from one institution to another and this is another reason why it is not possible for them to identify with the progress and well being of the students of a particular institutions.

Freedom of Management

The D.A.V. institutions, some of which have been in existence for about 100 years, had always enjoyed this freedom and their managing bodies have always been composed of persons having faith in the Arya Samaj. For example, the Constitution of the Arya Samaj Shiksha Sabha, Ajmer, makes it clear that at least two-thirds of its members must be regular members of the Arya Samaj (Rule 4 *ka, kha, sa*) and others also should come from either donors or members of the general body. The persons who manage the D.A.V. institutions and those who are responsible for its internal administration and teachings have been generally those who share the ideology of the Arya Samaj and that is why the Arya Samaj educational institutions have been able to maintain their great traditions.

Sense of Duty

Most of the teachers of non-government schools spend their lives in the same institution and thus develop a kind of vested interest in them.

The D.A.V. institutions generally are noted for some of these special features. Their results in the public examinations, their discipline and a general atmosphere of nationalist and progressive thinking in social as well as religious matters, have all been appreciated and acknowledged. If these institutions are now deprived of their distinguishing features they would no longer be able to maintain their long and well established record of service which would be a great loss not only to the cause of education but also to the national interest. It is generally, admitted that there should be greater individual freedom and initiative in the field of thinking, and educational institutions are the only place where freedom of thought can thrive and develop.

Religious Education

Religious and moral education has been a regular feature of these institutions. Havans and functions connected with the life and teachings of Svami Dayanand are special features of these institutions. There are regular textbooks for each class called *Dharma Shiksha* which are used for giving the religious instruction. In actual practice it is the principal or the headmasters, and the teachers who are supposed to implement and keep up these traditions. Obviously, therefore, the management must have a free hand in selecting suitable teachers for this purpose, provided they are otherwise qualified according to the academic standards prescribed by the universities or the Board of Education.

Countermining the denationalising influences of Macaulay's education was one of the objects of the D.A.V. movement. How admirably the D.A.V. institutions succeeded in their aim, may be seen from the observations of a well-known detractor of the Arya Samaj Sir Valentine Chirol, who says:

Their influence has been constantly exerted to check the marriages between mere boys and almost infant girls which have done so much physical as well as moral mischief to Hindu society, and also to improve the wretched lot of Hindu widows whose widowhood with all that it entails of mental degradation often beings before they have ever really been wives. To this end the Aryas have not hesitated to encourage female education, and the girls' orphanage at Jullandar, where there is also a widows' home, show what excellent social results can be achieved in that direction. Again in the treatment of the 'untouchable' low castes, the Arya Samaj may claim to have been the first native body to break new ground and to attempt something akin to the work of social reclamation of which Christianity and in a lesser degree, Islam had hitherto had the monopoly. Schools and especially industrial classes have been established in various districts which cannot fail to raise the status of the younger generation and gradually to emancipate the lower castes from the bondage in which they have been hitherto held. These and many other new departures conceived in the same liberal spirit at first provoked the vehement hostility of the orthodox Hindus, who at one time stopped all social intercourse with the Arya reformers. But whereas in other parts of India the idea of social reform came to the associated with that of western ascendancy and therefore weakened and gave way before the rising tide of reaction against that ascendancy, it has been associated in the Punjab with the cry of 'Arya for the Aryans,' and the political activities of the Arya Samaj, or at least of a number of its most prominent members who have figured conspicuously in the anti-British agitation of the last few years, have secured for it from Hindu orthodoxy a measure of tolerance and even of goodwill which its social activities would certainly not otherwise have received. That the Arya Samaj, which shows the impress of western influence in so much of its social work, should at the same time have associated itself so intimately with a political movement directed against British rule is one of the many anomalies presented by the problem of Indian unrest.[2]

These remarks were obviously made in support of the then prevailing suspicion against the Arya Samaj as a political organisation, but in the light of subsequent developments leading to the freedom of the country, they are not only a tribute, through a grudging one, to the Arya Samaj and its educational work but also show how it was successful in its mission.

A Doubtful Future

These very Arya Samaj institutions which pioneered the national basis of our education are facing discrimination and that too under our national government. While Article 30 (1) gives the Christian missionary institutions full freedom, the Arya Samaj institutions are denied similar facilities merely because they did not claim separate political rights to qualify for being a religious minority in the so-called technical sense. It is obvious that these institutions of the Arya Samaj cannot exist now without aid and assistance from the government. In fact it is their right to expect and claim such assistance from their own government which they once refused to take from a foreign government in order to preserve their freedom. It is therefore unfortunate if the government of free India should compel them to sacrifice their autonomy and utility in return for state aid and assistanc. ' hich are guaranteed under Article 30 (1), to educational institutions ot other religious minorities. In the face of the High Court decisions and the verdict of the highest judicial authority, the Supreme Court, there can be no doubt that the institutions of the Arya Samaj are entitled to similar protection under Article 30 (1). However, even if there is any doubt it is merely a technical one which can and should be set aside as is being done in the case of the Aligarh Muslim University. The claim of the University is even weaker than that of the Arya Samaj in view of the fact that the Supreme Court has already declared that neither on facts nor in law is the Aligarh University covered under Article 30 (1). As a matter of fact there is no moral or legal justification for denying the Hindus at least an equal right with the minorities only because the Hindus are in majority.

A Way Out

The late Shri Kumaramangalam representing the State of Kerala in the case of *Mother Provost versus the State* (AIR, 1970, SC 2977) had given an assurance that if any restrictions and conditions are considered ultra-virus and therefore, inapplicable to the Christian institutions because of Article 30 (1) then such conditions and restrictions would not be forced on the educational institutions of the majority community also. This assurance besides being just and proper is the only way to remove this discrimination against the majority community in a sensitive matter like the freedom of religion in its educational institutions.

EDUCATION AS A PART OF RELIGIOUS FREEDOM

Religious freedom is now universally recognised as an inviolable right. The declaration of human rights by the UN therefore, specifically includes this right in clause XVIII and XIX. The late Shri K.M. Munshi who prepared the draft of these rights of our Constitution, had pointed out that freedom of religion is included in most of the constitution.[3]

Background of Article 30

The various aspects of religious freedom are grouped under Articles 25 to 30 of the Fundamental Rights. There is a close connection between Articles 25, 26 and 30. In fact they have a common origin under Article 16 of Munshi's original draft[4] under the common title "Religious and Cultural Rights."[5] The Article was later on split up to give effect to the various aspects of the same right. Item No. 3 under Article VI of the draft was split into Articles 26 and 30. And item No. 1 is the present Article 25. The original clause VI was again split as under:

Sub-clause (i) is Article 29.

Sub-clause (ii) is Article 29 (i).

Sub-section 3 (a) is Article 30 (1) and 3 (b) is 30 (2).

Thus Article 30 (1), though now under the separate head "Cultural and Educational Rights," basically constitutes a religious and cultural right. In fact it says so by referring to minorities based on religion and language.

The present Article 30 reads. "All minorities whether based on religion or language shall have the right to establish and administer educational institutions of their choice."

It is thus clear that the establishment of educational institutions is an essential part of the religious freedom given under Article 25 which guarantees the right "to profess and even to propagate religion." This is admitted by the Supreme Court in 1958 SC 960,[6] where it is held that all these Articles belong to the same category. Article 26 gives the right to religious denominations in respect or religious and charitable institutions and education has been considered a charitable purpose. The various Religious and Charitable Trusts Acts passed by the state legislatures include education under the definition of charitable purpose as would be clear from the Trust Act of UP, Rajasthan and Bombay. In the ancient Indian tradition education has been called the best form of charity—*sarvesham dananam brahmadanam vishishyatey.*

Dr. Ambedkar had pointed out that Article 19 included the right to form associations based on religion also and this right is conceded under Article 19 of our Constitutions.[7] Therefore, the right of religious freedom given to individuals in Article 25 is equally available to religious associations like the Arya Samaj, even if it is considered to be a part of Hindu community. The term "religious" under Article 30(1) in respect of educational institutions should therefore be given wider and liberal meaning in the context of Articles 25 and 26 so as to include well defined religious organisations like the Arya Samaj, in their purview.

Education has always been one of the chief aims of the Arya Samaj. Swami Dayanand made specific mention of it in his will.[8] We have already seen how he placed great emphasis on suitable education of both boys and girls, in the eighth article of the Samaj. He also wrote a separate chapter on education in his *Satyarth Prakash*.

Right of Hindus

If educational institutions are considered essential for the preservation and propagation of the religion of the minorities under Article 30, how can this same right be denied to other religious organisations, even if they are supposed to be parts of the Hindu majority community. Giving protection to the minorities in the matter of religion does not and should not mean that the majority has no such right to preserve and preach its religion when even individuals have been given the right under Article 25. It should be remembered that it is religion which is the basis of the right given under Article 30 (1) and not any political, social and economic concession or considerations. The Right to Propagate Religion was specifically added under Article 25 on the demand of the Christians and the Muslims because they claimed to be proselytising religions and consequently it has been held by the Supreme Court that educational institutions are necessary and effective means of preserving and propagating their religion and culture.[9] Judicial decisions 1958 SC 961 (h) as also 1974 SC 1939 sum up the laws in this respect. Justice Mathew specially emphasised the importance of educational institutions in the context of religious freedom, Justice Dwivedi also endorsed his view in para 274 of this judgement.[10]

Arya Samaj and Propagation of Religion

The non-Arya Samaj Hindus who are in majority and are called *Pauranic Hindus* may not feel concerned so much, because they do not believe in coverting other people to their religion. As Mahatma Gandhi pointed out, Sanatan Dharma is not a missionary religion.[11] It is argued that the Sanatan Hindu Dharma is very Catholic and liberal which believes all religions to be true and follows different paths for the realisation of the same goal. Obviously, therefore, proselytisation may have place in it. The Arya Samaj on the other hand believes that the only true religion is its Vedic religion and, therefore, like the Muslims they consider it their duty to preach and propagate it amongst others. Thus if the Arya Samaj is denied similar rights as are given to the Christians or the Muslims under Article 30(1), the would not be able to enjoy the religious freedom guaranteed under Article 25.

It may be noted that the Sikhs, Jains and the Buddhists are now considered eligible for this right to administer their educational institutions under Article 30(1) as religious minorities, not so much because they are distinct or separate religions but because they claimed or supposed to have claimed certain separate political rights.[12] At least the Jains do not practice proselytisation and, therefore, may not need educational institutions for propagating their religion, although they are also entitled to give religious instruction to their own followers.

Propagation of Vedic Religion

The Arya Samaj on the other hand claims this right, exclusively on the basis of its religious beliefs and doctrines which clearly enjoin upon it to propagate its religion through educational institutions. It is their fundamental right also under Article 25 to provide facilities for religious instruction to their children for which purpose they may, and have actually, set up educational institutions. The Arya Samaj has always been a missionary organisation from the very beginning. Its founder Svami Dayanand had himself spent the best part of his life in preaching the Vedic religion of his concept. He toured a most the whole of north India and wherever he went, he did not only deliver sermons, and enter into religious disputations with the followers of other religions but also established schools and pathshalas for the purpose of teaching Sanskrit and Hindi as well as for propagating his religious doctrines. In his lectures in Poona as well as in his Will he has emphasised the need of sending missionaries all over the world to preach the message of the Vedas. Thus the Arya Samaj claims this right not on the basis of any extraneous political consideration, like other minorities, but solely on the basis of its obligation to propagate religion through educational institutions. Its claim is therefore founded on the sole argument that religion and religion alone should be the sole basis of this right under Article 30(1) besides of course the language. In any case this article guarantees cultural and religious freedom and should have nothing to do with any political consideration as wrongly held by Delhi High Court.

We have discussed how freedom of religion has been interpreted to include the right to profess and propagate religion through educational institutions as well. It would, therefore, be worthwhile to analyse the relevant judgment of the Supreme Court, which forms the basis of this aspect of religious freedom. My contention is that instead of conferring this freedom to establish and administer educational institutions for the students of their own religion or for giving religious instruction to them, the right to establish such institutions for general secular education for the followers of other religions also, is based entirely on the judicial interpretation rather than the intention or the language of the framers of the Article. It is also held by several High Courts and the Supreme Court that these institutions will be entitled to receive financial assistance from the state and would still be free from the control of the Government or the Universities to which the educational institutions run by the majority community are usually subject.

Education and the Minorities

The first and perhaps the basis judicial verdict on Article 30(1) is contained in the advisory opinion of the supreme Court on the Kerala Education Bill.[13] The views expressed in this judgment have been followed in all the subsequent decisions on Articles 26, 29 and 30.

In this important pronouncement it was held that the educational institutions are essential and necessary means or religious freedom given to the minorities, who have the freedom to propagate their religion. It is observed by the court that "The minorities evidently desire that education should be imparted to the children of their community in an atmosphere congenial to the growth of their religion." "The Constitution makers recognised the value of their claim and conferred on them the fundamental rights under Articles 29 and 30."[14]

, Again it says, "The educational institutions protected by Article 30(1) might impart purely religious instruction. Indeed, it seems likely that it is such institutions that the primarily to be protected under Article(1)."[15] Then again at the end of the same page it says, "Article 30(1) belongs to the same category as Articles 25, 26 and 29 so that their educational institutions may be administered without interference and the minorities be allowed to live their own cultural lives as regards religion and language. It is further held that "A minority community can effectively conserve its language, script or culture by and through educational institutions and, therefore, the right to establish and maintain the educational institution of their choice under Article 30(1)." In Note J at the it is remarked, "Indeed the object of conservation of the distinct language, script and culture of a minority can be better served by propagating the same amongst non-members of the particular community."[16] Further it is observed, "The Articles leave it to their choice to establish such educational institutions as will serve both the purposes, i.e., the purpose of conserving their religion, language and cultural and also the purpose of giving a thorough good education to their children.[17]

The latest and the most comprehensive verdict of the Supreme Court on this point is given in the case of the St. Xavier's College, Ahmedabad.[18] This important judgment confirms, and even extends further, what was held in the Kerala Education Bill case.

Religion at the Basis of Education

Justice Mathew on his own and on behalf of Justice Chardrachud (now the Chief Justice of India) has dealt with this religious basis of educational institutions vividly and in detail in paragraphs 135, 136, 137, 145, 147 and 183. Quoting from Ronald Eugene Smith, *Is India a Secular State?* Justice Mathew observed in para 136, "It is important to examine the raison d'etre of educational institutions administered by religious groups...such schools are started with a primary religious objective." We may add here another significant part of Smith's quotation, "In other words a religious body establishes and maintains schools in order to create a total environment which will be favourable to the promotion of its particular religious values." In para 114, Justice Mathew observes, "The religious minority should have the guaranteed right to establish and administer its own educational institutions where it can impart secular education in a religious atmosphere."

Views of the Pope

Justice Dwivedi is, therefore, right when he says, "in para 274 on the authority of the Pope himself, that the Catholic educational institutions believe that education belongs to the Church and the Catholic dogma categorically denies the premise that secular general education can be isolated from religious teachings." Pope Pius XI is quoted to have said that "Catholic educational institutions are those where Catholic religion permeates the entire atmosphere and where all teachings, organisations, teachings, syllabuses and text-books are regulated by Christian spirits."

In fact almost all judges of the Supreme Court while concurring with the majority judgment delivered by the Chief Justice Ray have emphasised the religious objects of these institutions run by the minorities and have held that any conditions of recognition or for grant-in-aid which result in the surrender of their rights under Article 30 would be improper and ultra-vires.

Right of the Majority

Justice Khanna (in para 17) referring to Article 25 about the right to profess and propagate religion and to establish religious charitable institutions under Article 26 quotes Articles 28, 29 and 30 and observes in para 73 that in spite of the use of the word minority in the marginal note, Article 29 gives that right both to the majority and the minority and in para 74, he agrees with the view that the management must be free to mould the institution in accordance with the ideals of the founders.

He observes (on para 1414, Col.. II) that the object of Articles 25 to 30 was to give the right to preserve and propagate religion for which purpose Fundamental Rights under Articles 25 to 30 are given.

The important question which arises in view of these observations is, what about the right of the majority community to similar freedom of religion? The justification for special protection for the minorities is said to be the fear that the majority may suppress or interfere with their religious freedom. Therefore, it is necessary that there should be no discrimination against the minorities but discrimination is one thing and special or exclusive privilege is another thing. The ideal situation, therefore, would be that the minority should enjoy their freedom without depriving the majority of its similar freedom, specially when there is no conflict as in the case of religious freedom.

Article 30 Abused

However, Article 30(1) goes beyond a mere safeguard against any interference in the religious affairs of the minorities. It confers on them a positive right to establish separate educational institutions, to give religious instruction in their educational institutions run practically at the cost of the state because sub-clause (2) of Article 30 guarantees state assistance also to these institutions and this financial assistance comes to 90 to 95 per cent of the total expenditure and in some cased 100 per cent of the teachers cost which is the major portion of their budget. What is significant is that the minorities are not only free to give religious instruction to their own children but also to the students of other communities as has been held in the matter of the Kerala Education Bill.

Why Not Hindus?

Now the question is how the majority community can also enjoy the freedom of their religion through educational institutions unless it is argued that they have no such right in spite of what is said in Article 25 which gives equal freedom to every minority and majority. The Hindu Community with religious divisions cannot possibly make use of their majority for giving religious instruction through the state educational institutions for obvious reasons. Therefore, the only way out is that all religious organisations, associations and denominations like the Arya Samaj which run their educational institutions should have the same freedom as given to the minorities under Article 30(1). However in actual practice Article 30(1) has result in depriving the Hindus of equal and similar religious freedom. This was never intended by the farmers of our

Constitution, not it is necessary to do so to safeguard the religious interest of the minorities. The claim of the Arya Samaj educational institutions, therefore, is a test of our secular ideal as well as of the religious freedom guaranteed to everyone under Article 25.

Three Aspects of Administration

In order to ensure that these minority educational institutions are able to fulfil the objectives for which they were established, the Supreme Court has held in a series of judgements, beginning from the advisory opinion in the Kerala Education Bill Case to the latest decision in the St. Xavier's College, Ahmedabad case (1974 SC 1389), that there are three indispensable spheres in which these educational institutions should have full freedom. They are (1) the appointment of the teachers and the principals and their recruitment and their dismissal; (2) the composition of their governing bodies; and (3) full freedom to impart religious instructions. In para 40 and 41 of 1974 SC 1389, it has been held that there should be no outside element in the managing committees and they should consist entirely of persons having faith in the object for which these institutions were established. Similarly, in para 42, it is observed that the management should be free to recruit the principals and headmasters and members of the teaching staff, so that persons who are suitable from the point of view of the special features of the institutions are appointed. In para 43, the right of the management to enforce its discipline including the dismissal and punishment of the employees has been considered a necessary part of their right of administration. Even a provision for referring any dispute between the management and the teachers to a tribunal prescribed by the University has been held to be ultra-vires in these words: "This would introduce an area of litigious controversy inside the educational institution and vitiate its atmosphere. The governing body should, therefore, be free to have its own discipline."

Needless to say that if the Arya Samaj institutions also do not have similar freedom in their administration, they cannot fulfil the aims for which they were established as has been rightly held by their lordships of the Supreme Court in respect of the Christian educational institutions. So far as the Arya Samaj is concerned it is not making any new claim. The D.A.V. institutions, some of which have been in existence for about 100 years, have always cojoyed this freedom and their managing bodies have always been composed of persons having faith in the Arya Samaj. For example, the Constitution of the Arya Samaj Shiksha Sabha, Ajmer, lays down that at least two-third majority of its members must be regular members of the Arya Samaj (Rule 4 ka, kha, sa) and other also should be either donors or members of the general body. The same was the case with the first D.A.V. institution, i.e. D.A.V. College, Lahore, as Lala Lajpat Rai has pointed out while speaking of the history of the establishment of that College that "It was provided in the rules that the management should be in the hands of the elected representatives of such Arya Samajees as contributed to its funds with the addition of a few Hindus representing the professions and the classes and that rule has been acted upon without exception. No non-Hindu had been associated with the 'management of the college.'

Managing Committees

The managing bodies of these institutions have been enjoying so far full freedom of internal discipline such as the appointment of teachers subject, of course, to their being qualified.

It is only recently that some of the state governments and their education departments as well as some of the universities, have begun to interfere in the internal administration of these institutions by claiming to put their nominees on the managing bodies irrespective of the fact whether they are Arya Samajists or not.

Teachers

Similarly, the right to appoint principals and teachers is either greatly reduced or is made subject to the approval of these authorities. It may be noted that the Supreme Court has already held in 1971 SC 1737 that the claim of the Guru Nanak University to put its nominees on the managing body of the D.A.V. College, Jullunder, or to limit the right of the management in the matter of appointment of teachers is a violation of the fundamental right of the Arya Samaj institutions. It is obvious that the principal or head master is the key figure and the teachers are equally important factors in fulfilling the aim and objects with which these institutions were established. Similarly, it is the managing body which lays down the policy and guides the teaching staff. The persons who managed the D.A.V. institutions so far and those who were responsible for their internal administration and teaching have been generally those who shared the ideology of the Arya Samaj and that was the reason why the Arya Samaj educational institutions have been able to keep up its traditions by providing regular religious instructions in them.

Right of Recognition

The Arya Samaj educational institutions are now faced with a serious problem as a result of the growing tendency on the part of the government to interfere in their long established freedom of internal administration. The universities and education boards threaten them with withdrawal of their recognition unless they submit to their new control. They are warned that the financial aid given to them was likely to be withdrawn if they fail to submit to the increasing interference by the State Education Department in their affairs.

Chief Justice Dass has, therefore, rightly observed that "without recognition the educational institutions established by the minority cannot fulfil the real objective of their choice and the right under Article 30(1) cannot be effectively exercised." This view has been confirmed by the Supreme Court which says that "Although affiliation or recognition is not a fundamental right, any conditions which will deprive these institutions of affiliation or recognition is tantamount to denying them the right given under Article 30(1)." Justice Dass further observes that "no educational institution can in actual practice be carried out without aid from the State and if they will not get it unless they surrender their right, they will, by compulsion of financial necessities, be compelled to give up their right under Article 30(1).

Justice Mathew quotes with approval the observations of Chief Justice Dass that financial aid is a compulsive need of these institutions. He also defends the unfettered right of appointing principals and teachers in these words, "The management has a right to assess their outlook and philosophy in making their appointments."

Financial Assistance

As is well known the Arya Samaj educational institutions cater mostly for students from the middle and lower middle class families. Women and the so-called untouchables have always been given preference in these institutions. Therefore, the fee-income in these institutions is not at all sufficient to run them without the aid of the government. The position of the Christian missionary schools is very different. As a common knowledge, they cater for more affluent students and charge a free which only upper classes can afford to pay. Obviously, therefore, the Arya Samaj institutions cannot exist without financial assistance from the government. It may, however, be remembered that the D.A.V. institutions have a tradition of considerable sacrifice in the national cause. They had even refused any financial assistance from the foreign government, primarily in order to escape its interference and keep up their freedom and independence to pursue their objective of inculcating a spirit of nationalism and patriotism and for this, they were always suspected of being disloyal to the British Government. Of course, today the Arya Samaj has and can have no objection to accept financial assistance from our own free government as their is no question now of any hindrance in propagating the spirit of nationalism as was the case during the British days.

Apart from these relevant considerations, the actual working of Article 30(1) has been a source of particular difficulty for the D.A.V. institutions and the discrimination invoiced has put them on the horns of dilemma. If they submit to the discrimination and the growing interference, they cannot continue to serve their special objective, for which they were established, and if they refuse to submit to government control their very existence might be endangered for want of funds. It would be ironical if these institutions have to close down in free India and that too because they did not claim any separate political rights or anti-national privileges as the other minorities did which would have made them eligible for freedom from these invidious restrictions and undue interferences. This was the strange ground on which the Delhi High Court actually refused to accept the Arya Samaj as a religious minority under Article 30.

—D. Vable

REFERENCES

1. Lala Lajpat Rai, *The History of the Arya Samaj*, New Delhi, Orient Longmen, 1967, pp. 140-42.
2. Valentine Chirol, *Indian Unrest*, London, Macmillan and Co., 1910, pp. 110-11.
3. Shiva Rao, *The Framing of India's Constitution,* (FIC), New Delhi. Institute of Public Administration, 1966, p. 266.
4. *Ibid.*, p. 76.
5. *Ibid.*, p. 275.
6. *AIR*, 1963, Supreme Court, Nagpur, pp. 540-44.
7. *Ibid.*, Note—1, p. 87, items 18 and 19.
8. *Constitution of the Paropkarini Sabha, Ajmer*, Vedic Yantralaya, 1920.
9. *AIR*, 1974, Supreme Court, p. 1889, Paras 135, 136, 138, 145, 146, 147.
10. *AIR* 1974, Supreme Court, para 274.

11. M.K. Gandhi, *Hindu Dharma*, Ahmedabad, Navajivan Press, 1950.
12. *AIR*, 1974, Delhi High Court, p. 207.
13. *AIR*, 1958, Supreme Court, p. 956.
14. *Ibid.*, Col 1 Last Para, p. 959.
15. *Ibid.*, p. 960.
16. *AIR*. op cit., p. 961.
17. *Ibid.*, pp. 22 and 23.
18. *AIR*. 1974, Supreme Court, p. 1389.

Dayananda—An Apostle of Universal Brotherhood

In the words of Romain Rolland Dayananda came like a flood. Never since Śankara, such an apostle of Vedism appeared: he possessed an unrivalled knowledge of Sanskrit and the Vedas, but none of the European languages. In all disciplines of activity the towering personalities born in the Nineteenth Century were those who belonged to the European soil—they contributed to modern sciences, technology, the modern philosophy and sociology. Max Müller, Max Planck, Karl Marx, Darwin, J.J. Thomson, all the great names were from the European Continent. In the galaxy of such world figures, the name of Dayananda stands alone and unique. His emergence was unexpected and sudden. He spoke in Sanskrit as if he belonged to an age, prior to the age of all our prophets, the age of those ancient Rsis who spoke for all nations and for persons of all creeds or cultures. While he was speaking, the learned Brahmans in the country got comfounded. He told them that what they had learnt so far, and what they had practised was not the sense of the Vedas and Shastras; what they had been teaching to others was in entirety misleading. Dayananda focussed the attention of Hindus, Jains, Buddhists, Muslims and Christians, all alike to the eternal truths; Till now, in India none had opposed Muslims of Christians since the Sixteenth Century.

But here was a personality, who wanted Muslims, Christians, Jews or for that reason people of any creed or cult to listen to him and see, for themselves what they upheld had any sense or rationalism. To Dayananda—there is nothing like a Hindu God, a Christian God or a Muslim God. God is ONE—the same for all. There is nothing like Christian Science, Hindus Science or Muslim Science; the Science is ONE and is meant for all; and similarly, there is nothing like a Hindu religion, the Muslim religion or the Christian religion—there is ONE Dharma and that Dharma is for all. It is the bounden duty of all of us to find out what that Truth is, what that God is, what that Science is and what that Dharma is. To Dayananda, Truth God, Science and Dharma then become synonymous terms, Dayananda throughout his life stood alone for this type of synthesis.

As an academician, Dayananda worked out this type of integration in several fields in which traditional Indians got confounded. To Dayananda, all the FOUR Vedas, represent one common thought, one philosophy and one discipline. Such terms are misnomers—the Yajurveda school, the Atharva-Veda school, the Sama Veda, school and so on. The Indian philosophers got divided into the Mīmānsakas, the Vaiśeṣikas, the Vedāntists and so on. Dayananda gave a synthetic philosophy in which the four vedas, the six Shastras, and all the ten or eleven Vedic Upanisads were one and the same.

Dayananda was really a Yuga Puruśa. Such persons are not born always. Once in millennia they come to serve us. Dayananda had many facets of his life. Gandhi admired him for his Brahmacharya. Late K.M. Munshi said that India got her freedom by following the path of Dayānanda. To some Dayānanda was a great social reformer, who championed the cause of women and the down-trodden. According to Dayananda, a child born in the family of a Sūdra, could, by his personal efforts, become a Brāhamaṇ. It is the 'guṇa, karma or svabhāva of a man that decides one's position in the society. To some, Dayānanda was an unparalled grammarian with a great insight into the mysteries of the Vedas. As a philosopher, he could be ranked with Śankara. He stood for the philosophy of dynamic, realism; against the Advaitavāva of Śankara. To some people, it was he who stood for a common natinoal language, and in that respect, he adopted the Arya Bhāṣā (now known as Hindi) as the language of the country. He is one of the architects of the modern Hindi prose.

We are told that Max Müller, the great philologist and linguist of his times was contemplating of writing of Biography of Dayānanda, he said; "To Svami Dayānanda, everything in the Vedas was not only perfect truth, but he went a step further, and by their interpretation, succeeded in persuading that everything worth knowing, even the most modern inventions, were alluded to in the Veda."

By far the greatest of his works consists in his efforts to establish Universal Brotherhood. His immortal work Satyarth Prakash contains 14 Chapters. In the first ten he has dwelt upon own doctrine. In the eleventh he has discussed and pointed out the short-coming of prevailing Hindu sects. Similarly in the 12th he has dealt with Buddhism and Jainism and in the 13th Christanity and in the 14th Islam. His aim in the writing of the Satyarth Prakash was not destructive but constructive. He had no animosity (ill-will) against any one. He wanted the people to see and realise the truth, which is one and only one and discard falsehood which comes in many attractive forms. In his introduction to the Satyarth Prakash, he says:

"The world is fettered by the Chain forged by superstition and ignorance. I have come to snap asunder that chain and to set slaves at liberty. It is contrary to my mission to have people deprived of their freedom."

"Though I was born in Aryavarta (India) and live in it, yet just as I do not defend the falsehood of the faiths and religions of this country, but expose them fully: in like manner, I deal with the religions of other countries. I treat the foreigners in the same way as my own countrymen, so far as the elevation of the human race is concerned."

"Therefore the purpose of my life is the extirpation of evils: introduction of truth in thoughts, speech, and deeds; the preservation of unity of religion; the expulsion of mutual anmity; the extension of friendly intercourse; and the advancement of public happiness by reciprocal subservicence of the human family, May the grace of the Almighty God and the constant co-operation of the learned soon spread these doctrines all over the world to facilitate everybody's endeavour in the advancement of virtue, wealth, godly pleasure, and salvation, so that peace, prosperity, and happiness may ever reign in the world." AMEN!

To attain this object he wrote in the short span of 10 years 16,000 pages, restoring Vedas to their intrinsic purity and glory. He invited a conference of the representatives of all religion on the occasion of the Delhi Durbar in 1877. Keshav Chandra Sen, Sir Syed Ahmed and Munshi Alakhdhari were among those who responded to the invitation. The Rishi's idea that the exponents of various faith should put their heads together to evolve a formula of United activity was unique in those days when ideas of Jehad and Crusades prevailed and signified the true conception of religion that it was a unifying and not a dividing force. This Conference paved the way for the later religions, parliaments and conferences in which preachers of different faiths met on a common platform and offered to one another alive branch of goodwill and peace. To Swami Dayananda, truth, whenever found is of the Vedas. He founded Paropkarini Sabha as his successor to whom he bequeathed the whole of his literature, his personal clothes etc. He enjoined on its to carry on his work by publishing literature, training missionaries for propogation of his ideals in India and abroad.

He gave the clarion cell of कृण्वन्तो विश्वमार्यम् i.e. making everybody in this World pure, and noble and uprooting miserliness.

T.L. Vàswani Says:—

"My hope is in the nation's youth. And may you, the youth of the Arya Samaj, have the courage and strength from Ishwara to stand boldly forward for the great Gospel of Spiritual and National Freedom. Many are, I am afraid, still moving in old grooves, and the Great Message of Rishi Dayanand remains undelivered. He is not of this Samaj or that. He is of Humanity. It is this Dayanand, the Greater Dayanand of the Spirit, I seek to interpret."

—Rai Saheb Chowdhury Pratap Singh

Is the Arya Samaj Another Religion?

Zealous defenders of the Arya Samaj wish to dissociate the Samaj from Hinduism. It is said Dayanand was India's Luther fighting against orthodox Hinduism. It cannot be denied that Dayananda was bitter against certain aspects of Hinduism like costly rituals in various ceremonies connected with marriage, death, birth and so forth, the exploitation by greedy priests, superstitions like belief that a dip in the Ganga river would wash off one's sins and the debasement of its gods, like the amorous deeds attributed to Lord Krishna and so forth. For that matter he also came down equally heavily on the evil aspects of other religions too. It is often argued that Hinduism itself is not a religion. Even if this were so, it does not thereby follow that the Arya Samaj is one. There has been a lot of hair-splitting over the term 'Hindu' and 'Hinduism'. It is said that Dayanand himself was averse to the use of the term Hindu, and cited Persian. Arabic and other sources to show that the term meant an infidel etc. At one place Dayanand is reported to have said the Aryas should give up the name 'Hindu' and take pride in the terms 'Arya and 'Aryavarta'. On another occasion when introduced as a Hindu, he said, 'it is a matter of insult and disrespect to introduce me as a Hindu. Again Pandit Lekhram is said to have quoted Persian and Moslem sources to show that 'Hindu' means a kaffir, a highwayman and so forth. Thus, it is argued that 'Hindu' is a term of contempt and Hinduism does not denote any 'organised' religion. If one says that Hinduism is not a militant religion like Islam, or one that prides itself on obtaining converts, like Christianity, that would be correct. But Hinduism is very much a religion, and a tolerant one at that, like Buddhism. When Lord Krishna finished explaining the *Gita* to Arjuna he ended by telling him. 'Reflect on it fully and do as you choose to'— '*yathe chasitatha kuru*'. That expresses the true spirit of Hinduism. It is not a religion, which says 'Hinduism or the sword' as Islam does, or which sends out missionaries to allure people and convert them into Christianity. Hinduism is a resilient religion and its very resilience makes it unassailable. Religions, or for that matter, civilizations, do not thrive on militancy. The very fact that Moslems killed thousands of Hindu 'infidels' shows the strength of Hinduism. Those persons could have easily adopted Islam–the alternative and saved their lives. But they considered their religion more precious. What greater proof can exist about the solidarity of Hinduism? Writers, who, in their enthusiasm for their own faith, scoff at it as a weak and disorganised religion, do not know what they are talking about.

The claim made about Arya Samaj is that it has no moorings with Hinduism and is a separate religion, as different from it as the east is from the west. The scriptures of the Arya Samaj are the Vedas, as Dayananda himself asserted several times. Now the point which arises is whether the Vedas are Hindu scriptures or not. Here we have to pause and examine what has been called 'the Arya-Hindu controversy'. A distinction is drawn between Aryas and Hindus. If we look back towards Indian history it will be clear that some kind of civilization existed before the Aryans come to India from the north. The excavations of Harappa and Mohenjodaro have put this beyond doubt. Moreover the civilization was of a superior type showing great sophistication and development. The people living then had a separate script using signs and combinations and development. The people living then had a separate script using signs and combinations of pictographs. There was a highly organised community under the administration of a powerful central government, which controlled both production and distribution. There were organised municipalities, tolls, customs and guides. It is also historically true that when the Aryans came from the north, they wrecked this civilization and slaughtered and laid waste the land, pillaging treasures, burning, raping young women—all the usual concomitants of the wars of those times. In the *Satyarthaprakash,* Dayanand uses the term dasyu (slave) for a 'wicked man'. This, it is said, refutes the claim that the Aryas conquered the dasyus who were the inhabitants of Bharat (India) before them. Nevertheless it cannot be denied that there was bitter fighting.

The god Indra, is frequently invoked in the Rig Veda to help in the war, 'destroying castle after castle with your strength', tearing away their (the enemy's) cunningly built defences' and 'praised by the Angirasas helping in the slaughter'. There are other references too, 'Indra has made the dasyus devoid of all virtues...he destroyed five hundred and a thousand dasyus...Indra cuts the dasyus in twain. It is for this fate they were born...O destroyer of foes slay them. Exterminate their race'. Thus the Aryans were not the first inhabitants of Bharat, or Aryavarta or India by whatever name one chooses to calls this country.

Coming to Dayanand's own observations, it is said that he issued a directive to Arya Samajists to enter themselves as Aryas, in the community column in the census of 1881, and to mention their religion as 'Vedic dharma'. In one of his lectures at Poona he is said to have called himself a Hindu, and forthwith corrected himself, saying it was a mistake. He appealed to one of his audiences to give up the name 'Hindu and take pride in calling themselves 'Aryas'. Then (as already stated) in Calcutta he observed it was an insult to him to be introduced as a Hindu. We have seen that in his early contact with Hinduism, Dayanand got involved with pandits and priests of Benares and other citadels of orthodox Hinduism. Much of the controversy was on the subject of idol worship, which Dayanand repeatedly said was not advocated by the Vedas. He was also irked by the exploits of Shri Krishna as stated in the *Bhagavata Purana*, and by the many beliefs of orthodox Hinduism based on blind superstitions. Finding in Dayanand a formidable opponent, the pandits, too, were rather acrimonious in the utterances. There was, thus, no love lost between the fundamentalists and the reformists. Therefore, when Dayanand spoke of 'Hindu' and 'Hinduism' the idea lingering in his mind was of these Hindus, who formed mostly the priestly class. And he got so disgusted of their foul practices in debates and in their rampant corruption, that his bitterness vent itself upon Hinduism in general. Nonetheless what is the Veda if not a Hindu scripture? It finds mention in the *Gita*, the *Ramayana* and other Hindu religious books. The Upanishads are the third division of the Vedas attached to the Brahmana portion, forming part of the shruti (revealed word). Thus the Vedas are the foundation of Hindu religion, and their language too is Sanskrit, the script of other Hindu scriptures. The rishis to whom they are ascribed were Hindu sages such as Vasishtha, Vishvamitra, Bharadvaja and so forth. Jordens emphasises that Dayanand made the Vedas (only the mantra portions) the corner-stone of the Arya Religion because he wanted to have one authoritative scripture forming the basis of Arya Samaj, just as the Christians had their Bible and the Moslems their Quran. Nevertheless, as, stated above, the Vedas were also the foundation of Hinduism. Hence we arrive at the rather intriguing position that while decrying the Hindu faith, Dayanand was relying on the scriptures which formed their very basis! One can wriggle out of this dilemma only by assuming that Dayanand's target of attack was just ritual Hinduism, which had been debased over the centuries by over-zealous and rapacious priests, and not against the spiritual aspect of Hinduism. The Arya sect could have formed a separate religion, had it based itself on an exclusive scripture, as the Buddhist Pitakas (Vinaya, Sutta and Abhidharmma) and their various divisions, the Nikayas of the Sutta Pitaka (Digha, Majjhima, Samyutta, Anguttara and Khuddaka); the Christian Bible, the Moslem, Quran, the Zoroastrian Gathas, Yasna (has sections including the Gathas of Zarathushtra); the Jain 14 Purvas and 11 Angas, the Pangas, Prakirnas, Chedasutras, Nandi and Anuyogadvara and the Mula sutras, the Granth Sahib of the Sikhs, and so forth. The Arya Samaj has mainly principles of good living, rules which are mandatory and an organisation like that of the Ramakrishna Mission. It would probably be more difficult therefore to establish that the Arya Samaj is a religion, than to do the same for Hinduism.

Who is a Hindu? Some writers on the Arya Samaj have pointed out the vagueness of Hindu beliefs. As we have stated elsewhere also, certain positive features and beliefs are common to all Hindus. These may be summed up as follows:

1. The acceptance of the eternal cycle of Nature without beginning or end–the Kalpa, the hundred years of Brahma, Mahapralaya, the hundred years of chaos and thereafter re-creation.

2. The belief in rebirth, and its corollary, the doctrine of moksha (liberation) and the law of karma (judgement according to one's deeds).

3. The acceptance of dharma as the moral law. There are three worldly pursuits–artha (possessions), Karma (delights) and dharma (virtue). These are called the trivarga. Beyond them is the other worldly goal of moksha. These four are known as purusharthas 'what is sought by men.'

4. The aim of all life is liberation (moksha).
5. The universality of sufferings—this is of three kinds: adhyatmika (disease and mental grief); adhibhautika (suffering arising from the world of living creatures); and adhidavivika (arising from) the supernatural, like the influence of natural calamities, floods, earthquakes etc.

   It is acknowledged that life involves suffering and one of the aims of Indian philosophy is to remove this suffering.
6. All Hindi schools of philosophy recognise the Vedas and the Upanishads, and have them as their base. (The Gita's comment on the Vedas is that following the Vedic injunctions only result in repeated rebirths, but it does not negate the Vedas).

The belief in idol worship and that in avataras, though quite universal among Hindus, are not essential ingredients of Hinduism. These will be discussed in relation to Dayanand's concept about them, later on, but it will be clear from the above that none of the essential requirements of Hinduism is adverse to Dayanand's view of the Arya Samaj. To say that 'the two' [Pauranic Hinduism and the Arya Samaj] are so conflicting that one is reminded of Kipling's famous couplet "East is East, West is West. Never the Twain shall meet", shows a complete misunderstanding of Hinduism.

Apart from the beliefs common to all Hindu schools, there were of course many variations in these beliefs. We have already pointed these out at the beginning of this book. Mainly the trends were two—dvaita, the belief that there are two, the worshipper and the worshipped; and advaita, the existence of the one without a second. The advaitist believed in an impersonal God, a God without form, and the dualist in the worship of a personal God having some kind of form. Dayanand took the stand of the believer in the formless.

To deny that the Arya Samaj was a religion, in the sense of its having a following a set of beliefs and an entity, would be unfair to it. But to say that it was poles apart from Hinduism, would be equally unfair. No Hindu would quarrel with the broad principles enunciated by it. In fact following the ten rules of the Lahore Arya Samaj would make any Hindu a better Hindu. Even the clause about the Veda, which gives the Samaj its exclusiveness, would be welcome to a Hindu, for Hindus revere the Vedas. Where the protagonists of the Arya Samaj err is in isolating it from Hinduism–at least from Hinduism in all its forms. Being a reform movement, the Arya Samaj sets right many of the bad practices of ritual Hinduism–the tyranny of pandits, the social ostracization of widows, the ban to reconversion, the cruelty of the caste system, the complicated rituals whose main objective is to enrich crafty priests, the hypocrisy of external observances like pilgrimages, bathing in rivers to escape sin and so forth. The cleansing breeze of the Arya Samaj removes much of the pollution of Hindu religious rites. Many Hindus would therefore adopt the Arya Samaj to escape such evils. There would be quite a fair proportion of Arya Samajist Hindus, but very few Arya Samajists who would disclaim Hinduism. And in this respect Jorden's analysis is justified that towards the end Dayanand realised that it would be disastrous to cut off all relations with Hinduism. With the third rule existing— 'the Veda is the book of true knowledge. It is the highest duty of all Aryans to study and propagate the Veda' —the doors of the Samaj would be shut to all except to Hindus. People of all faiths, but not this would welcome the other rules. Hinduism did not militate against the Arya Samaj. On the contrary it gave it strength.

Another thing about religion that has been misconceived by many critics, is that it exists on reason not on faith. It was Dayanand's constant effort to rationalise, the concepts of God, the soul and so forth. This has been spoken of as his 'greatest contribution'. What cannot be understood by the five senses of human beings can only by inferred. For example we know death in the sense that everyone dies. We see it all around us. The doctors can perhaps tell what caused it. But what is, no one can really say. Or, for example, God. We may believe there is one, or not believe. But one simply can't reason it out. So is it with the soul, afterlife, rebirth, and the doctrine of karma and so forth. How can that which is beyond reason, be rationalised? Dayanand's real contribution appears to be to expose the duplicity and rapacity of those who exploit faith and spirituality to their own pecuniary advantage. Religion has always been irrational and it will always remain so.

That is why the religion of one is meaningless to another, whose religion it isn't. A rational religion cannot have much appeal. This is because men want to conceive of a God who is all-powerful, to whom nothing is impossible, who can accomplish miracles and who is the master of the universe. Unless God is all-powerful he cannot command the love and obedience which one should give him. In fact much of Dayanand's criticism of other religions stemmed from this misconception.

The Arya Samaj is a religion in the sense that it has a set of beliefs so broadbased that almost anyone can subscribe to them—all except the one about the Vedas. If that was not there the door of the Samaj could be open to men of other faiths too. But the provision about the belief in the Vedas being essential for Aryas, makes it open to Hindus only. Another essential quality of the religion which is absent in the Arya Samaj, is that apart from the Vedas it has no scriptures. The concepts of a formless God, the Samkhya element and so forth in Dayanand's philosophy are essentially Hindu in the import, though he does interpret these terms somewhat differently. Moksha, artha, kama, prakriti, sanskara, yajna, terms of Hindu religion, figure in the *Swamantavyamantavya*, albeit they are in a greatly different sense. Dayanand gave new and novel interpretations to Hindu beliefs, and it is only in that sense that the Arya Samaj can be called a religion apart.

DAYANAND AND IDOL WORSHIP

Perhaps the greatest attack Dayanand made on Hindu practices was the one against idol worship. The root of this obviously goes down to the incident in the Shiva temple when keeping awake, despite all other (including his father) not being true to their vows and falling asleep, a mouse crept out of its hole and ate away the offerings. Dayanand was fourteen years old then—an impressionable age. And this small incident seems to have made an indelible impact on his mind, as he records in his autobiography: 'I feel it impossible' he told his father, 'to reconcile to the idea of an omnipotent, living God, with this idol which allows the mice to run over his body and thus suffers his image to be polluted without the slightest protest.

Thereafter Dayananda's quest to find a yogi proved futile. He encountered many mahants and pujaris (temple priests) who had enriched themselves through the offerings made to idols by over-credulous people. He saw for himself the hypocrisy of priests, the dirty temples, which served as 'God's abode', the rapidity of pandas and the corrupt practices that were connected with Hindu religion. All that set his mind against idol worship. The Christian missionaries, needless to say, encouraged him to oppose idolatry. It provided them with an opportunity for creating a schism in Hindu religion, one of the foremost practices of which was idol worship. The Muslims, too, welcomed it, for they were not only haters of idols but also their breakers. Dayanand found himself challenged by orthodox pandits in religious debates at which the issue was mostly murtipuja (idol worship). These debates, in many of which the pandits stage-managed victory for themselves, turned Dayanand's mind even more against image worship. In his stand he usually took the Vedas as his support. In *Sayarthaprakash* he quotes from the Upanishada and the *Manusmriti* also.

The quotations are as follows (from the Yajur Veda):

1. Andhantamah pra vishanti ye sambhutimupasate tato bhuya 'iva te tamo ya'u sambhutyacch am ratah.
2. Na tasya pratima' asti

From the *Kenopanishad* Yadvachana bhyuditam yena vagabhyuddte yanmanasa na manute yenahur mano matam yaccashush na pasyati yena chakshunshi pashyanti yat pranena na praniti yena pranah praniyat [Common second line to all mantras 1.4-8] tadeva brahma tvam vidhi nedam yadi damupasate/

The import of the quotations from the *Yajur Veda* is:

1. They who worship the bhutas (the sentiment and insentient) in this world instead of Brahma the cause of beginingless primordial nature, are drowned in the sea of darkness [i.e. ignorance]. So too those who worship lifeless things [like trees and so forth].
2. This is in praise of Hiranyagarbha, the 'golden-womb' which is said in the Rig Veda to have arisen in the beginning, 'the one lord of all beings, who upholds heaven and earth, who gives life and breath, whose command even the Gods obey, who is the god over all Gods, and the one animating principle of their being'. The Vedic mantra says that it is this Hiranyagarbha who is to be worshipped, not a pratima'.

The whole controversy follows from the sense assigned to the word 'bhuta' and 'pratima' in these mantras. Dayanand takes these words in the sense of image worship. 'Bhuta' means 'what is moving or unmoving, sentient or insentient'. Thus worship of 'bhutas' does not imply just image worship but is used in the wider sense of animism. It implies that trees, snakes, evil spirits, plants, animals, and so forth, should not be worshipped. The word does not specifically relate to worship of idols. Similarly the word of 'pratima' means in the context 'form' or 'shape', (pratibimba or chhaya). The idea is that the formless Brahman is worthy to be worshipped not the God with form.

As we have stated, both the schools form part of Hinduism, Shankaracharya is the protagonist of the formless God [nirankara rupa

Brahman] while Madhav and Ramanuja believe in God with form. There remains the quotation from the *Kenopanishad*. The relevant word in the second line of each of these verses is yadidamupasate (i.e. yat-idam-upasate) and 'na' meaning 'not'. The sense is: What speech cannot reveal, but what reveals speech—know that alone as Brahman: and not this that people worship here. What mind does not comprehend, but what caginess the mind—know that to Brahman: and not this that people worship here. What sight fails to see, but what perceives sight, knows that alone as Brahman and not this that people worship here. What hearing fails to grasp, but what perceives hearing—know that alone as Brahman: and not this that people worship here. What smell does not perceive, but what directs smell to its object—know that alone as Brahman: and not this that they worship here. It is obvious that these verses are meant primarily to convey the import of Brahman, and to define what it means.

Again 'this that people worship here' means the God with form or worship of creatures, spirits, trees and so forth. Madhva interprets the word 'upasate' as upas=near, te=this i.e. jiva, implying that Brahman is not the jiva. Thus it is the relation between the soul and Brahman, which is, meant here, not image worship. The worship of idols is not implied by these verses of the Upanishad. The *Bhagavadgita* also says: 'Worshippers of the gods go to the gods, worshippers of the manes go to the manes, sacrificers of the spirits go to the spirits, and those who sacrifice to me come to me'.

Manu has been quoted as saying. 'Decrying the Vedas, dishonouring them or not following them is atheism. Those scriptures that are contrary to the Vedas emanate from contemptible persons and drawn the people of the world in the ocean of sorrow. They are without fruit, untrue, of the nature of darkness and make people miserable in this world and in the next'. We have already before mentioned Dayanand's condemnation of those scriptures, which he says were not written by the rishis (anarsha). But as regards worship of God through his image, as we have endeavoured to show, neither the Vedas nor the Upanishada prohibits it. They may not advocate it in so many words, but they do not prohibit it either.

The *Bhagvadgita's* views are very clear on the subject. It does not condemn any form of faith whatsoever. Lord Krishna says 'As men approach me so do I accept that: men on all sides follow my path, O Arjuna'. There is no condemnation of other religions here, nothing against the form in which a man may worship God. Besides the Gita does not look down upon any degree of faith. All men are striving, and in the race for salvation they are in various stages. Some are nearing the goal, some are just beginning, others are somewhere in the middle, and yet others—a sizeable lot-have not even begun. But there is no going back.

Lord Krishna says: tan akrtsnavido mandan krtsnavin na vichalet i.e., 'but let no one who knows the whole, unsettle the mind of the ignorant who knows only a part. Those who know only the part, are obviously those who have not yet been able to conceive of the formless state and falsely identify the self with the ego. In fact, as we have said elsewhere, the Gita believes that to grasp the formless is difficult for human beings. Therefore even those who worship other Gods with faith, they also worship the one God. Whoever offers the divinity, with devotion and with a pure heart, a leaf, flower, fruit or water, that is acceptable to the Lord. The Gita does not castigate worshippers of images. What is needful is faith and purity. That alone, Dayananda obviously does not fall in line with this teaching of the Gita, even though he nowhere renounces it.

The arguments given in the *Satyathaprakash* against image worship apart from the Vedic and Upanishadic testimony discussed above are as follows:

While the mind is engrossed in forms, it is in bondage. When it is yoked to the formless it become free. Illustrating his point he says, 'if we assume that the mind becomes steady in fixing itself on the forms, then it follows that the minds of all in the world will be steady. In this world, men are attached to wives, sons, wealth, friends, etc., but we do not find the mind of anyone steady'. Yet, curiously enough, quoting the *Manusmriti* he says a little further on: 'First a man should keep his mother and sons happy in every way. Second, like his mother, his father should also receive his service. Third, so too, the teacher, fourth, the guest who is wise, moral, free from guile wanting the advancement of all, who, wandering about, keeps everyone happy by his true counsel. Fifth, a man should revere his wife and a woman her husband...' How can these two views be reconciled? On the one hand the Swami rules out being attached to wives, sons and so forth and on the other he advocates service to them! The second argument against image worship is wastage of money on temples. This sounds reasonable, except for the more moneyed and flourishing business class to whom spending money to build temples is so much an act of charity as to get round income tax! Thirdly, when there are crowds at temples, there are fights, the practice of immortality, and the spread of epidemics. Fourthly, men foolishly spend all their lives worshipping images in temples and considering that to be the means of artha (wealth), kama (pleasure) and mukti (emancipation).

Fifthly, by encouraging worship of different denominations [according to the image worshipped, like Shiva, Vishnu, Hanuman etc.] the worshippers create division and discord and cause destruction of the country. Sixthly, relying upon these images their worshippers acknowledge their own defeat and surrender their freedom, wealth and happiness to the enemy, as if they [the worshippers of the images] were donkeys carrying bricks or earthen pots [an obvious reference to the British].

Seventhly, as though one might say 'I will place bricks on your name and your seat' and hearing him say so the person whom he thus insulted gets enraged and runs to beat him; even so when these worshippers place stone images on the abode of God, why should God not destroy these people of little intelligence? In other words images tarnish God's abode and his name. Eightly, these deluded people undergo trouble unnecessarily in roaming all over the country, visiting temples, forsaking dharma and virtue, and falling prey to thieves and thugs.

Ninthly, they give money to wicked priests. These priests squander it on prostitution, adultery, wine, meat and disputes; with the result that the giver loses that which can yield him pleasure, and instead reaps sorrow. Tenthly, these worshippers display their ungratefulness by neglecting their parents and elders and instead paying obeisance to these stone images. Eleventh, if anyone smashes or breaks these images, or steals them, they raise a hue and cry and weep. Twelfth, the purjaris [priest] disport with other women and the pujarins [priestesses] with other men, and thus defile and degrade the joys of married love. Thirteenth, not carrying out fully as necessary the commands of master and servant, the two do not achieve compatibility and the relationship is nullified [the idea apparently is that the true relationship between worshipper and worshipped is not achieved by worshipping stone images]. Fourteenth, by fixing the mind on an insentient object the mind too becomes dull and lifeless as the object mediated on. Fifteenth, God has created sweet-smelling flowers etc., to keep the atmosphere pure and disease-free. By plucking flowers for making an offering of them to these images, heaven knows for how many days these priests deprive the atmosphere of its perfume. Has god created these scented things for offering on stone images? Sixteenth, the flowers, sandal-wood, grain-offerings and so forth offered to these images form a mixture which flows into the consecrated hollow pit (kunda) and rots. Evil smell emanates and spreads all over. And thousands of small insects and creatures fall in the kunda and die in it, and give an evil odour.

Thus, concludes Dayanand, innumerable evils arise from the worship of images, it will be noticed that Dayanand's arguments against image worship are levelled mostly against the obeisance paid to them in temples in which priests, pujaris and pandas [a kind of go between betwixt the god's image and the devotee] exploit the worshippers by extracting money. There is another aspect of image worship however, namely the worship of the family deities which is a daily rite in most Hindu homes. The defects of image worship envisaged by Dayanand cannot be said to apply to such ritual worship, because in it there are on priests or temples.

As regards the shortcomings he points out, in fixing the mind on the sakara (with form) apart from the contradiction in his own argument as aforesaid, it is acknowledged by the *Bhagavadagita* and other such scriptures that it is very difficult for a human being to conceive of what is formless: avyakta hi gatir duhkham dehavadbhir avapyate ['the goal of the unmanifest is hard to reach by embodied beings']. Therefore, the worship of God with form, in the shape of an image, statue, picture of symbol, is a kind of half way house to the worship of the formless. In the *Satyarthaprakash*, the imaginary questioner says, 'image worship is for those not wise enough, because if one climbs up the stairway step by step, he reaches the floor he has to ascend to. If he wants to leave the stating step and climb up, he can't do it. Therefore image worship is like the first step in the stairway to God. That is sound reasoning. But Dayanand dismisses it by replying that image worship is not like a first step, but it is an abyss into which one sinks.

Another point made by Dayanand is that the mind acquires the nature of that upon which it is fixed. But is so? When one sees the photograph of a person, it is not the paper on which it exists which is material, but the person whose photograph it is. Of course seeing that person in flesh and blood, hearing him [or her] speak, move about and so forth is different, as the poet says: 'I love not pictures eyeless, soulless still, bereft of reason, passion, strength and will.' Even then one's picture or photograph does take one's thought towards that person. So too when one believes with faith that a certain embalmer image represents god, he may not see him, but certainly the mind is directed godwards. It is not the stone image, which matters, but the feeling it creates in the mind. As Tulsidasa says in the Ramacharitamanasa about persons who were beholding Lord Rama at the dhanusha-yajna [lifting of Shiva's bow].

Jaki rahi bhavana jaisi, prabhu murati soi dekhi taise- 'As was the feeling in one's mind, so did the Lord's image appear to him then.'

It is the mind which comprehends everything not as it is, but as one imagines it to be. For example one may see a rope lying ahead and imagine it is a snake. The feeling towards it, till such time as the reality is not realised, will be one of fear. Similarly, if he sees a piece of glass shining and imagines it to be a pearl, he will perhaps say 'Let me pick it up, what a lucky find!' and will discover his disappointment only when it dawns upon him that it is really a worthless piece of glass. We know that dreams have the same effect. A fearful dream may leave one trembling with awe, a pleasant one give pleasure.

Then there is the incident of the mouse nibbling the holy offering made to the image of Lord Shiva, which had such a great impact on Dayanand. Its just like termites attacking a photograph. This would not mean that they have in any way affected the person whose photograph it is. The photograph and the person whom it represents are connected mentally in the observer's mind, but not so factually. The two are not identical. So, too, the image of God is not identical with God. And if Dayanand, who was then only fourteen, conceived that the God was powerless to drive away the mouse, and therefore the image was not worthy of worship, he was assuming an identity where there wasn't one which was of course pardonable in a youth of fourteen. But it was strange that he should have persisted in imaging such an identity later too.

Dayanand also believed that taking the name of God was fruitless, as he says, "by repeating 'sugar' one does not taste it sweetness, nor by saying 'nim', one feels the taste of bitterness'. This way of thinking is also rather unconventional, for in almost all religions the rosary is an essential item of prayer. Taking the name of God is believed to be one of the ways in which he is to be worshipped. Among the ways of devotion, which Shri Ram relates to Shabari, one is mantra japa-man dhrirh vishvasah i.e., 'taking the name of the Lord with faith'.

The questioner is made to ask a very relevant question in connection with image worship in the *Satyarthaprakash* namely 'As desire arises in the mind by dwelling on the stone statue of a woman so why should not an image of God, from which peace and clam emanate, create that feeling in the worshipper'. Dayanand answers that point in a roundabout manner carrying much the same import as Lord Krishna says in the Gita: 'For the uncontrolled, there is no intelligence; nor for the uncontrolled is there any peace, and for the unpeaceful, how can there be happiness? But the question remains unanswered. The true idea of image worship is not to worship the image itself, but through it the one God of whom Dayanand speaks.

In the *Satyathaprakash* itself Dayanand gives God many names, like Shankara, Prajapati, Swayambhu, Ganesh, Indra and so forth. It is believed that he indicated these names as the different functions of God. The same is the concept of Hindu mythology which postulates the trinity as Brahma-Vishnu-Mahesh i.e. 'Creator-Presever-Destroyer'. Thus there is hardly much difference in Dayanand's concept and that of orthodox Hinduism. Shankara, Shiva or Mahesh is worshipped by Shaivites, Vishnu and Krishna, Rama and so forth by Vaishnavities. True, Dayanand waged a crusade against both, particularly against the Vaishnavas. But he still includes Shankara as one of the names of God.

When one gives God various names-and Dayanand gives a hundred— it is just a short step to worshipping them in a particular form. Thus most of Dayanand's trade against image worship does not have a strong foundation, despite it being one of the points which he often emphasised, on many of his shastrarths. Nor does his stand seem to have made any marked impact. Image worship continues both in the form of daily worship of the family deity and also worship in temples. Unfortunately the evils mentioned by Dayanand and the greed and corruption of temple priests, the unhygienic atmosphere prevailing in them and the gullibility of worshippers also remains. One would wish Dayanand's criticism and deprecation regarding this had been taken seriously. He was rightly critical about it and we owe him a great debt for condemning these. The temples with their inherent corruption and dirty look are the bane of Hinduism. They are quite a contrast to the neatness, orderliness and serenity of Christian churches and Buddhist shrines.

THE SOUL, WORKS AND EMANCIPATION

Every religion believes in a afterlife; the concepts, however, differ. Death is a universal phenomenon, and all creatures who are born, and bound to die sometime or the other, only their life spans differ. In the *Bhagavadgita* Lord Krishna says: jatasya hi dhruvo mrtyur dhruvam janma mrtasya cha. Buddhism also emphasises the point that everything in the world is subject to decay, but it does not seem to speak much about future life except that, like the Hindu concept of moksha, it speaks of nirvana. Let us recapitulate the various concepts of jiva, the soul. According to the Hindu concept, the Vedanta conceives the organs of the soul to be as follows:

1. Manas and the indriyas (the organs of relation).
2. The five pranas—the organs of nutrition associated with the upadhis of the soul.
3. The Sukshma sharira (the subtle body).
4. A factor that changes from birth to birth based on karma, the actions of each of the many existences.

When the soul departs from the body the subtle body (sukshma sharira) accompanies it in its wanderings. It is also accompanied by the ethical substratum (karma-ashraya) which determines the character of the new body it will inherit. This ethical substratum is formed of actions done in the course of each of the several lives and is therefore different for each soul.

The three states of the soul are waking, dream and deep sleep, and the fourth state-the-turya-in which the disappearance of the manifold universe and the union with Brahman, on which deep sleep depends, takes place not unconsciously but with continued and perfect consciousness. Then there are the 'envelopes' of the soul, the koshas, as they are called. These are, progressively, tha anandamaya, vijnanamaya, manomaya, pranamaya and fifth the gross of sthula sharira.

The Upanishads believe in the doctrine of rebirth. Rebirth is determined by one's deeds in various existences. But the idea of God's grace also exists in them. Whoever god wishes to raise, he makes him perform good deeds, and whomever he wishes to cast down, he makes him perform evil deeds. Moksha means, according to the Vedanta, release of the soul from worldly existence. The soul becomes one with Brahman:

'When every passion vanishes

That finds a home in the human heart

Then he who is mortal becomes immortal,

Here already he had attained to Brahman.

Of course, there are minor differences in the various schools of Hinduism, but fundamentally the soul suffers the consequence of its deeds, the power of wiping out karma resting with God, and on attaining moksha the soul does not return to worldly existence. It casts off its subtle body then and becomes merged with Brahman.

The Buddhist and the Jain views may be briefly mentioned, although Dayananda rejects them outright. The Buddhists do not believe in an eternal changeless soul. According to them the human being is formed of five khandas or skandhas. These are forms, i.e. the body; sensation (vedana) i.e. mental and physical feelings; perception (sanna), man's cogent medium with the outside world, mental tendencies and conditions (sankhara), and consciousness (vinnana) i.e. mental cognition or thought. Buddhism doctrine is an-atta or 'non-self', i.e. nothing material, but only the abstract character is reborn. Hence there is no eternal soul. 'Void is the world' says the Buddhist of self, or of thought of that nature. God cannot set aside the natural law of justice that men are judged according to their deeds. Even the gods are governed by karma. There is therefore no scope for God's grace in Buddhism. He, too, cannot suspend the law of karma. Moaka, called Nibbana by Buddhists, means literally 'blowing or going out of fire'. But it is not emptiness. The Auguttara-nikaya says of it: 'This is good, this is excellent, to wit, the calming of all knowledge, of all karma-activities, the renunciation of all the bases (of rebirth), the destruction of craving, passionlessness, ceasing, nibbana.'

Coming to the Jain view, it is quite different and radical. There are two divisions of all things jiva (living) and ajiva (non-living). The pure soul has infinite perception, knowledge, bliss and power, but other souls (samsarin), have their purity covered by a veil. They are infinite in number (not limited) but their size is limited. They are not all pervasive, nor are they atomic. The soul occupies the body as a lamp illuminating the whole room, though remaining in a corner. When 'karma matter' is once produced it is 'discharged' from the soul. This purging process is called nirjara. After death the soul along with the karmic body goes to find a new body. Even elements like earth, water, air and fire are believed to have souls. Also all around are minute soul-clusters packing the whole space like powder in a box. These replace souls, which attain moksha. The actual connections of karmas with the soul are like the sticking of dust on the body of a person smeared all over with oil. Moksha implies infinite knowledge, infinite perception and omniscience. It is a state of pure happiness.

Dayanand regarded the soul as eternal [along with prakriti and God]. The jiva had no beginning or end and moksha too was endless. To start with, Dayanand believed the soul to be of God's creation. Later he found it difficult to define the relationship between the soul and God. He had already rejected the Vedantic theory that the soul was of the same nature as Brahman. If the jiva was not Brahman, then how did it stand in relation to Brahman? To this question Dayananda had no answer. If he denied the jiva's divinity, it would be reduced to a position as low as that of the gross body. And that would be almost the position of the Charvakas, whom he reviled. If he held the soul to be divine it would be admitting that it was of the nature of God, the theory expounded by Shankara and the advaitas. Though he believed this initially, he had already discarded it, and couldn't possibly go back to it now.

Dayananda wriggled out of this dilemma by saying that the soul was eternal in its own right, even as God and primordial nature. Thus discarding the concept of Shankaracharya, as well as the bhedabheda concept of difference in non-difference i.e. God is the material cause of the universe, but at the same time the two are different; Dayananda formulated the traitavada-theory of three eternal entities—God, prakriti and the soul. He thought he had thereby solved the problem. God was not the 'creator' either of the material world or of the soul. Creation was the coming together in an orderly manner, of various substances. God was only the shaper or organiser. But if the soul is eternal it must eternally take rebirth, and if that happens there cannot be anything like moksha.

Dayananda did not choose to revise his theory about the soul. So he had to fit in the concept of moksha with it. That led him to the rather outlandish theory that the soul can never achieve emancipation in the sense of freedom from rebirth. Thus, taking an unconventional stand about the jiva. Dayanand was forced to take an even more startling view of moksha. One might call it 'limited moksha'. Thus the jiva, which had been emancipated, was freed from human existence for the duration of a cosmic cycle. At the end of the cycle (mahakalpa) it returned to the world of life and death again. The argument he advanced was that man is finite in his works and powers, and therefore cannot have infinite bliss. The problem that he leaves unsolved is the relation of the soul to man. The entire human personality consists of the spirit inside acting on matter. In other words the spiritual soul is enmeshed in the body. If one did not believe in a spiritual entity as part of man, death could not be explained.

The Vedantists explained the relationship as a temporary material imposition on the spiritual. A piece of transparent glass *assumes* the colour of the cloth on which it is placed. If placed on a red cloth it seems red. But it does not thereby lose its transparency. When lifted from the cloth it is again transparent—as indeed it ever was. Thus Dayanand's argument, 'how can man who is finite in actions and powers, ever have eternal bliss?' is not really a cogent one. It is the spiritual soul, which is entitled to bliss, not the gross body that encloses it. The body only helps the soul towards right works, which constitutes dharma. Once a man reaches the roof, the leader by which he did it loses its importance in so far as the ascending is concerned. So too, the body is the ladder to emancipation. And to carry on the metaphor, one might say that, as to reach the very top of a multi-storied building, one has to climb not one, but many flights of steps, so too one has to undergo many existences to achieve moksha. Dayananada does not seem to have adequately distinguished between the spiritual soul and the material body, and so fell into the error of holding that 'man is finite in his works and powers'.

As regards works (karma), Dayanand is on firmer grounds. He avoids the great pitfall of Hinduism by which reward and punishment may not remain the final judgement. Hinduism makes a mockery of the law of karma by introducing grace. The wind bloweth where it listeth. Even so God can, out of his mercy, condone the evil deeds of man. Dayananda saw the absurdity of this, and his final view was that works (karmas) alone determine human destiny. He is yet uncertain about works in the first *Satyarthaprakasha* in which he wrote that those sannyasis who have full knowledge [purna jnana] are not bound by works. Knowledge destroys karma and makes the knowledge omniscient. In the second edition of the book, however, he makes it clear that all-even sanyasis-are bound by works.

His argument is as follows: Moksha is for one who is bound, and the bond is ignorance and transgression of the moral law (ajnana and adharma). The Vedantic idea that the soul is never born nor does it ever die, nor is it bound nor desires to remove bondage, and being ever free, moksha has no meaning for it; is discarded by Dayanand. In this respect he approaches the Buddhist concept that refuses to grant any eternality or unchangeability to the soul. The soul is not the witness of deeds (sakshi) but the actor taking part in works and suffering their consequences. The soul is not the reflection of Brahman. The soul is indeed bound by its deeds, and this relation between the soul and work is an eternal one.

Emancipation can be got by right actions alone. These consist of carrying out God's commands; remaining removed from evil company, evil desires, evildoers, adharma and ignorance; speaking the truth, doing good to others, acquiring knowledge, being equal-minded and just and furthering dharma; prayer, singing God's praises, and yoga; increasing knowledge and education, and following noble practices which are just and without prejudice. Since moksha is only a change in the soul's condition effected by human works, works can also undo it. It is a kind of gift, which can also be withdrawn. Moksha is therefore, limited in time. There is no eternal bliss for the finite soul. Even in the state of moksha, the taint of sin can cause the soul to return to the earth. God only administers the law of karma, he cannot transcend it.

Despite Dayanand's condemnation of Buddhism, in his view about karma and moksha, he follows very much the same ideal. Buddhism did not deny the existence of the gods, but at the same time held that, like all mankind they too are governed by the law of karma. They did not create the world-order, nor can they destroy it. Brahman is all right as an impersonal principle, but only as the world soul. There is no affinity between it and the human soul. 'Void is the world' the Buddhist holds, of self or aught of that nature'. There is, according to him, no unchanging spectator, agent or seer, as the Vedantist believed. The *Samangala-vilasini* says: 'Anything whatever within the soul, who sees, who moves the limhs etc., there is not'. No outside force incites one to good or evil. Pain automatically follows immoral living, and pleasure moral living. This natural law of justice cannot be suspended even by God.

Dayanand believed that the soul can never be equated with God. This as we have discussed, negates the Vedantic concept of the identity of Brahman and atman. He says: 'God is eternal, and having power, he cannot be bound by ignorance and by the bonds of sorrow. The jiva, even when emancipated, is of limited knowledge and qualities, and it can never be like God'. When the imaginary questioner asks that if emancipation too is like birth and rebirth, what is the point in labouring for it. Dayanand puts his view thus: 'Emancipation is not like birth and death, because it is the soul remaining free of sorrows, which enjoys the bliss of moksha till creation and destruction does not take place 36000 times. Is this of no consequence? When you have enough to eat, why do you not still arrange for where withal to cook a meal, thinking you will need to eat in the future? When you consider it necessary to arrange for hunger and thirst, money, land, repute, wife, sons etc., then why should't try for emancipation. When one knows death to be certain, yet he makes arrangements for living, so too, even if you have to come back from the state of emancipation to the world, to make an effort for it [moksha] is essential.'

There appears to be some change in this view of Dayanand from the usual concept as contained in Hinduism about swarga. According to the traditional Hindu cosmogony, there are different lokas, or divisions, of the universe, for example, bhur-loka (the earth) bhuvar-loka the space between the earth and the sun (where munis and siddhas live), swar-loka (the heaven of Indra, between the sun and the polar star), mahar-loka (the abode of Bhrigu and other saints who are believed to be co-existent with Brahma), jana-loka (the abode of Brahma's sons, Sankara, Sananda and sanat-kumara), taper-loka where the deities called vairagis live, and satya-loka or brahma-loka (the abode of Brahma) from which there is no rebirth.

There are various other divisions. Dayanand, however, as we have seen, did not believe in the existence of heaven or hell. Heaven or hell was here on earth and implied joy and suffering. In the place of swarga we have the Swami's idea of 'limited' moksha where the soul enjoys bliss till its return to earth at the end of a cycle. But apparently this enjoyment is not like the pleasure other religions have to offer. The *Satyarthaprakasha* draws a distinction between the concept of limited moksha for a cosmic cycle and the Jain concept of enjoyment in Shivapur; the Christian one of the residence of the soul in the fourth heaven along with 'marriage', musical instruments, clothes etc., the Mohammedan heaven on the seventh firmament, the Shripur of Vama-margis, Kailasha of ahaivites; the Vaikuntha of vaishnvas; Goloka etc., of the Gokuliya-gosains, where they enjoy beautiful women, food, clothes, residence and so forth; and the Pauranikas who enjoy proximity with God. Dayanand criticises these concepts in the part of *Satyarthaprakash* which deals with these religions.

As regards rebirth, Dayanans seems to agree with the Hindu view. The soul undergoes many repeated births on the earth, as Lord Krishna says in the *Gita* 'As the soul passes in this body through childhood, youth and age, even so is its taking on of another body', and many are my lives that are past, and thine also, O Arjuna. In the *Satyarthaprakasha*, when the hypothetical questioner asks pointedly if there is one birth or several the reply is, many births. Dayanand also considers the related question of man's first sin.

According to the Christians man's first sin was to break the Lord's commandment. After God had created Adam and Eve. 'They were both naked and were not ashamed'. God had asked Adam not to eat 'of the tree of knowledge of good and evil'. Eve, tempted by Satan in the shape of the serpent, broke God's command and ate the fruit of the tree, and also gave it to Adam to eat. That opened their eyes and they discovered that they were naked. For their sin, God drove them out of Paradise inflicting punishment on the serpent, Eve and Adam all of whom had partaken of the sin of breaking his commandment. 'Unto the women, he said, I will greatly multiply thy sorrow and thy conception; in sorrow thou shalt bring forth children; and thy desire shall be to thy husband and he shall rule over thee.' To Adam, the Lord said: 'Because thou hast hearkened unto the voice of thy wife, and hast eaten of the tree, of which I commanded thee, saying thou shalt not eat of it: cursed is the ground for thy sake; in sorrow shalt thou eat of it all the days of thy life; thorns also and thistles shall it bring forth to thee; and thou shalt eat the herb of the field; in the sweat of thy face shalt thou eat bread, till thou return unto the ground; for out of it wast thou taken; for dust thou art, and unto dust shalt thou return.'

Dayanand, of course, scoffs at the idea of eating of the fruit of the tree of knowledge of good and devil, being a sin. It is queer, he says, that knowing the difference between good and evil should be counted as evil, when it is the mark of wisdom. In the *Satyarthaprakasha* a similar point is taken up. Why should people suffer for past works without having knowledge of them? The soul is incapable of knowing what deeds were done by it in past lives. He says: 'The jiva has limited knowledge and cannot have knowledge of the past, present and future, so it can't remember its past deeds. Also the mind cannot have knowledge of two things simultaneously. Leave alone events of past lives, why can't the jiva remember events from the time of birth to when the child was five years old? Also why cannot it remember in deep sleep, all its experiences in the sleeping and the waling state? And suppose one were to ask you [the hypothetical questioner] what you did at one minute past ten on the ninth day of the fifth month of your thirteenth year; what was the position at the instant of your face, hands, ears, eyes and body, and what was your mind thinking of? [Can you tell?] When this is so in this very life then to speak of past lives is mere childishness.

'And, in fact, the jiva is happy just because it cannot recollect its past deeds. Otherwise knowing the sorrows of past lives it would not be able to bear them, and the man would did. Even it one wants to know the events of the life before and past lives, he can't because the knowledge and nature of the jiva is limited. God can know them, but not man'.

The questioner then goes on the question which an obvious corollary of this 'When one has no knowledge of one's past deeds and God punishes him for them, this cannot act as a corrective; for when he knows that he had done such and such a deed and this is the punishment for that deed, then only can he realise his fault'.

Dayanand's answer to this does not really convince. He explains punishment and reward for past deeds on the basis of incompatibility between human beings in regard to wealth and poverty, ignorance and knowledge, but one can obviously not thereby conclude that the incompatibility is due to acts done in past lives. How much of it is God-made and how much man made, is anybody's guess. The questioner goes on to argue that placing any restriction on God's power would not make him supreme. As a gardener plants small and big trees in his garden and of these some he tends, others he cuts or uproots; so too the person to whom a thing belongs may keep it as he likes.

There is no one above God, so why should he fear [i.e. be restricted]. In reply Dayanand says 'God does as seems just to him. He is never unjust. That is why he is worth adoration and is great. If he acted unjustly he would not be God. As a gardener is a fault if he plants trees without adequate space and approach, cuts those trees, which are useful, and trends the useless ones; so also if God acts unreasonably, he would be at fault. God is by nature pure and just, so he must act justly. If he were arbitrary without reason, he would be worse and more dishonourable than a human judge. Is he not to be condemned in this world who does not reward one who does good work and punishes an evildoer? Therefore God does no injustice, and that is why he fears no one'.

The accident, or destiny of birth has been explained by Hindu philosophers as springing from works done in previous lives. How else, they say can one explain why one is born with the proverbial silver spoon in his mouth and another in abject poverty. No one bothers to consider such differences man-made. There is also the very significant factor of human endeavour. Without effort nothing is possible, and as a *Bhagavadgita* says one cannot even exist without working: sharirayatra' pi cha te na prasidhyed akarmanah. However, Dayanand falls in line with other Hindu thinkers in attributing differences of birth to the good or evil works performed in previous lives. In the *Satyarthaprakash* he says: 'See one child is born from the womb of the queen of a learned, virtuous king and another from that of a very poor grass-cutter's wife. One gets happiness always, the other sorrow... Secondly, if these things were not governed by karma, there need not have been hell and heaven thereafter. For, if we believe God gives happiness and sorrow arbitrarily not according to one's deeds, then he can send anyone to hell or heaven as he chooses at his own will. This will lead to all beings becoming shorn of dharma, for what will then be the incentive for good works? They will doubt if there will be no fear of retribution for immortal works. Sin will increase in the world and dharma will be extinct'.

As regards the question whether there is the same soul in all living creatures or different ones Dayanand says the soul is the same but it is sin or virtue, which creates the differences. The sinful soul falls, while the virtuous one rises.

AFTER LIFE

Dayanand believes in rebirth. In the *Satyarthaprakash* he goes into the question of the mechanism of rebirth, and the factors that contribute to the kind of future existence one has, according to his deeds.

We will recapitulate in brief, here the Vedantic concept about rebirth. As soon as a human being dies, the soul withdraws into itself all the permanent atoms, beginning with speech and ending with prana. The whole region of the heart lights up. This illumination takes place in the case of all persons at death, whether they are wise or ignorant. But in the case of the wise man, the soul is able to see and select the sushumna artery (the hundred and first one) by which the soul can depart. In this the wise soul is assisted by devotional knowledge, by the Lord's favour and through the memory of the gods who have conducted it on the god-ward path. Other souls go out of other arteries. When the soul goes forth, speech is merged with mind, the mind in the breath in fire, and fire in the highest god. According to its deeds the soul passes either by the way of the Gods (devayana) to the worlds of Brahman, or by the way of the father (pitriyana) to the moon. The path of the gods is through the world of the gods to the sun, then to the moon, the path of the gods is through the world of the Gods to the sun, then to the moon where the soul is tested, and if found worthy, continues its journey on to lighting. From lighting the soul proceeds to the world of Brahman, being led by a person made of mind, not human. In the course of its progress the soul sheds its good and evil deeds, the former falling on the relatives he loved, and the latter on the relatives he hated. The way of the fathers is to the atmospheric world (bhuvarloka) where the soul becomes a disembodied ghost till the death ceremonies are completed, when he goes into a suitable body and takes his place among his fathers in their realm. From there again the soul enters space, and then to the moon, where he remains till his merit is exhausted. Thence he goes again into space, from there respectively to the wind, smoke, mist cloud, rain, earth and vegetable life. The Soul then passes into the destined form through anyone who eats the vegetables. Those good are born in higher castes, and those not so good in the lower forms like worms, moths, pigs, dogs and so forth. There are others who being very wicked, dwell in hell and suffer age-long torments;

and if even then their wicked deeds are not exhausted, the are hurled into regions lower, below the earth. Whose children fail to perform the funeral ceremonies become ghosts.

In some manner other religions too believe in an afterlife, heaven, hell and so forth. The Christians have their Day of judgement when everyone will be judged, the Muslims the Barzakh and the Day of Reckoning, the Zoroastrians believe in judgement and punishment or reward. The righteous should according to the Zoroastrians are met by a fragrant wind and a supremely beautiful maiden—the Conscience of the soul. The wicked souls encounter a lithesome old hag. They also believe in heaven and hell.

Dayanand's account is not so comprehensive as the Hindu one, but in essence it is the same. The soul, he says, may, after abandoning a human body, enter that of an animal or other creature. This happens when the sins committed by the soul are great and its virtue little. When dharma is predominant and sins very much less, then the soul gets the body of a learned and virtuous person. When virtue and evil are evenly balanced, it attains the life of an ordinary human being. Thus the kind of rebirth for the soul depends on sin and virtue being predominant, deficient or middling. When, after suffering the consequences of great sin by assuming the body of a beast the soul's punishment is complete and virtue and sin balance each other, it takes the body of an ordinary average human being. The soul then enters a human body through the wind, grain, water or through the holes of the body, according to the will of God. It then enters the semen, and through that into the womb of a woman. If its deeds are such as to necessitate a female body, it is born as a girl or else as a boy. The soul of the man who commits theft, adultery, the murder of good, persons and such evil deeds, gòes into trees and other such stationary objects; the should of those who commit sin by speech are reborn as animals, deer etc.; and due to sins committed through the mind one gets the body of a chandala and so forth. Thus the soul undergoes many births, till having attained enlightenment, it achieves moksha. In line with his thinking, Dayanand speaks of this moksha as 'mahakalpa parayanata', that is to say 'lasting till a mahakalpa (the great cosmic cycle)'.

As we have already said Dayanand believes that even in the state of moksha, the soul remains separate from God. If it merges with Brahman, he argues, it would not be there to experience the pleasure of bliss. It appears Dayanand is not very certain about his concept of bliss. At one place, as we have already said, he believes that to confer eternal bliss on the soul, would be to place a burden on it too great for it bear. Yet he says that the jiva remain separate from Brahman to be able to enjoy bliss. The two stands do not seem to be very consistent. To differentiate between 'eternal bliss' and 'limited bliss' is to make too find a distinction.

The Samkhya Element

Dayanand held the traitavada theory according to which there exists three eternal substances namely God, Jivas (souls) and prakriti (Primordial nature). The cosmic cycle was in the beginning conceived by him to be subject to evolution and dissolution. But as we have seen he modified many of his concepts later, and this was one of them. The cosmic cycle was finally declared by him to be eternal. There is no beginning or end and it maintains a progress from evolution to dissolution and them again from dissolution to evolution forever and ever. Its association with the gunas (qualities) brings about the evolution of the dormant and undifferentiated prakriti. According to Samkhya all things animate and inanimate (bhutas from 'bhava' meaning' existent') are comprised of the gunas. These gunas are three, namely sattva (purity), rajas (activity) and tamas (dullness). Sattva leads to knowledge, purity, goodness and pleasure; rajas are the root of ceaseless activity, and tamas produced apathy, indifference, ignorance and sloth. The gunas are extremely fine in texture and are continually changing. When their equilibrium is disturbed, we have evolution. One of the three guans is preponderant in all phenomena. The others are also there but in a subdued form. The preponderant guna determines the type of creature existing in creation. In prakriti, before evolution, all the three gunas remain equal and in a balanced state, like a tug-of-war in which both sides are pulling the rope with perfectly equal strength. While prakriti is non-consciousness (achetanam) purusha (which is akin to the Vedantic atman) is consciousness (sachetanam). Prakriti is active and ever revolving, purusaha is inactive (akarta). Purusha is unalterably constant, while prakriti is so alterable. Purusha causes movement in the quiescent prakriti, not deliberately like a footballer kicking the ball, but by its very nearness, like a magnet attracting iron-fillings. Gaudapada's example is, as that of a blind man (prakriti) carrying a lame man (the soul). The soul having consciousness can see, but not move. The body has no consciousness but can do things. Hence the two combine to produce a living, moving, thinking and acting creature.

In another way, which is very relevant in view of Dayanand's theory of 'limited moksha', in which Samkhya had a positive influence, is in the fact that according to it when release (emancipation) is achieved, there is only disappearance of things, not destruction. This leaves the chance that ignorance and passion may reassert them in the released soul. On release, the Samkhya philosophy says. "The purusha unmoved and self-collected as a spectator contemplates prakriti which has ceased to produce." The Samkhian idea might have spurred on Dayanand to reject the Vedantic theory of moksha as union with Brahman, and instead substitute the one of bliss till mahapralaya.

In the *Satyarthaprakasha*, Dayanand invokes Samkhya to explain the differences in the accomplishment of various persons and consequently the characteristics of their deeds and of the fruits of those deeds. He says: 'The guna, which is predominant in these jivas, makes it like itself. When the soul has knowledge then it is sattva [which predominates]; when ignorance then tamas; and when the soul is influenced by desire and aversion, then it should be known to be overpowered by rajas. These three kinds of gunas pervade all worldly things.

One should understand this thus: when the mind is contained in the atman in a state of happiness and purity, then one should know that sattva is on the rise and the other two gunas are in small measure. When the soul and the mind shorn of happiness, sorrowfully wander about seeking sensual pleasures, then one should know rajas to predominate. When the mind and soul are lost in delusion and enslaved by worldly things, have no power of discrimination, and are attached to sensual joys and know not what is wrong and what is right; one should then know for certain that the tamas guna is uppermost.

'Now I will tell you what the signs are by which one can know the presence of these gunas. When there is knowledge of the vedas, the arising of dharma, increase in knowledge, desire for purity, control over the senses, following of the moral laws, meditation the arman—that is the sign of sattva. When rajas is predominant there is interest in starting projects and ventures, relinquishment of peace of mind, carrying out of false works and the constant use of things which bring sensual pleasures. The signs of the tamas guna are increase in sins, great greed, laziness and sleep, destruction of calmness, cruelty, disbelief in God and the Vedas, a wandering mind which cannot stay at one place, begging for money, drinking and indulging in sensual pursuits'.

The character of the man of sattva guna is that he puts his effort in good works and in what gives happiness to the mind. The man in whom rajas is one the rise delights in showing prominence, and even if he is in want of money, he will give charity just to show off. The person in whom tamas prevails, does things with selfish desire, shame and suspicion in his mind, Briefly the sign of tamas is carnal desire, of rajas gathering wealth, and of sattva—moral and social service. The highest place belongs to the sattva guna, then comes rajas and the lowest is tamas.

Dayanand goes on to explain what the result of acting according to the gunas is, on rebirth and future life. In doing this he divides each guna into three categories—low, middling and high. The sattvic persons are learned and wise, the rajasic are ordinary and the tamasic are of the low kind.

Those who, are greatly tamasic are reborn, as trees, worms, insects, fishes. serpents. tortoises, beasts and deer. The middling, tamasic, and reborn as elephants, horses, shudras, lions, tigers, boars and pigs. The best among the tamasic persons are reborn as bards, loverly birds, braggarts demons and evil spirits. The lowest kind of rajasic people are reborn stupid men, boatmen, acrobats and wielders of arms who are drunkards. The middling rajasic people are reborn as kings, priests of kshatriya rajahs, debaters, messengers, lawyers and barristers and heads of the departments of defence and war. The best classes of rajasic persons are reborn as singers, players of musical instruments, wealthy persons, servants of the wise, and lovely women. The ordinary sattvic persons are reborn as sages, ascetics, sannyasis, chanters of the Vedas drivers of vimans (air-chariots), astrologers and vaidyas i.e. those who help in the maintenance of the body. The middling sattvic persons and those who carry out yajnas, knowers of the meaning of the Vedas i.e. those who write commentaries on the Vedas, wise men, the knowers of scientific knowledge, learned persons and teachers of men who are keen to acquire knowledge are who are accomplished.

Those who having the loftiest sattvic nature, do noble deeds, knowing all the Vedas and the knowledge of how creation came about and are the planners of projects for making vimans and so forth (technicians). They are reborn as the knowers of the eternal, and obtain special powers. Those who have no control over their senses, ignorant, and seekers of sensual pleasures, obtain low bodies and lead sorrowful lives. Thus in brief the fruit of one's deeds are according to the guna which is predominant in him, and also according to works. When the mind becomes steady and pure, then the soul is established in the nature of God. Therefore one should strive for emancipation. Quoting an aphorism from the Samkhya, Dayananda concludes: 'it is very necessary that one should free himself from the three types of sorrows, namely adhyatmika adhibhautika and adhidaivika, and obtain mukti (moksha). This is the ultimate aim of life'.

CREATION

We have seen that Dayanand gives God a hundred names, implying that there is only one God, and men call him by various names, as the *Rig Veda* says; ekam sad vipra bahudha vadanti. God is sat-chit-ananda i.e. being-consciousness-bliss. He is formless (nirakara), and the four Vedas are his word. God taught their texts and meaning to four rishis—Agni, the *Rig Veda;* Vayu, the *Yajuraveda;* Aditya, the *Samaveda;* and Angirasa, the *Atharva Veda*. The Vedas contain all that needs to be known. Arts, science, philosophy, the mode of government and all knowledge finds place in them. But, according to him, the Vedas include only the mantra (hymns) portion and not the Brahmana scriptures.

Further he believed—though other religionists would hardly agree with him in this, even the indigenous religions of Buddhism and Jainism refute their authority—that the Vedas were the gospel of all mankind. Sanskrit, in which the Vedas were written, he believed was chosen to reveal God's word. Dayanand discusses the world's origin and creation in the eighth chapter of *Satyarthaprakash*.

In the beginning, he says, the worlds were enveloped in darkness and akasharupa i.e. pervaded by space. The same is the Upanishadic concept. The world, says the *Mahanarayana Upanishad*, was enveloped in darkness; 'In the beginning of creation the mortal world, enveloped in gloom, received its divine brilliance from the sun shining in the glory of paramatman' So too the Bible: 'And the earth was without form, and void; and darkness was upon the face of the deep. And the Spirit of God moved upon the face of the waters'. Other Upanishads (like the *Aitarya,* and *Brihadaranyaka*) however, do not subscribe, to the darkness theory. The *Rig Veda* says that there was nothing 'aught nor nought' and 'gloom hid in gloom'. Maybe Dayanand got his idea from this passage of the Rig Veda.

Thereafter, says Dayanand, God, by means of his power, converted 'cause into action'. God was present and existing before the creation of the universe, and he was its Maker. That maker or parmatman is known as Brahman. When the questioner asks whether the universe has been produced from God or from some other, he says 'Its efficient cause (nimittakarnaa) is God, but its material cause (Upadana-Karana) is primordial nature (prakriti)'. As we have already said, according to Dayanand's concept prakriti is eternal. Thus according to Dayanand's theory of creation, two eternals have a hand in the fashioning of the universe—God and prakriti.

God can, therefore be only a kind of primus inter pares in regard to nature and the soul. It is as it were, the playing of an orchestra. There are the musical notes denoted by the various signs appearing in the music which the players see and are guided by—the bass, trebles and so forth. Its composer composes the music. It has to be played according to the orchestral score. The conductor only directs it. He cannot change a note, or in any way alter the music sheet. God is like the music conductor. The various notes are as the works or deeds done by human beings. The players are the gunas of prakriti, and the orchestral score the soul (jiva). Thus God has no power to alter the notes or the karmas (deeds). All he can do is to conduct the drama of life according to the deeds of beings living in the world. He has no authority like that of the Vedantic grace which can nullify the evil influence of bad deeds.

Besides, as the music conductor, the music sheet and the players all exist as of their own right, so too God, the soul and primordial nature are eternal and unalterable. Dayanand's theory of creation has much of the samkhian element in it. The Samkhya too, does not believe in any universal destruction, or mahapralaya, which cannot occur in the sense of complete destruction of the soul and prakriti, as the two share co-eternality with God. The *Samkhya Karika* says: 'Once nature exhibits herself to the soul it is never joined to matter. When the linga (the soul's vehicle) dissolves at moksha, nature has no capacity to produce. The soul having got supreme knowledge looks on as spectator on an actress. All things retire into consciousness; consciousness into intellect; and intellect into prakriti. Soul and matter continue to exist, but isolated and independent of each other. But there is a difference. According to the Karika after the drama of life is thus ended, no new character can be assumed and the actors retire from the stage forever.

Dayananda mentions the cause of the creation of the universe as three, later on in the *Satyarthaprakash*. In essentials this does not change his stand but only elaborates it. He says; 'There are three causes, one the efficient, second the material and third the ordinary (sadharna). That is known as the efficient cause by the making of which something is made and by its not making it is not made, but which does not itself become that which is made, only gives form to another. Second, is the material cause. This is that without which nothing can be made. It takes the required form, and also again turns the form into the original state. The third is ordinary or common cause, which assists in the making. Efficient cause is of two kinds. One is God who is the chief efficient cause. He creates creation from cause; sustains it, destroys it, and maintains order.

As stated before, this is the same concept as that of the Hindu trinity, Brahma-Vishnu-Mahesh. The other efficient cause is the soul, which takes the various ingredients of God's creation and makes them active in various ways. The material cause is prakriti—the paramanus (infinitely small particles like atoms)—which is the material from which all things in the world are made. Dayanand says that 'one Arab, ninety-six crores many lakhs and many thousands of years have passed since creation began'. The basic substance, which goes to make it, is the indivisible paramanu. Sixty paramanus combine to form an anu. The gross air is made of two anus (which form one 'dvayanuka'). Fire consists of six anus, water of eight anus and ten anus from the earth [i.e. three, four and five dvayanukas respectively].

Being lifeless, creation can't make or unmake itself, but by another's making it is made, and by another's destroying it is destroyed. Sometimes a lifeless thing can also assist in making or destroying another lifeless thing, as the seeds made by God fall on the earth and on getting water, turn into trees; and by coming into contact with fire etc., are also destroyed. But their making and destruction is controlled by God according to a definite pattern.

The elements by which things are made are its ordinary cause. For example knowledge, appearance, strength, hands, and various things that help in the making like direction, time and space. As for a potter working at his wheel, the potter is the efficient cause, the clay from which the pots are made is the material cause, the wheel etc., are the common-efficient causes, and the hands, eyes etc., are also the efficient and the common-efficient causes. Nothing can be created or destroyed except by these three causes—efficient, material and common.

Dayanand discards the Vedantic concept of God being the efficient as well as the material cause of the universe, as for example, a spider weaving a web from its own body. His argument is that if we accept this God would be insentient, false and devoid of bliss. Brahman is limitless, while the world is limited. If we believe substances like earth etc., are produced from God, the same lifeless quality would have to be believed to reside in him also. And if we insist that God is sentient, such lifeless things as earth, stones and so forth, would also have to be so. In both cases we reach as absurd conclusion.

Apparently Dayanand could not rise to the level of the concept that there could be fullness even if something was taken from it. As for example the rivers flow down from their sources in the mountains and even though continually discharging their water into the sea, and never empty. Water forms clouds and that water comes from the ocean, yet the ocean is always full. The snow melts on snow-clad peaks, yet they are always clad in snow. The wind blows and blows and never exhausts itself, and fire is always latent and comes into existence just by striking a match stick on a match box. Despite being eternally produced it never exhausts itself.

As the Upanishads put it: purnamadah purnamidam purnat purnanamudachayate purnasya purnamadaya purnamevavashishyate. From the full take the full and yet the full is lef behind; for this is full and that is full, and in the full we fullness find'. Dayanand does not depict his usual clarity on this point, perhaps because he could not effectively refute the Vedantic stand. He harnesses the Vedantic metaphor of the spider and the web to his own advantage, saying that apart from the spider there is no other creature which can produce the substance which makes the web from its own body. He is not even factually right, as he forgets creatures such as bees which convert pollen into honey and then deposit the honey into honeycombs.

However, the conclusion he ultimately reaches is almost the same as that of the Vedanta. 'In the same way the pervasive Brahman has made the gross universe from Prakriti and the infinitestimal atoms (paramanus) existing in him; and making it thus gross-shaped, himself pervading it, enjoys bliss as a witness looking on. This has an Upanishadic ring "Two birds, always united, of equal name, dwell upon one and the same tree. The one of them enjoys the sweet fruit of the tree, the other looks on as a witness'. Besides, if the paramanus exist within Brahman the argument about Brahman being gross if it is considered to be the material cause of the universe, is not forceful at all. Dayanand goes on to say that God can't be said to have any desire for gaining reputation by producing the world, for any advantage to be so gained in creation will be of no account when pralaya or destruction overtakes the worlds.

Why Creation?

Answering a hypothetical question, why should there be creation at all, Dayanand answers, why not? The Vedanta considers Brahman's creative activity as mere sport (lila). It is not any desire or motive, which makes him create the world, it is just his pastime, as a rich man or prince would do something just to amuse himself, or as children play for mere fun. This is much like Shakespeare's famous lines. 'As flies to wanton boys are was to the gods. They kill us for their sport'.

Nonetheless a man's deserts are according to his deeds. Dayanand denies that the world was created for letting human beings experience joy and sorrow. What sorrow or joy exists to creatures in pralaya (the world's destruction), he asks? Besides joy is many times more than sorrow. Many persons of pure souls try for emancipation, achieve it, and with it, bliss [contrast this with his view that the emancipated soul cannot bear the burden of supreme bliss]. God has created the world for perfecting mankind. Human beings get sorrow or joy according to their deeds. God does not give it to them arbitrarily. One might as well ask, what is the use of eyes? The answer would obviously be, for seeing. So what can be God's purpose in creating the world by his power, act of creation and his knowledge, except to bring if forth?

There can be on other reason. And God's qualities of justice, mercy and so forth can only made manifest when there is creation. His eternal power lies in creation of the world, its existence, its destruction and in its organisation. As the inherent quality of the eye is to see. God's purpose in creating the world is to give countless gifts to human beings and thus bring about their redemption.

Dayanand says that the cause precedes the effect as the seed is cast first and then grows into a tree. When the questioner says, "When God is all-powerful why can't he create the two [cause and effect] simultaneously"? Dayanand's answer is that being all-powerful does not imply that one can accomplish even that which is impossible. So God is not all-powerful in that sense. He cannot produce sentient things from what is insentient, or the other way about. He cannot produce another God and then himself 'die' [i.e. cease to exist]. God's ways are perfect and true, and he cannot act otherwise. Being all-powerful only means that God can carry all his tasks unaided, and by his own self-alone.

THE WORLD IS NOT UNREAL

God, according to Dayanand, is without form. He can't be with form because if we assume him, to be so he would be limited, without power, defined by country and time, and subject to hunger, thirst, being cut and pierced, cold, heat, pain and so forth. Without the spirit, God-like qualities can never dwell in him. As neither do human beings have bodies that they cannot have control over prakriti and minor atoms of infinitesimal size, nor can they catch hold of those subtle things and make them gross; so too, a gross form-endowed God cannot make the gross world from subtle elements.

But being subtler than prakriti and pervading it, he can by controlling prakriti, create the universe, and be the dweller in all and the destroyer too. Without cause there cannot be effect. God too cannot create or make anything unless he sees existence of a cause. Dayanand's view is different from that of the Advaita Vedanta. According to Shankaracharya it is Brahman which is the cause of the universe. Dayanand's argument is that Brahman cannot be the material cause, because while it is non-material the universe consists of matter. The nature of the two is different, so one cannot be the cause of the other.

The Vedanta says it can. As for example, worms in insentient putrefying matter like cow-dung. We evil are of themselves produced in wood and grain, insects and worms in fruit which rot. At the same time nails and hair growing in the body are lifeless. Vedanta believes cause and effect to be one. The earthen pot is in essence clay, even after it is made. The effect is not different from the cause. So there does not exist the world (effect) different from Brahman (cause). As we have discussed before, Dayanand's argument in favour of his view that God cannot be the material cause of the universe, is also that if this were so, at the time of dissolution (pralaya) the world of effects, would dissolve back into Brahman, the cause. The impurities of the worldly state might then also make the causal state of brahmahood impure. The Vedanta's answer to this is that it is not necessarily so. For example, when gold or silver articles are melted, the resultant god or silver does not become impure. When the magical creations of a magician are no more, they cannot affect him.

Another Vedantic concept, which Dayanand refutes, is that only Brahman is true and the world is false (Brahman satya, jagat mithya). He says, 'if every substance's immutability is eternal how can it be no-eternal'. To this the objector says 'The immutability of all things is also transient. As fire burns up firewood and then is consumed [dies out]'. To this Dayanand's answer is: 'That which appears as it is, can never be said to be transient in the present and so too its greatly subtle cause cannot be said to be transient. If the Vedantists consider Brahman to be true, the world, which proceeds from it, cannot be false. Even if dreams are said to be imaginary like the "snake-in-the-rope" and so forth, the cannot stand scrutiny, because imagination is a quality; and substance and quality can never remain separate from each other. If we believe the one who imagines to be eternal, what he imagines must also be eternal; otherwise you have to consider the one who imagines to be transient also. In other words either the imaginer and what he imagines must both be eternal or both transitory. One can't be eternal and the other transitory.

As dreams never come without the dreamer seeing and experiencing them, those objects, which exist in waking, are seen and their knowledge established in the soul. These are then seen again in dreams. As even in deep sleep when a person is unaware of anything, the objects of the waking world are still there, so also in dissolution (pralaya) cause-matter [seed of cause] remains existent. If dreams are not caused by mental impressions, then even a man blind by birth would be able to see forms. So in dreams we have only mental impressions, while in the waking world the objects exist in their reality.

Dayanand goes on to say that it can never be conceded that the waking world does not exist in deep sleep or dreams. When a person is soundly asleep or dreaming he may not see the objects around him, but that does not mean they have no existence. Its, as a person is looking in front of himself cannot know what things are there behind him. So it must be acknowledged that the cause of Brahman, the soul and the world are beginningless and eternal.

By saying this, however, Dayanand was not contradicting the Vedanta stand in its entirety. The illustrations of the world was certainly a Vedanta concept. The Vedanta said in general that what is real is present at all times. It ever was, and ever will be. The world of experience is not present at all times, and therefore unreal. Only Brahman is real. The *Brihadaranyaka Upanisha* says that as the notes of a drum, a conch-shall or a lute have no existence in themselves, and can only be received when the instrument that produces them is struck, he who knows the atman knows so all objects and relations of the universe. Nevertheless it must not be supposed that Dayanand's view can count to the Vedantic concept in its entirety.

In some schools of Shankar Vedanta everything is held to be illusion. Objects are said to exist only when they are perceived, and dissolve into nothingless when they are not perceived. This is the drishti-sroti school, which perhaps takes its inspiration from the *yoga Vasistha*. The world of waking is akin to dreams and is mere awareness with any right, as of itself, to existence. (Vijnana-matra or bhava-matra). According to Gaudapada, the guru of Shankara's guru, the world is a dream, and existence is unreal. There is no production, destruction, no one is fettered, on one liberated. All that one sees, feels, or experiences is mere imagination.

As Tulsidasa says in the *Ramayana* 'dekhiye, suniye, guniye mana mamhi, moha mula paramaratha nahim' [Whatever one sees, hears or imagines in the mind is illusion, and has no reality']. Appearances are only relatively produced, not in reality. They are like dreams, which come and go. In the beginning Shankara, too, was inclined to this view. But the Buddhist idealists like Vasubandhu, made him revise his view. Between his commentary on the *Karika* and that on the *Brahma Sutras*, there was a visible change. If there is nothing outside the mind, he wrote, how could objects exist as they do? It was wrong to say that the appearance of worldly objects in wakefulness is like dreams. Dreams are contradicted on waking, experiences are not contradicted. It is only one's view about the world, which change. When one is bound to the world, he is lost in sense pleasures, and when he is not so bound he achieves liberation. The world is there, it is not non-existent like the horns of a hare. The real error is in taking the transitory to be eternal, the painful as the pleasure giving, the unholy as the holy and the body as the soul. As soon as this error is removed, one sees truth as it really is (yathartha). Thus Dayanand's view in this respect may be contrary to certain schools of the Vedanta, but not contrary to Shankaracharya's philosophy.

THE RELATIONSHIP OF GOD WITH THE SOUL

Dayanand does not concur with the Vedantic view-aham brahmasami 'the soul is Brahman'. The objector poses the question of the eternality of the universe. Dayanand expounds his view that without a maker nothing that has the quality of becoming can be made. Those elements, which we see, go to produce the world, like earth etc. They can never be beginningless. And what the union of various things brings about cannot exist before such union, nor can it exist when such union ceases. Atoms unite to make elements and so they can also separate at some time. We have stated that when Dayananda wrote the first *Satyarthprakash*, he was greatly influenced by the Nyaya philosophy. According to the Nyaya's atomic theory a particular body was the product of a particular atom. When two material substances combined to form a new product there was both samayaya (intimate relation) and samyoga (coming together). The material dravyas, earth, water, fire and air, were believed to be derived from atoms (anu).

The universe thus consisted firstly of atoms that were the ultimate substances and so could not be further sub-divided, and secondly the sub-stratum built on them, which is the world we ordinarily see and know. Dayananda, however, denies the soul to have the same status as

Brahman. No soul, however much it tries, however great wisdom it may gain, can ever be like God. If God had not endowed the soul with a body and with the five senses, how could it ever strive for perfection? And if it could not so strive how could it attain that perfection? The soul can never be equated with God in whom there is infinite perfection. However great the soul's knowledge may be it will be limited, and so too its power. The soul cannot have limitless knowledge and power. No one has yet been born and no one will ever be, when can change the order or law of God's creation.

The earth and the elements were created first, according to Dayanand, and thereafter—human beings. Also many human beings were created in the beginning, not just one like the Adam of the Christians. This was a natural corollary to Dayananda's concept of moksha, according to which souls, which have achieved liberation, are again reborn on the earth after the end of the cosmic cycle. If he propounded the theory of their being one man and one woman only in the beginning of creation, how could he fit in with that of the rebirth of all these liberated souls? He also says that after creating the earth. God inhabited it with young men and women, for if he created them old how could they copulate and produce children? Creation is beginningless and endless. As day follows night, night follows day and so on, so too before creation there was dissolution, and after dissolution, creation and so forth. In this way creation goes on eternally, although, it may appear to be non-eternal. As day and night follow each other eternally in succession, yet one day has an end, and a particular night and end too, so too creation and destruction. It is as the flow of a river. The river goes on. It may dry up in summer, yet as the rains come, its bed fills up again and it brims with water.

TRUTH AND UNTRUTH

The foundation of the Arya Samaj by Maharashi Dayanand Saraswati on 6 April 1875 at Bombay was commemorated with great enthusiasm during its centenary celebrations held in 1975 all over India and at many places abroad. The colourful processions and mammoth meetings held on that occasion proved that the Samaj continues to be a popular and effective organisation in India. Glowing tributes were paid by the President, the Prime Minister, and other eminent persons to the great services rendered by the Arya Samaj in the sphere of national and political awakening, social and religious reforms, the spread of education and the emancipation of women and the downtrodden depressed classes, and its role in attempting to free the people from the shackles of caste, purdah and priesthood.

However, this record, glorious as it is, is not and should not be an excuse to make us complacent. It is necessary to evaluate the past achievements in order to formulate its future programme which may ensure yet another glorious century of greater service and success. Before we venture to think of the future it is essential to understand and delineate the actual position of the Arya Samaj because of the many misconceptions and misinterpretations about its historical background, real mission and scope. Unless this is done its future work is likely to be either hampered or misdirected.

There is no doubt that the Arya Samaj began as a revolutionary movement of all-round reformation and reawakening in the peculiar circumstances of the nineteenth century India. The advent of Swami Dayanand has been rightly described as a baffling historical phenomenon in the unlikely conditions of those days. But it was not and was never meant to be merely a reform movement, otherwise it should have come to an end like all other movements when its immediate object was realised. There was no need to have branches in India and abroad and thousands of institutions of a permanent basis.

Did the Arya Samaj complete its mission? There are people both inside and outside the Arya Samaj who have already begun to say that it has achieved its objective of paving the way for reforms in Hindu society. Modern Hinduism is a proud achievement of the teachings and sacrifices of Swami Dayanand and the relentless efforts of the leaders of the Arya Samaj. They point out that the constitution of free India enshrines in its Directive Principles as well as in the Fundamental Rights almost everything preached and advocated by the Arya Samaj. Untouchability has been made unlawful, caste distinctions have no legal recognition, women have been granted equal status, child marriages, purdah, dowry are all on their way out. Swadeshi and Swarajya, the twin dreams of Swami Dayanand have been realised.

It was he who, although, himself a Gujarati, first declared that Hindi should be our national language.

All this is true and very satisfying; but if we remember the real aim of the foundation of the Arya Samaj and the scope of its mission, we would not fail to realise that its aim and mission were of far more abiding nature. The reform of Hindu society and freedom of India were only its immediate objectives. Perhaps a revitalised Hindu society was a necessary base for its onward march. Similarly, a politically enslaved India could not claim to preach a universal religion to the world.

A World Religion

It is significant that from its very inception the horizons of the Arya Samaj included the entire world. The ten principles are so broad-based and universal that they could easily become the basis of a world religion. The sixth principle says that, "The chief object of the Arya Samaj is to do good to the entire world, and to bring about physical, spiritual, and social progress of entire humanity". The ninth and tenth principles contain the ingredients both of socialism and democracy. They insist that the individual good can only be achieved through the good and welfare of all. Similarly, every individual has been remained that while he is free in his personal affairs, he is bound to act according to the general will of the society in all other matters. Neither in these principles nor in any of his books is there any reference to the emancipation of Hindus only. In fact the word seems to have been deliberately avoided. Everywhere, the word "Arya" has been used and that too not in the popular sense of any race or colour, but in its original Sanskrit sense of a good, honest and a brave human being irrespective of caste, creed or nationality.

The aims and by-laws of the Paropkarini Sabha founded by Swami Dayanand, speak of "desh deshantar" and "dweep dweepantar" i.e. all the countries and islands and habitations of the universe as the sphere of its work. Conversion of the whole world to Arya Samaj was the lofty ideal which Dayanand put before his followers. The Arya Samaj today is an international organisation with its branches and temples in India and abroad, it has over one thousand educational institutions for boys and girls and other institutions of religious and charitable nature.

It is a misconception to consider the Arya Samaj either as a reformed sect of Hinduism or only as a movement or timely organisation. At one time it was even dubbed as merely a political or even a seditious society. According to Ramsay Macdonald, former Prime Minister of England, the British Government looked upon the Arya Samaj as a secret political movement. It is well known how Sir Valentine Chirol in his book '*The Indian Unrest*' alleged that the violent and revolutionary activities against British rule were the direct results of the preaching of Swami Dayanand and the activities of Arya Samaj leaders like Lala Lajpat Rai and Bhai Parmanand and others. Sir Valentine, after a visit to India early in the nineteenth century, wrote in *The London Times*, "The whole drift of Dayanand's teachings is far less to reform Hinduism than to rouse it into active resistance to the alien influences, which threatened in his opinion, to denationalise it". This may be and is certainly true so far as the fact goes that before the foundation, ten years later in 1885 of the Indian National Congress, the Arya Samaj founded in 1875 was the only organisation which stood for nationalism and took pride in our ancient culture and civilization. Dayanand's teachings were bound to inspire national and political awakening. But, he intended the Arya Samaj to play a more abiding and permanent role in human affairs.

As he explained, during the hectic period of his wanderings and preaching throughout India and also in the vast literature left by him, Dayanand's mission, as well as that of the Arya Samaj founded by him, was to re-establish the universal religion of the Vedas.

The history of world religions show that every existing religion is either a revival in modified form or an improvement on some earlier old religion and therefore, even if Swami Dayanand did not claim to be the founder of any new religion, the Arya Samaj as it has grown or developed after his death, is undoubtedly a distinct religion in the same sense in which Islam and Christianity are. A comparative study of Vedism, Buddhism, Zaurastrianism, Judaism, Christianity and Islam proves that every founder of a new religion was only a reformer of some old religion and Dayanand was undoubtedly one who aimed not only at reforming but replacing the Hindu religion with the ancient Vedic religion.

Arya Samaj as an Organised Religion

The Oxford Advanced Dictionary defines religion as a "brief in the existence of a supernatural ruling power, the creator and controller of the Universe who has given to man a spiritual nature which continues to exist after the death of the body".

As explained later in this work, the very first two principles of the Arya Samaj fulfil this essential condition of a religion. The first principle declares that God is the source of all true knowledge and the second affirms the faith of the Arya Samaj in God and defines in detail its monotheism. Belief in God is only the general though indispensable requirement of a religion. An organised religion must have some separate scripture or book of God. The third principle of Arya Samaj fulfils this condition. It declares the Vedas to be such books.

Thirdly, there must be some founder or discoverer of a religion. Maharashi Dayanand occupies this position in a special sense. Anyone wishing to join the Arya Samaj has to declare in writing that he believes in the teachings of Dayanand besides accepting the ten principles. In the words of Lala Lajpat Rai, the beliefs of Swami Dayanand from the creed of Arya Samaj. Lastly, the Arya Samaj is a separate organisation with its definite and written constitution. Thus, it fulfils all the essential conditions of a separate religion more than any other accepted or established religion of the world.

There is, therefore, no question of the Arya Samaj being a sect or part of Hinduism or any other religion. This misconception requires to be removed at the outset because it is as widespread as it is baseless.

The popular confusion is the result of the use of the word "Hindu" in a loose sense. It is also incorrect to confuse the terms "Hindu", "Hinduism" and "Hindu religion", because one can be a Hindu without being a follower of Hinduism or the Hindu religion. Scholars agree that Hindu is a geographical term and originally referred to all inhabitants of Hindustan, irrespective of their religion. There cannot be any religion based on geography. We have no "Americanism", "Germanism" or "Japanism" as the religion of the people of these countries. Similarly, there is no Hinduism as the religion of all the Hindus living in Hindustan. It is significant that till recently the Americans used to call everyone from India a Hindu. Even Sir Syed Ahmed, the founder of Aligarh Muslim University, claimed to be a Hindu because he considered all those who lived in Hinduism as Hindus.

Many competent foreign observers and a large number of our own, have often credited the Arya Samaj with reforming and consolidating Hinduism. Some have even called it militant and reformed or modern Hinduism. Sir Herbert Risley had warned that, "The flame of patriotic enthusiasm will not readily arise from the cold grey ashes of philosophic compromise of Hindu religion. Before Hinduism can inspire an active sentiment of nationality, it will have to undergo a good deal of stiffening and consolidation. "He further says, "The Arya Samaj seems to be striking out a path which may lead in this direction, but the tangled jungle of Hinduism bristles with obstacles and the way is long". In this context the following observations of Mr. Blunt are also significant. He says, "Orthodox Hinduism is too apt to lead to irreligious dogma. A religion which gives rituals in place of a creed and unintelligible mantras in place of religious instructions, is bound to have such a result. And a thoughtful man will often be driven to other creeds. Amidst, all the religions, such a man has the choice of four. Brahmo Samaj is nothing but a limp eclecticism. It has discarded the Vedas and put nothing in their place. It has adopted a belief here and a doctrine there, and when doubt arise, leaves the individual to decide for himself. Such a religion has little vitality. Christianity and Islam are utterly irreconcilable with Hinduism in any shape or form but Arya Samaj is different".

Lala Lajpat Rai quotes Mr. Blunt to say that "An element of the strength in the Arya Samaj is its freedom from the formlessness and indefiniteness of Hindu polytheism on one side and the weakness of the Brahmo Samaj on the other. The Arya Samaj alone has provided a manly and straightforward creed". While it is correct and also a matter of great satisfaction for the Arya Samaj that its religious teachings and doctrines have been acclaimed and considered to be the basis of new and modern Hinduism yet we have to be careful in the assessment of these tributes and avoid confusing the reality with more wishful thinking, however well meant.

ETHICS

Dayanand's great significance is not in the propounding of his religious philosophy, which, despite some fundamental departures, is based mainly on the Samkhya Nyaya, the Vedas and some aspects of the main Hindu non-denominational scriptures such as the *Bhagavadgita*, the *Yoga Sutras*, the Six systems, and of course, the Vedas which are his main prop. His greatest contribution lies in defining the ideals of relationship between parents and children, teacher and student, guru and disciple, the duties of householders and sannyasis, right conduct and the proper way to conduct oneself in the world. In this respect his writings have much of the idealism of the *Ramayana*, where too we find such directions of good conduct and the ways in which worldly duties should be discharged.

Evils for Men and Women

The evils the Swami enumerates for women are of six kinds, namely drinking, the use of bhang (intoxicating hemp, incidentally as we have related, Dayanand himself fell into this bad habit), also the use of other such intoxicants; the company of evil persons; remaining away of the wife from her husband; going alone to have darshan of imposters and hypocrites [the indication is towards bad-charactered temple-priests, vicious persons in the garb of sadhus etc.] and sleeping or living in someone else's house [implying immortality]. The evils for men are also these [substituting 'wife' instead of 'husband'].

Education

Dayananda lays great stress or proper education, which to him is not merely acquiring knowledge, but building character also. Thus education should be comprehensive. The mother should teach the child the correct should of the various Hindu alphabets as soon as he begins to speak. He should be taught to speak in a sweet tone, and be encouraged to listen to the talks of wise men, to his mother and father and so forth. He should not be allowed to waste time in useless amusements, fighting, deriding others, greed, jealousy etc. When the child is five years old, he should be taught the devanagri script [Hindi], and also the scripts of other regional languages. He should be taught how to behave towards his parents, teachers, wise man, guests, people, family members, relations, sisters, brother and so forth; also reverence to God and acquiring education and following dharma.

The main duty of educating the child falls on the parents. There are three main persons who educate him—the mother, the father and the teacher. The mother ought to educate him from birth till he is five years old. The father from the sixth year to the eighth year, and from the ninth year onwards the boy [or girl] should attend school and study under the guidance of learned teachers, both men and women.

Dayanand is not in favour of pampering and doting on the child by parents and teachers. Instead, they should reprimand and punish them when occasion demands. He says: 'Those who reprimand the child are, as it were, giving them nectar with their own hands. And those who pamper them are, so to say, making them drink poison and are spoiling them'. By doting on children, they develop faults and by punishing them they develop good qualities. But, he cautions the parents and teacher not to chide the boy with any revengeful attitude or hatred or because of jealousy. They should outwardly chide and reprimand him but in the hearts there should be love and kindness. This is salutary advice, and Dayanand's insistence on it at an age when the child can still be moulded, shows his far-sightedness. Many parents fail to mould their children when they can yet be moulded and then when the boy's personality is hardened with the passage of years, they try to impose firmless. But then it is too late, and the parents have missed the bus.

The boy should be taught to abstain from theft, laxness, the use of intoxicants, useless speech, cruelty, jealousy, hatred, illusion etc., and to cultivate truthfulness. The lad should be told to keep his word always. Dayanand particularly cautions against arrogance and egotism in particular, as long before him Shankara did. Angar, cunning and guile also come in for his condemnation. Elders he says should be respected and given a seat higher than the one on which one sits. Another very sensible and useful observation of the Swami is that one should sit in an assembly or social gathering according to one's station, so that he is not made to vacate the seat when someone of greater importance comes. This is salutary advice, particularly in our country in which everything conforms to status and the high and low remains high and low whatever the function or occasion. Quite often one forgets this and is made to suffer the humiliation of having to get up and make way for a greater VIP than he thinks he is.

Dayanand also gives us tips about food. One should eat less than what his appetite is, abstain from meat, and eat what will keep him healthy, not what is merely tasty. He cautions people not to venture deep into the waters of a river or pond, perhaps a reflection of his own experience. Water, he says should be drunk after consecration. One who walks should also keep his gaze on the ground so that he avoids falling due to unevenness of the terrain—a useful hint even today for pedestrians who walk on our bumpy roads, littered with cow-dung and banana skins and holes dug (and left uncovered) for welcome arches for VIP's.

The Asharmas

Family Life

Dayananda goes on to describe the education and way of living of the grown-up youth. He follows the Hindu pattern of the four asharamas—student life, family life, and the later stages of a fort dweller and a hermit, which in our times are merely theoretical. Dayanand's views about marriage and revolutionary. He is liberal and insists on the mutual consent of the boy and the girl. He even believes in the meeting of the two and a frank talk between them in the presence of elderly respectable people. Much less sanctioning marriage of minors, Dayanand's view about the right age for marriage is rather unusual and more prevalent in western countries than in our own. The girl should be from sixteen years to twenty-four and the boy from twenty-five to forty-eight. The age difference, however, is bound to be considerable between the two in that case, particularly at the higher age limit [48 minus 24 i.e. 14].

Another rather out-of-the-ordinary view of his is that marriage should be in different sub-castes and the prospective couple should be living in places far away from each other. If the two have lived together in childhood have played and quarrelled, or have had love for each other, have known each other's qualities and faults, or have seen each other in the naked state; they should not marry. He gives various reasons for the girl and the boy living far away, for example those who have been familiar can never develop love for each other. Most of his arguments are based on the motto familiarity breeds contempt. If the married couple have their homes near, the wife will go away to her father's house on the slightest pretext. Thus Dayanand is all for arranged and intercaste marriages and certainly not in favour of local marriages. It must be said that from the medical point of view he is right, and there is much to support his contention. Though he mentions the eight kinds of marriages sanctioned by Manu, he rejects all except brahma-vivah, the nuptial ceremonies in the mandap [marriage pavilion] ought to end by ten in the night or at the most at midnight. This again simplifies the usual orthodox Hindu procedure, and is one of the gifts of the Arya Samaj. More and more Hindus are adopting this practice. The same is of course true for other practices, too, connected with birth and death ceremonies. He prohibits sexual intercourse from the time of conception for a year thereafter.

Speaking the truth means, according to Dayanand, speaking truth, which does not hurt. For example one should not call a one-eyed man, one-eyed [kana] to his face. Nor should one speak a lie merely to praise someone. Speech should be gentle and pleasing, keeping the good of others in mind. Never should one disparage or revile another. He should follow dharma, and act according to scriptural injunctions. The way of dharma only can redeem a person. In the other world (after death) neither mother nor father, nor wife nor son can be of any assistance. Only dharma can plead for the soul when it is before its maker.

We have already spoken about niyoga, which was favoured by Dayanand to do away with the odium attached to widows. In his view, men and women when young, cannot suppress the sexual instinct. So instead of its leading them into vicious channels, it could be chanelised into some kind of sanctioned union. Another object of niyoga was to have children or a son, which, according to Hindus was essential, for only thus could the family be continued. A son was necessary not only because of this, but also for carrying out the funeral rites of his father.

If the husband has gone away to distant lands in pursuance of dharma, the woman may enter temporary sexual union with another, under niyoga after waiting for his return for eight years. The husband's absence for other purposes makes the wait different depending on the object of his going—if for acquiring knowledge and fame, six years; if for seeking wealth, three years. When the husband returns after these periods of waiting, the nigoya relation ends and the wife and the husband revert to married life. So too, the man may take a woman in nioyga if he cannot get a son from his wedded wife—if she is barren, eight years after marriage; if a son is born but thereafter dies, the tenth year after marriage; if a girl is born repeatedly, after the eleventh year and if the wife speaks improperly without any affection, he may forthwith take another women. Niyoga has its good points as well as bad, just as any other institution. On the plus side there is the social upliftment of widows, and prevention of moral depravity. But it would certainly appear that it is rather like sanctioned adultery. Dayanand's argument is that it is not, because it is approved by the shastras as much as marriage is. Nevertheless when practiced after marriage, it loses much of its authority in as much as it negates something, which is more authoritative than it. Among Hindus [as among many other races too, like Christians], marriage is a sacrament, while niyoga can at best be something which finds mention in a particular shastra. Secondly, niyoga can also be misused, for the terms which bind it are rather loose. Then there is the question of the children born from niyoga. Disclaimed by the husband, and disowned by the temporary partner, they would have a very dubious status in the family.

Post-family Life: "Sannyasa"

After having lived a virtuous family life and conquered the senses, those belonging to the higher castes, namely the brahman, kshatriya and vaishya should depart for the forest. This should be done when grey hair and folds on the skin appear. It should be remembered that for Dayanand, brahman, kshatriya and vaishya do not have their usual connotation. They are not castes but divisions of human beings according to nature and works. In the forest they should subsist on fruits and roots and grain which can be grown there. If the man's wife accompanies the forest dweller, the two should not have any conjugal relations. They should sleep on the ground and under a tree. Thereafter, when the man has the desire to take sannyasa, he should send his wife to her sons and become a sannyasi. This should be from the fiftieth to the seventy-fifth year. The person who has gained victory over his senses earlier, may adopt sannyasa earlier too, straight after the student life. The sannyasi should acquire knowledge, wean the mind from other thoughts and fix it in the atman. God cannot be reached by mere action. So he should seek a guru who is knower of Brahman, and remove all his doubts.

The duties of the sannyasis are as follows: freedom from partiality, love of justice, truthfulness, rejection of falsehood, carrying out the commands of God according to the Vedas, doing good to other, saying what is correct and so forth. Dayanand also gives a detailed account of how a sannyasi should behave. When he walks, he should keep his eyes fixed to the ground and not look this way or that. He should drink water after straining it, he should always speak the truth, and even if one reviles him he should not show anger towards him and always think about his good. This recalls the famous observation of Tulsidasa about a saint: 'the doing of a saint and an ordinary person resembles the axe and the sandlewood tree. When the axe falls on the sandlewood tree the wood imparts to the blade of the axe its perfume. But the ultimate consequence is that the blade of the axe is beaten after being heated in the fire at the forge, and the paste of sandalwood adorns foreheads'. The saint's main duty is to increase dharma and knowledge in the world. Outward observances and signs like donning the ochre robe, bearing a staff and water-bowl and so forth are not so relevant, although the sannyasi should adopt them.

The virtues to be practiced by the sannyasi are the usual ones mentioned as yamas and niyamas in Patanjali's *Yoga Sutras*. These are: tolerance, forgiveness, shaucha i.e. purity of mind, asteya i.e. non-stealing, not appropriating what is another's keeping to the path of dharma (damā), abandonment of intoxicants and so forth, knowledge, truth and non-anger (akrodha). Dayanand believes that only brahmans have the right to adopt sannyasa. Of course, for him a brahman means, as we have already said, a brahman by works and deeds, not by birth. He quotes Manu in holding the view that only brahmins are entitled to sannyasa. He condemns other sadhus, vairagis and so forth, who wander about in the garb of sadhus, but are really impostors. They do not have any of the characteristics of sannyasis. Theydo no have knowledge of the Vedas, and in fact go against its precepts. They praise their own practices and hoodwink others. They beguile people for their own selfish interest. They cannot be counted among sannyasis. Although Dayanand himself took sannyasa early, he does not speak about the subject as exhaustively as one would have expected him to do. He devotes only about seven pages to it in his *Satyarthaprakash* and disposes of vanaprastha in just a page. Perhaps he realised that in the Kali-age the grihastha asharama (family life) was of primary importance because adopting the two other asharamas required such determination as could not be expected from people in the Kali-age.

PRACTICAL CONDUCT AND VIRTUE

Works

Dayanand's concept about works and their significance appear to be akin to that of the *Bhagavadgita*. The view held by its has already been stated. Man has the right to work, but not to their already been stated. Man has the right to work, but not to their fruit. Nor must work be abandoned, for without them even existence is not possible. In the eighth chapter of the *Satyathaprakasha* he says 'the jiva' (soul) is free in doing work, but dependent on God in the fruit of works'. The test of right and wrong, he says, is one's own conscience. That, which the heart concedes as right, is the true dharma.

In the world, he says, extreme desire and absence of desire (i.e. desirelessness) both are not to be preferred. Work done according to the Vedic injunctions fulfils all desires. If one says, I will become desireless and not expect any fruit (reward) from work, that cannot be, because all works like yajnas, fasting, vows and true speech—follow from having the desire for them. All the motions of the hands, feet, eyes and so forth are possible because of desires (willing). If there is absence of desire, one can't even open or close one's eyes. There appears to be some confusion of thought here, for this view somewhat contradicts the one mentioned earlier.

There is a difference between works and desire. Works are prompted by volition (exercise of the will). Desire means expectation that the act done will bring some advantage or reward. The Gita is not against works as volition. It goes so far as to say that even God works to maintain the world-order. But it is against expecting reward from works or that a particular act must bring one what he seeks.

The difficulty before Dayanand obviously was that the Vedas, which he set much store by, favoured works for accomplishing certain ends. The yajnas, sacrifices, oblations and acts mentioned therein were for achieving some specific desire. There was no concept in them, which raised a man above works. That's why the Gita speaks of them as flowery words but not bearing fruit-pushpitam vacham. There are two stages of wisdom. The Gita says there are those who have not risen to the higher knowledge, and a very few who have achieved knowledge of Brahman. For the latter, works lose their significance: 'The man who delight in the Self alone, who is content with the Self, who is satisfied with the Self, for him there exists no work that needs to be done'. For the others, however, the way of works is essential.

It is true that the Gita also says that the scriptures should be the guide for our works: jnatva shastravidhanoktam karma kartum iha rhasi. But this does not imply that work should be done with desire of reward. There are three stages, firstly 'the prompting of desire, the guidance of the law and the spontaneity of the spirit'. Dayanand's enthusiasm for the Vedas was due to his disgust with the various schools of Hinduism decrying one another in their bid for supremacy and he goes as far as saying that 'those who speak ill of the Vedas are atheists!'

Recalling the famous Upanishadic metaphor of the chariot whose horses are under control. Dayanand says that one should subdue his senses which run after sense-pleasures and thus forcibly carry away the mind-studd (chitta). *The person who has gained victory over his senses, does not rejoice on being praised, nor is grieved on being disparaged; does not gladden at the pleasant or shrink from the unpleasant; is not happy at having good food to eat, or miserable on getting bad food; is not pleased by good odour or repelled by an unpleasant one.*

The man of wisdom should keep quiet when his counsel is not asked, or is asked with an evil or cunning intent. But he should teach those who are eager for knowledge. Five coveted objectives are mentioned by Dayanand, namely wealth, relations, family and clan, position, excellent works, and superior knowledge. These are in ascending order of importance, with wealth at the lowest end and knowledge at the top. Dayanand's stand regarding what make man learned or experienced (vriddha) is peculiar, in as much as he believes this varies with the class. A brahman should be considered vriddha because of knowledge, a kshatriya by his strength, a vaishya by his wealth, and a shudra by his years. This concept appears to be based on the caste division made according to occupation. But it is rather uncomplimentary to shudras, because he does not give any reason for the shudra being considered vriddha, except age, which of course is a common factor for gaining experience, whatever a person's caste.

Dayanand was not in favour of image worshipper-worship of God with form. We have already discussed about this before. He considered true worship to be serving one's mother and father, teacher and guest. It is the duty of human beings to do those works by which others are benefited [i.e. public service], and to avoid doing what is harmful to living beings. The company of non-believes in God, voluptuaries, betrayers of trust reposed in them, thieves, hypocrites, persons who are selfish, cunning cheats and so forth; should be shunned. Those who are truthful, followers of dharma and who do well to others, should be befriended.

Foreign Travel

In Dayanand's time a great deal of stigma was attached to going abroad. Anyone who did so was ostracised and had to undergo shuddhi ceremonies which were cumbersome and expensive before he was taken back. Dayanand opposed such an attitude, which he said, was illogical and not conducive to a country's development. Inner and outer purity, speaking the truth and so forth developed virtue, wherever one may be, he reasoned. And if one did vicious deeds, even though he remained in Aryavarta, he would be considered to be of evil conduct.

Dayanand proves by historical examples that the ancient Indians went abroad. He says: at one time the sage Vyasa used to live in Patala i.e. modern America, along with his son, Shuka, and his disple. In ancient times Iran and other countries which were north of Meru (the Himalayas) were known as Harivansha 'Hari' means 'a monkey'. The people of this country are still of red faces i.e. of faces like monkeys with brown eyes. These countries are now known as Europe. From there the Huns (Yayudis) came to China. From China they came to Mithila through the Himalayan passes.

Shri Krishna and Arjuna went to Patala (America) on the ship known as 'Agniyana' and brought Uddalaka rishi to participat in the yajana of King Yudhisthira. Dhritashtra married Gandhari princess of Gandhara, also known as Kandhara. Madari, wife of Pandu, was the daughter of the King of Iran. Arjuna married Ulopi, daughter of the king of the Patala country i.e. America. Thus Arjuna took an American wife. When Emperor Yudhisthira performed the rajasuya yajana, Bhima, Arjuna, Nakula and Sahadeva were sent by him to all the directions of the globe. The *Manusmriti* mentions ships, which were used by the inhabitants to sail the oceans. This shows that it was considered necessary for the development of Aryavarta to go out to distant lands. How could there be any evil attached to such voyages?

Dayanand believed that it was only fools who thought tht going to foreign lands destroyed one's dharma. In fact such contact was necessary for trade and development of the country. The good points of other races ought to be adopted. But he cautioned against Indians going abroad and taking to meat eating and the use of alcohol.

Swamantavyamantavya:

My Beliefs and Disbeliefs

That faith[1] (*dharma*) alone is really worthy of credence which is accepted by the *apata*, i.e., the persons who are true in word, deed and thought, and who promote public good, and are impartial and learned. Similarly, what is discarded by such man (i.e., the *apata*) is unworthy of belief and is not authoritative. It is not at all my purpose to found a new system or religion. My sole object is to believe in what is true, and help others to believe in it, and to reject what is untrue and help others to do the same. If I had been partial, I would have championed any one of the religions prevailing in India, but neither I accept the demerits of different faiths whether Indian or alien, nor reject what is good in them.

He alone is entitled to be called a human being who, keeping his mind cool, feels for the happiness and unhappiness, profit and loss, of others, in the same way as he does for his own self, who does not fear the unjust, however, powerful he may be, but fears the virtuous though weak. And not only this: he should always exert himself to his utmost to protect and promote the cause of the virtuous people even if they are extremely poor and weak and to discourage, suppress and destroy those who are wicked and unrighteous, even though they be the mightiest sovereigns of the whole world. In other words, a man should, as far as it lies in his power, constantly endeavour to undermine, the power of the unjust and to strengthen the power of the just, even at the cost of great suffering. He should perform this duty which devolves on him as a man, and which he should never shirk, even if he has to sacrifice his life.

I subjoin here some relevant verses which *Bhartrihari* and others have written in this regard:

निन्दन्तु नीतिनिपुणता यदि वा स्तुवन्तु,
लक्ष्मीः समाविशतु गच्छतु वा यथेष्टम्।
अधैव वा मणरमल्तु युगान्तरे वा,
न्याय्या पथः प्रविचलन्ति पदं न धीराः ।।
।। भर्तृहरि।।

"*The wordly-wise may praise them or censure them; fortune may smile on them or frown on them; death may overtake them today or after ages, but wise men do not severe from the path of justice.*"

Let no man ever renounce dharma (*righteousness*) *either through lust or through fear or through greed or even for the sake of his life.* Dharma *is eternal while pleasure and pain are transitory. The soul is eternal, while the body is perishable.*

एक एव सुहृद्धर्मो निधनेप्यनुयाति यः।
शरीरेण समं नाशं सर्वमन्यद्धि गच्छति।।
।। मनु ।।

"Dharma *is the friend that follows one even after death. All else perishes with the body.*"

सत्यमेव जयते नानृतं सत्येन पंथा विततोदेवयानः ।
येनाक्रमन्त्यृषयो ह्यात्प्तकामा यत्र तत्सत्यस्य परमं निधानम्।।
।। उपनिषद् ।।

"*Truth alone conquers; untruth never. It is the path of rectitude alone that men of learning and piety have followed; and it is by treading this path that the great sages of righteous desire have reached the highest citadel of truth.*"

नहि सत्यात्परो धर्मो नानृतात्पातकं परम्।
नहि सत्यात्परं ज्ञानं तस्मात् सत्यं समाचरेत्।।
।। उपनिषद्।।

"*Verily there is no virtue higher than TRUTH; no sin greater than falsehood. Verily, there is no knowledge higher than TRUTH; let a man, therefore, follow truth.*"

Every one should hold convictions in accordance with the teachings of the above verses.

I now proceed to describe briefly various things as I believe them to be. Their detailed expositions have been given in my books (*Satyaratha Prakash* etc.).

1. There are many names of God, such as *Brahma* (the most High), *Parmatma* (the Supreme Spirit), etc., and He possesses the attributes of Existence, Consciousness, Bliss, etc. His attributes work and characteristics are pure. He is Omniscient, Formless, all-pervading, Unborn, Infinite, Almighty, Merciful and Just. He is the maker of the whole universe and is its sustainer and dissolver. He awards with absolute justice to all souls the fruits of their deeds as they deserve, and is possessed of the like attributes. Him alone I believe to be the Great God.[2]

2. I hold that the four *Vedas* (the Divine revealed knowledge and religious truth comprising the *Samhita* or *Mantras*) as infallible and as authority by their very nature. In other words, they are self-authoritative and do not stand in need of any other book to uphold their authority; just as the sun or a lamp by its light is self-luminous and illuminates the earth and other objects, even so are the *Vedas*. I hold the four *Brahmanas* of the four *Vedas*, the six *Angas*, and *Upangas*, the four *Up-Vedas*, and the eleven hundred and twenty seven *Shakhas* of the *Vedas* as books composed by *Brahma* and other *Rishis*, as commentaries on the *Vedas*, and having authority of a dependent character. In other words, they are authoritative in so far as they are in accord with the *Vedas;* whatever passages in these works are opposed to the *Vedas*; I hold them an unauthoritative[3].

3. I accept as *Dharma*[4], whatever is in full conformity with impartial justice, truthfulness and the like (virtues); that which is not opposed to the teachings of God as embodied in the *Vedas*. Whatever is not free from partiality and is unjust, partaking of untruth and the like (vices), and as opposed to the teachings of God as embodied in the *Vedas*—that I hold as *Adharma*.

4. I hold the soul as that enternal entity which possesses the attributes of desire and hatred, repulsion, feelings of pleasure and pain, and as possessing limited knowledge and such other things.[5]

5. God and the souls and distinct entities, being different in nature and characteristics: they are, however, inseparable being related as the pervader and the pervaded, had having certain attributes in common. Just as a material object has never been and shall never be, separable from the space in which it exist; nor has it ever been or shall ever be one and the same or identical with it; even so, I hold that God and the souls are related as the pervader and the pervaded, worshipped and worshipper, father and son, and having other similar relations.[6]

6. There are three things beginningless: namely, God, Souls and *Parkriti* or the material cause of the universe. These are also ever-existing. As they are eternal, their attributes, works and nature are also eternal.[7]

7. Substances, attributes and works come into existence by combination, cease to exist after dissolution. But the power by which they first integrated is eternally inherent in them, and will lead to similar unions and disunions in future. I hold these three to be eternal by succession.[8]

8. *Creation* is that which results from the combination of different substances in various forms in an intelligent manner and according to design.[9]

9. The object of creation is the exercise or fulfilment of the creative energy, activity, and nature of the deity. When a person asked another, "what is the use of the eyes", the other person replied, "to see with", similarly, the fulfilment of God's creative energy is in creating the universe, and in making the souls reap the fruits of their deeds properly.[10]

10. *The world is a creation*, and its creator is the aforesaid God. From the display of design in the universe and the fact that dead inert matter is incapable of moulding itself into seeds and other various requisite forms, it follows that the world must have a creator.[11]

11. Bondage (of the soul) has a cause. This is ignorance. All sinful acts such as worship of objects other than God result in suffering, which has to be borne through no one desires it. Hence it is called *bondage*.[12]

12. *Moksha* or salvation is the emancipation of the soul from all woes and sufferings, and to live bondfree, a life of liberty and

free movement in the all-pervading God and His creation, and resumption of the earthly life after the expiration of a fixed period of enjoying salvation.[13]

13. The means to attain salvation are, contemplations of God, i.e., practice of *yoga*, performance of virtuous deeds, acquisition of knowledge, practising *brahmacharya* associating with wise and pious men, true knowledge, purity of thought, a life of (benevolent) activity and the like.[14]

14. *Artha* or true wealth is that which is righteously acquired; while that which is acquired or achieved by vicious means is called *anartha*.

15. *Kama* or enjoyment of legitimate desires is that which is achieved by righteousness or *dharma* and honestly acquired wealth or *artha*.

16. I hold that the *verma* (caste or class or order of an individual) is determined by his merits (qualifications) and actions.[15]

17. He alone deserves the title of a *raja* or king, who is illumined with excellent qualities, works and disposition, who follows the dictates of impartial justice, who treats his subjects like a father; considering them as his own children, always strives for promoting their advancement and happiness.[16]

18. *Praja* or subjects are those who, by cultivating excellent qualities, works and disposition, and by following the dictates of impartial justice, and being ever engaged in furthering public good, are loyal to the sovereign whom like children they regard as a parent.[17]

19. He, who after careful thinking, is ever ready to accept truth and reject falsehood; who puts down the unjust and promotes just things, and strives for the happiness of others as he does for his own self, to him I call the just.[18]

20. I hold that *devas* are those men who are wise and learned; *asuras* are those who are ignorant; *rakhshasas* are those who are sinful; *pishachas* are those who are wicked in their acts.[19]

21. *Devapuja* consists in showing honour to the wise and the learned, ton one's father, mother and preceptor, to preachers of truth, to a just ruler, to righteous persons, to whom who are devoted to their husbands, to men who are devoted to their

wives. The opposite of this is called *Adevapuja*. I hold that worship is due to these living persons and not to the inert images of stone etc.[20]

22. *Shiksha* or education is that which promotes knowledge, culture, righteousness, self-control and such other virtues, and eradicates evils like ignorance.[21]

23. I hold that the *Puranas* are the *Brahmanas* such as *Aittiriya* and others written by *Brahma* and others. They are also called *Itihas, Kalpa, Gatha*, and *Narashansi*, but not the *Bhagwat* and other books of that sort.[22]

24. *Tirtha* is that by means of which the ocean of misery is crossed: In other words, I hold that *tirthas* are good works such as speaking the truth, acquisition of knowledge, society of the wise and the good, practice of the *yamas* and (other stages) of *Yoga*, life of activity, spreading knowledge and similar other good works. *No places or water of rivers are tirthas*.[23]

25. Activity is superior to destiny since the former is the maker of the latter, and also because if the activity is well directed, all is well but if it is wrongly directed, all goes wrong.

26. I hold that it is commendable for a man to treat all others in the same way as he does his own self; sympathise with them in their happiness and sorrows, their losses and gains. It is reprehensible to behave otherwise.

27. *Sanskara* (ritual) is that which contributes to the physical, mental, and spiritual improvement of man. From conception to cremation there are sixteen *sanskaras*. I hold their performance as obligatory. Nothing should be done for the dead, after their remains have been cremated.[24]

28. *Yajana* consists in showing due respect to the wise and the learned; in the proper application of the principles of physical and mechanical sciences and chemistry; in the dissemination of knowledge and culture and the performance of *agnihotra* which, by contributing to the purification of air, rain, water and medicine plants, promotes the well-being of all sentient creatures. I hold its performance as highly commendable.[25]

29. The word *Arya* means virtuous man, and *Dassue* as wicked man. I hold the same opinion.

30. This country is called *Aryavarta*,[26] because it has been the above of the *Aryas* from the dawn of creation. It is, however, bounded on the north by the Himalayas, on the south by the Vindhyachala mountains, on the west by the river Attock and on the east by the river Brahmaputra. The people who have been living in it from time immemorial are called *Aryas*.

31. One is called *Acharya*, who teaches his pupils the science of the *Vedas* with the *Angas* and *Upangas* and helps them to adopt right conduct and relinquishment of wrong conduct.[27]

32. One is termed as *shishya* (pupil) who is fit for acquiring true culture and knowledge, possesses a virtuous character, is eager to learn, and is devoted to his preceptor.[28]

33. By the term *guru* is meant father, mother and any one who imparts truth and makes one reject falsehood.[29]

34. He is a *Purohita,* who wishes well to his *Yajman*, by preaching truth to him.[30]

35. An *upadhayaya* (Professor) is one who can teach any portion of the *Vedas* or the *Angas*.[31]

36. *Shistachar* consists in leading a virtuous life in acquiring knowledge while observing *brahmacharya,* in testing truth by reasoning, such as direct cognition, and other ways, and then accepting truth and rejecting error. He who practises *shishtachar* is called a "*Shishta*" (gentleman).

37. I believe in the *eight kinds of evidence*[32] (as described in the *Shastras*) such as direct cognition, etc.

38. I call him alone an *Apta* who always speaks the truth, is virtuous and strives for the good of all.

39. There are five kinds of tests of knowledge. The first is the attributes, works and nature of God, and the teachings of the *Veda*. The second is eight kinds of evidence such as direct cognition, etc. The third is "Laws of Nature". The fourth is conduct and practice of *aptas;* the fifth is purity and conviction of one's own conscience. Every man should sift truth from error with the help of these five tests, and accept truth and reject, error.[33]

40. I call that *paropkar* (philanthropy) which helps in freeing all men from their vices and sufferings, and promotes the practice of virtue and happiness.

41. The soul is a free agent in his works; but is dependent inasmuch as he has a to enjoy and suffer the fruit of his works awarded by the justice of God. Likewise, God is independent in doing his good works.[34]

42. *Swarga* (heaven) is the enjoyment of special happiness and the possession of the means thereof.[35]

43. *Narka* (Hell) is undergoing great suffering and the means thereof.

44. *Janma* (birth) is the soul's assumption of the body which I hold to be three-fold, viz, past, present and future.[36]

45. Birth is the name given to the union of the soul with the body, and Death is only their separation.[37]

46. *Marriage* is the acceptance of the hand, through mutual consent, (of a person of the opposite sex) in a public manner and in accordance with laws or rules.[38]

47. *Niyoga* is the temporary union of a person with another of the opposite sex, of the same or higher class, as a measure in exceptional or distressing conditions, for the raising of issue in widowhood, or when he or she is suffering from some permanent disease, like importance or sterility.[39]

48. *Stuti* (adoration) is reciting divine attributes or hearing them recited, and meditating on them. It results in love for God and similar pious feelings.[40]

49. *Prarthana* (Prayer) is requesting God to grant knowledge (and similar other boons) which can come only from communion with Him and what is beyond one's own power and capacity after one has exerted his utmost. Its result is humility and similar things.[41]

50. *Upasana* (Communion) consists in purifying our attributes, works and nature to become similar to those of God, and in feeling that god, pervades us also, and that we are the pervaded. Also in realising through the practice of *yoga* that we are near to God and he is near to us. This results in the advancement of our knowledge.[42]

51. *Saguna* and *nirguna stuti* consists in praising God as possessed of the attributes which are inherent in Him, and also as devoid of the attributes which are foreign to His nature,

Saguna and *nirguna prarthna* (Prayer) consists in praying for God's help for the attainment of virtuous qualities and elimination of vicious qualities.

Saguna and *nirguna upasana* consists in resigning one-self to God and His will, realising Him as possessed of all good attributes, and as devoid of all evils.

I have thus briefly explained my beliefs here: their detailed exposition is to be found in *Satyaratha Prakash* in their proper places, and is also given in other works such as *Ṛig Vedadi Bhashya Bhumika* (An Introduction to the exposition of the *Vedas*).

In short, I accept universal maxims: for example, speaking of truth is commended by all, and speaking of falsehood is condemned by all. I accept all such principles. I do not approve of the wrangling of the various religions, against one another for they have, by propagating their creeds, misled the people and turned them into one another's enemy. My purpose and aim is to help in putting an end to this mutual wrangling, to preach universal truth, to bring all men under one religion so that they may, by ceasing to hate each other and firmly loving each other, live in peace and work for their common welfare. May this view through the grace and help of the Almighty God, and with the support of all virtuous and pious men, soon spread in the whole world so that all may easily acquire righteousness, wealth, gratification of legitimate desires and attain salvation, and thereby elevate themselves and live in happiness. This alone is my chief aim.

May God, the Lord of justice, the mightiest of all, the Lord of the Universe, the Omnipresent, be the giver of happiness to us. Salutations to *Brahma*, the Supreme Lord of infinite power, the Great God, whose true knowledge I have preached. I have spoken the Truth. You have, therefore, given protection to me, the Truth Speaker. May you, Lord, save us from three kinds of sufferings.[43]

ओइम् शान्तिः शान्तिः शान्तिः।

—Dayanand

REFERENCES

1. This is called 'Eternal Religion' by Dayananda. It is based on cosmopolitan and universal doctrines, agreed upon by all wise men throughout the world.
2. For details see *Satyaratha Prakash*, Chapter I, pp. 11-41.
3. See *Ibid.* Chapter VII, pp. 245-88; *Rigvedadi Bhashyabhumika* (Banares: 1878).
4. He gives ten characteristics of Dharma in *Satyaratha Prakash: Dhrti, Karma, Dharma, Asteyya, Shanchya, Indirya, nigraha, Dhi, Vidya, Satye* and *Akrodhya*. See Chapter V, pp. 189-90.
5. See *Ibid.*, Chapter III. 88-97.
6. *Ibid.*, Chapter VIII, pp. 289-324.
7. *Ibid.*
8. *Ibid.*
9. *Ibid.*
10. *Ibid.*
11. *Ibid.*
12. *Ibid.*, Chapter IX, pp. 325-62.
13. *Ibid.*
14. *Ibid.*
15. *Ibid.*, Chapter IV-V pp. 114-97.
16. *Ibid.*, Chapter VI, pp. 198-244.
17. *Ibid.*
18. *Ibid.*
19. *Ibid.*, Chapter X, pp. 363-84.
20. *Ibid.*
21. *Ibid.*, Chapter III, pp. 55-113.
22. *Ibid.* Chapter XI-XII, pp. 387-682.
23. *Ibid.*
24. See his work *Sanskaravidhi* (Bombay: 1877) for details pertaining to sixteen *Sanskaras*.
25. See his *Sandhyaopasanadi Panchayana-mahavidhi* (Bombay: 1931 V.S.).
26. For the boundaries and description, see *Satyaratha Prakasha* Chapter VIII, pp. 315-16.
27. *Ibid.*, Chapter III, pp. 55-113.

28-31. *Ibid.*

32. Namely, institution, inference, comparison, verbal knowledge tradition, presumption, probability and negation as given in *Naya-sutra*, Chapters 1-2, see *Ibid.*, III, pp. 81-85.

33. *Ibid.*, 81-95.

34-37. These have been clearly discussed above at f.n. 5-15.

38. *Ibid.*, Chapter IV, pp. 114-78.

39. *Ibid.*

40-42. See *Sandhya Opasnadi Panchayajnavidhi* (Bombay: 1931).

43. The three kinds of suffering are: (1) *Adhyatmika*, those arising from ignorance, jealousy hatred, folly favour etc., (2) *Adidaivika*, those arising from excessive rain, cold, heat, earthquake, etc., and (3) *Adibhautika*, those arising from an enemy, predatory brutes, thieves, etc.

Swikarapatra: The Last Will and Testament of Dayananda

Dayananda made his will in 1880 while at Meerut and got it registered there. In the will in question he had appointed a Society called *Paropakarani Sabha* as his successor and defined its constitution and rules.

However, on his visit to Udaipur, 1883, he cancelled this will and got registered a new will on February 27, 1883, as under:

I, Swami Dayanand Saraswati, do give authority over my entire Property, i.e., Clothing, Books, Money, Press and Co. to a society of twenty-three Aryan gentlemen in accordance with the rules given below and constituting the same Society as *adhishtatha* (Manager) for the purpose of the applying the said property to works of public good, to execute this deed that it may be of use as occasion required.

This society is designated *The Paropkarini Sabha*, of which the under-mentioned twenty three gentleman are members. Out of them, the President of this Sabha being:

1. Shriman Maharaja Dhiraj Mahi Mahendra Yavadarya Kula Divakara Maharanaji Shri 108 Shri Sajjan Singh Ji Varma, Dhir Vir, G.C.S.I., Maharana of Udaipur, Raj Mewar.
2. Vice President—Lala Mulraj, M.A., Extra Assistant Commissioner, Vice-President, Arya Samaj, Lahore, born at Ludhiana.

3. Secretary—Shriyut Kavi Shamal Das Ji, Udaipur, Raj Mewar.
4. Secretary—Lala Ramsaran Das, Rais, Vice-President, Arya Samaj, Meerut.
5. Assistant Secretary—Pandya Mohanlal Vaishnu Lalji, residing at Udaipur, born at Mathura.

Members

1.	Shriman Raja Dhiraj Shri Nahar Singhji Varma of	...	Shahpura, Raj Mewar.
2.	Shrimat Rao Takht Singhji Varma of	...	Bedla, Raj Mewar.
3.	Shrimat Rana Shri Fateh Singhji Varma of	...	Delwara, Raj Mewar.
4.	Shrimat Rawat Arjun Singhji Varma of	...	Asind, Raj Mewar.
5.	Shrimat Maharaj Shri Gaj Singhji Varma of	...	Udaipur, Raj Mewar.
6.	Shrimat Rao Shri Bahadur Singhji Varma of	...	Masuda, Distt. Ajmer.
7.	Rao Bahadur P. Sunderlal, Superintendent, Postal Workshop and Press		Aligarh.
8.	Raja Jai Krishn Das, C.S.I., Deputy Collector		Bijnor, Moradabad.
9.	Babu Durga Prasad, Rais and Treasurer, Arya Samaj		Farrukhabad.
10.	Lala Jagan Nath Prasad, Rais of	...	Farrukhabad.
11.	Seth Nirbhai Ram, President, Arya Samaj	...	Farrukhabad.
12.	Lala, Kalicharan Ram-charan, Secretary, Arya Samaj	...	Farrukhabad.
13.	Babu Chhedilal, Commissariat Agent, Morar Cantonment	...	Cawnpur.
14.	Lala Sain Das, Secretary, Arya Samaj	...	Lahore.
15.	Babu Madhav Das, Secretary, Arya Samaj	...	Danapur (Behar).

16. Rao Bahadur P. Gopal Rao Hari Deshmukh, Member of Council of the Governor of Bombay and President, Arya Samaj, Bombay. Poona.
17. Rao Bahadur Mahadeva Govind Ranade, Judge ... Poona
18. Pandit Shyamji Krishan Varma, Professor of Sanskrit, Oxford University, England Bombay.

Rules

1. The aforesaid *Sabha*, as is at present and in time of difficulty does, according to the rules, take care of me and all my property and applies it to works of general good, so shall it contine to do after me, *viz*., after my demise also, in like manner:
   (a) In the dissemination of the *Vedas, Vedangas* and other like *sastras, i.e.*, by fostering the commentary, study, teaching, hearing and publication of these.
   (b) For teaching and preaching of *Vedic Dharma*, by organising a body of teachers and lecturers to work in India and other countries, so that truth may be accepted and false-hood rejected.
   (c) For the providing of means and institutions for the protection, maintenance and right training of the orphans and the destitutes of India.
2. This *Sabha*, as it is in my life-time making all arrangements, it shall after my death also, in like manner, depute one of its members every three or six months to examine and check the accounts of the *Vedic Yantralaya*. The said member shall after examining all the items of receipt and expenditure and the stock, affix high signature thereto and shall inform by letter every member of the *Sabha* of his having done so. In case he notes any defects or improvements in the management he shall send information of the same to every member with any suggestion that he may have to make. On getting the information it would be proper for every member, to submit his own opinion in writing to the President of the *Sabha*. The

President shall make the necessary arrangements, in accordance with the opinions of all the members. No member should in this matter give way to indolence or act improperly.

3. It is proper for this *Sabha*, and, absolutely essential, that as this is a work of the highest merit and universal benefaction, it shall be performed with similar zeal, energy, gravity, broad-mindedness.

4. This *Sabha* of the said twenty three Aryan gentlemen should, after my demise, be deemed to be my representative in every respect and shall have the same right and control over all my property as I myself have. In case anyone of the said members, influenced by selfish motives and contrary to these rule, or any other persons asserts any claim of his own, the same shall be considered to be altogether false.

5. Just as this *Sabha* has at present according to its capacity, the right to take care of my person, all my property and to improve the latter, in like manner shall it have the right to look to the proper disposal of my body when dead. In other words, when my life is extinct, the *Sabha* shall not permit my body to be buried or shown into the water or left exposed in the *jungle*. The *Sabha* shall make a pile entirely of sandal wood, but if this be not possible, it shall then take two maunds of sandal wood, for maunds of *ghee,* five seers of camphor, two *seers* and a half of *agar tagar* (aloe wood), and ten maunds of fuel, and having made a *Vedic* (pile) in accordance with the directions of the *Vedas* as described in the *Sanshkarvidhi*, shall reduce my body to ashes chanting the hymns as given therein. No ceremony apart from this shall be performed in any way opposed to *Vedic* rites. If the members of the *Sabha* be not present at the time, any time, any one who is present may perform the ceremony as above described and recover the costs from the *Sabha* and the *Sabha* shall pay the same.

6. This *Sabha* can during my life-time and after my death expel any member, if it considers such action proper and can appoint any other fit person who is a *Samajist* and an *Arya* in his place, provided that no member of the *Sabha* shall be removed from the *Sabha* unless and until impropriety of conduct is exhibited in his actions.

7. In my place, any action that may be taken by the *Sabha* in the following matters, *viz.*, the construction of this Will or the observance of its objects and rules, or the removal of any member and the appointment of another in his place, or the adoption of any measures for the removal of any trouble or difficulty of mine shall be with unanimous approval of all the members. In the event of there being difference of opinion amongst the members, the decision shall be in accordance with the opinion of the majority, the President of the *Sabha* always having two votes.

8. At no time shall it be within the power of the *Sabha* to dismiss more than three of the members after having judged of their misbehaviour without first nominating substitutes for those three.

9. Should any of the members of the *Sabha* die or, having renounced the above rules and the *Vedic Dharma*, should act in opposition, it would be proper for the President of the *Sabha* to remove the said member with the opinion of all the members, and to appoint in his place, another *Arya* person who is fit and is an adherent of the *Vedic Dharma*. Until then, save the ordinary business (of the *Sabha*), no new business shall be taken in hand.

10. This *Sabha* has full power to take all steps and devise original plans, but in case the *Sabha* has not full confidence in its own deliberations and counsels, it may call for the opinions of all the *Arya-Samajis* by letters, fixing a date for the purpose, and act in accordance with the opinion of the majority.

11. The President of the *Sabha* shall annually or half yearly, give information by printed letter, to all the members, of the changes in the management of the press, the approval and disapproval of work done, the dismissal and appointment of any of the members, the examination and checking of receipts, disbursements and stock and other matters of weal and woe.

12. No disputes connected with this Will shall be taken to the law courts. This *Sabha* should decide them itself accordance to justice. In case, however, it is beyond its power to do so, it may get the matter settled by resort to the law courts.

13. If, in my lifetime, I decide to give pension to any deserving *Arya* person and get a deed executed any registered to this effect, the *Sabha* shall accept it and give effect to it.

14. If some especial profit results, the reform or important considerations, of philanthropy or public welfare demand, I and after me the *Sabha*, shall be fully and at all times competent to add or to take out from the above mentioned rules.

—**Dayananda Saraswati**

Library Works of Dayananda

Dayananda possessed a robust intellect and encyclopaedic knowledge of the ancient Indian literature, both *Vedic* as well as non-*Vedic*. He had a wonderful command of Sanskrit language but preferred to speak and write in Hindi. A prolific writer, he has to his credit 66 books covering about 20,000 full-scap page.*

S. No.	*Book*	*Language*	*Publishers*	*Year of publication*
1	*2*	*3*	*4*	*5*
1.	*Sandhya*	Sanskrit	Jawala Prakash Press, Agra	VS 1920
2.	*Bhagavata Khandana*	Sanskrit	-do-	VS 1923
3.	*Advaitamata Khandana*	Sanskrit	Light Press Benaras	VS 1927
4.	*Gardabhatapani Upanisad*	Sanskrit	Unpublished	
5.	*Satyaratha Prakash*	Hindi	Star Press, Benaras,	First edition 1875
		Hindi	Vedic Yantralya, Benaras	Second Ed. 1884
6.	*Sandhyaopashnadi Panchamahayagyavidhi*	Sanskrit and Hindi	Arya press, Bombay	1st Ed. VS 1931
		-do-	Lajras press Benaras	2nd Ed. VS 1934

1	*2*	*3*	*4*	*5*
7.	*Vedantidhwantanivarana*	Hindi	Oriental Press, Bombay	VS 1931
8.	*Vedavirudha Mata-Khandana*	Sanskrit	Nirnaya Sagar Press, Bombay	VS 1939
9.	*Shikshapatridh-wantaniwarana*	-do-	Star Press, Bombay	VS 1931
10.	*Aryabhivinaya*	Sanskrit	Aryamandala press, Bombay	1876
11.	*Sanskaravidhi*	Hindi and Sanskrit	Asiatic Press, Bombay	1877
12.	*Rigvedadi Bhashyebhumika*	Hindi	Lajras Press, Bombay	1878
13.	*Specimens of Rigveda Bhashya* (1)		-do-	1878
14.	*Specimens of Rigveda Bhashya* (2)		-do-	1878
15.	*Rigvedabhashya* (9 parts incomplete)	Sanskrit	Vedic Yantralya	Different dates
16.	*Yajurvedabhashya* (4 parts)	-do-	-do-	-do-
17.	*Yajurvedabhasha--Bhashya*	Hindi	-do-	VS 1906
18.	*Aryodesharatnamala*	Sanskrit	Chashmanar Press, Amritsar	VS 1934
19.	*Bharanti nivarana*	Hindi	Arya Bhushana Press, Shahajehanpur (U.P.)	VS 1934
20.	*Ashthadhyai-Bhashya*	Hindi	-do-	VS 1935-36
21.	*Atmacharita* (VS 1936-37)	Hindi	Party published in *Theosophist*	Oct. 1879 Dec. 1879 Nov. 1880
22.	*Vedanga-Prakasha*, 14 Vols.	Sanskrit	Published from different places at different times.	
23.	*Sanskrita-Vakyaprabodha*	Sanskrit	Vedic Yantralya	VS 1936
24.	*Vyevahwarabhanu*	Hindi	-do-	1936
25.	*Gautma-Ahalya-Ki-Katha*	Hindi	-do-	VS 1937
26.	*Bhramochhedana*	Sanskrit	-do-	-do-

1	2	3	4	5
27.	*Anubhramachhedana*	Sanskrit	Vedic Yantralya	-do-
28.	*Gokaranunidhi*	Hindi	-do-	-do-
29.	*Prashnotra-Haldhara*	Sanskrit	-do-	VS 1926
30.	*Kashi-Shastrarartha*	Sanskrit and Hindi	Star press, Bombay	1886
31.	*Hugali-Shastrarartha aur Pratima-Pujanavichara*	Hindi	Light press, Benaras	1873
32.	*Stayadharma-Vichara*	Hindi and Urdu	Vedic Yantraleay	1937
33.	*Jalaushara-Shastrartha*	Hindi	Panjabi press, Lahore	1877
34.	*Satyasatya-viveka*	Urdu	Arya Press, Shahajahanpur	1930
35.	*Udeypura Shastrartha*	Hindi	Unpublished	
36.	*Chaturveda Vishya-Suchi*	Sanskrit	-do-	
37.	*Rigvedamantra-Suchi*	Sanskrit	-do-	
38.	*Yajur-Atharva-mantra-suchi*	Sanskrit	-do-	
39.	*Atharva-mantra-suchi*	Sanskrit	-do-	
40.	*Veda-Brahmana-suchi* (alphabetical)	Sanskrit	-do-	
41.	*Nirukta ki Vishya-suchi*	Sanskrit	-do-	
42.	*Aitriya-Brahmana-suchi*	Sanskrit	-do-	
43.	*Shatapatha-Brahmana-Vishya-suchi*	Sanskrit	-do-	
44.	*Taitiriyopanishad mishrita-suchi*	-do-	-do-	
45.	*Rigveda-Vishya smaranartha-suchi*	-do-	-do-	
46.	*Nirukta-Shatpathamula-suchi*	-do-	-do-	
47.	*Satapatha-Brahmana-suchi*	-do-	-do-	
48.	*Dhatupetha-suchi*	-do-	-do-	
49.	*Karika sanketa-suchi*	-do-	-do-	
50.	*Nighantu-suchi*	-do-	-do-	

1	*2*	*3*	*4*	*5*
51.	*Karuna-suchi*	Hindi	-do-	
52.	*Bible-suchi*	-do-	-do-	
53.	*Jainadharma-grantha-suchi*	-do-	-do-	
54.	*Vartikapatha-sabhushya*	-do-	Unpublished	
55.	*Manusmriti: Selected Shlokas*	-do-	-do-	
56.	*Vidurapraja: Selected Shlokas*	-do-	-do-	
57.	*Asthadhyayi Ka Yadipatra*	-do-	-do-	
58.	*Kurana (translation)*	-do-	-do-	
59.	*Prakrita-Sanskrit Anuvada* (unrevised)	Sanskrit	-do-	
60.	*Jaina Shlokas: A Selection*	-do-	-do-	
61.	*Ram Shehi Mata-ka Gutaka*	Hindi	-do-	
62.	*Aitryia Upanished-suchi*	Sanskrit	-do-	
63.	*Chhandogyaupanishad-suchi*	-do-	-do-	
64.	*Rigveda Sukta-suchi*	-do-	-do-	
65.	*Satapatha Shilashta Pratika-suchi*	-do-	-do-	
66.	*Mahabhashya: Sankshepa*	-do-	-do-	

* In this I have deprived much help from Pandit Yudhishtra Mimanska, a great living Sanskrit scholar. Inquisitive readers, eager to know more about Dayanand's work may consult his learned book: *Rishi Dayanand Ke Granthon Ka Itihasa* (Delhi 1949).

Appendix—I

FAMILY TREE OF DAYANANDA*

LALJI TIWARI

Krashanji Tiwari (1758-1853) + Yashoda Bai

1	2	3	4	5
Dayalji (1824-83)	Daughter (1827-42)	Vallabhji (1829-?)	Prembai (1831-?) Married to Mangalji Rawal (Successor to Krashanji Tiwari)	Son (1833-41)

Prembai → Boghaji Rawal → Kalyanji Rawal

Kalyanji Rawal:
1. Prabha Shankar
2. Pran Shanker

Prabha Shankar:

1	2	3	4	5	6
Manu	Mukand Rai	Jayntilal	Harsukh	Parvin	Arvind

Pran Shanker:

1	2
Keshav Lal	Son

* For details see Yudhishtra, Mimanska, *Swami Dayanand Ka Bhratrivansha tatha Swasrivansha* (Amritsar: 1959)

Appendix—II

CHRONOLOGY OF DAYANANDA'S LIFE

1824	Born at Tankara.
1829	Home-teaching began.
1832	Invested with sacred thread.
1837	Observed *Shivaratri* fast; lost faith in idol-worship.
1841	Sister's death; moved to unimaginable extent.
1842	Death of uncle; resolved to seek means to conquer death.
1846	Left home; wandered about in search of learned *Yogis*.
—	Initiated into *Brahmacharya* at Sayable and named Suddha Chaitanya.
July-Oct.	Visit to Kotgangara, near Ahmedabad.
Oct.-Nov.	Went to Sidhpura to attend *Kartika* fair; caught by father, but again escaped.
Dec. 1846-1847	Visited Baroda and heard *Vedanta* discourses from Brahmananda and others; gained certainty that "I was a *Brahma*"; also had scientific and metaphysical discussion with Satchitananda Paramahansa.
1847	Went to Chanoda Kalyani (on the bank of the Narmada); met Chida-sharma;

		studied *Vedantasara; Arya Karimide Totak Vedantapriksha* and other philosophical treatises from Parmananda Paramahansa.
	—	Ordained into *Sanyasa* by Swami Parmananda Saraswati; named Dayananda Saraswati.
1847-48		Went to Vyasha-ashrama; learned theory and practical modes of scientific *Yoga* from Swami Yogananda.
1848-49		Stayed at Sinoor; learnt a good deal of Sanskrit grammar under the guidance of Krishna Shastri.
1849-50		Returned to Chanoda Kalyani; met Jawalananda Puri and Shivananda Puri and practised Yoga with them for some time.
1850-52		Went to Dudheshwar (near Ahmedabad) where the two above mentioned *Yogis* had also settled after their coming from Chanoda; acquired from them the practical training in the science of *Yoga*.
1852-54		Visited Mount Abu in search of great *Yogis;* met on the peak of Bhawanigir "those whom I so eagerly sought"; learnt from them various systems and modes of *Yoga*.
1854		Visit to Hardwar on the occasion of *Kumbhamela*; practised *Yoga* at Chandee across the Ganga during the fair days.
	—	Went to Rishikesh after the fair; studied and practised *Yoga* in the company of good *Yogis* and *sanyasis*!
	—	Went to Tehri (Garhwal) along with a *Brahmachari* and two mountain ascetics; studied *Tantra* books.
	—	Went to Shrinagar (Garhwal) and stayed at Kedar-ghat temple for two

		months; befriended *Sadhu* Ganga Giri and discussed *Yoga* and other sacred subjects; criticised the local *panditas* for having faith in 'nasty *Tantras*'.
	—	Visited Rudraprayaga and other places; went to the shrine of Agastamuni.
1854 Oct. to 1855 Feb.		Went to Shivpuri, and spent cold season there with three followers.
1855 Feb. to Dec.		Visited Gupta Kashi (short stay); went to Triyugi Narayan shrine, Gauri Kund Tank and the Cave of Bhima (Bhima-gupha).
	—	Came to Kedarnath, discussed different subjects with *Pandits* and *Sanyasis*.
	—	Went to Okhi-math via Gupta Kashi; request of the wealthy *Mahants* to become his disciple declined.
	—	Went to Joshimath and enjoyed for a while the company of some *Maharashtrian Shastris, Sanyasis* and other *Yogis*; learnt more of *Yoga-vidya*.
	—	Visit to Badri Narayan; met the chief-priest, Rawalji.
	—	Toured the mountain country along the banks of the Alkhananda; reached the place of its rise, where hunger, thirst and freezing cold made him "more dead than alive"; passing through Vasudhara, a sacred bathing place and Mana village, reached Badrinarayana, stayed for a day and started downward journey.
	—	Visited Rampur; stayed with the celebrated *Sanyasi* Ramgiri.
	—	Visited Kashipur.
1855 Dec. to 1856 February		Went to Dronsagar (Nainital) and stayed there for the whole winter.

	—	Visited several places on the banks of the Ganga near Garhmukteshwar for some time; tested here theories of nervous system as given in *Shiva-sandhya*, *Hathpradipika*, *Yoga-Brijak* and *Kesarni Samhita*, by examining a 'corpse'; finding the theories wrong. Came to the conclusion that with the exception of the *Vedas*, *Upanishads*, *Patanjali* and *Sankhya* all other works upon science and *Yoga* were false.
	—	Visited Farrukhabad.
1856 5 April	—	Passing via Shringaranpur reached Kanpur.
	—	Visited several places between Kanpur and Allahabad.
1856 August	—	Visited Mirzapur and stayed at the shrine of Vindhiachal Asoolaji.
September	—	Came to Benaras and took up residence for 12 days in the cave at the confluence of *Varuna* and the *Ganga* with Bhumananda Saraswati; met Karta Ram, Raja Ram and other *Shastris*.
	—	Wandered on the banks of the river Ganga.
September & October	—	Stayed for ten days at Chunar in the shrine of Durga-Koho; left eating rice altogether, lived on milk alone; practised *Yoga* night and day.
1857 April to 1859	—	Toured the Narmada valley, meeting learned *Sanyasis*, practising *Yoga*.
1860	—	Visited Hathras and Mursan.
1860, 14 Nov. to 1863	—	Came to Mathura to study the *Vedas*, grammar, etc. at the *ashrama* of Swami Vrijananda Saraswati; stayed here for about 3 years until 1863.
1863 May	—	Finished education and took a solemn vow to devote the life to spreading the *Vedic* faith and removing the superstitions prevailing in India; left Mathura.

1863 May to 1864 October	—	Lived at Agra, making preparations for the future life; practised *Yoga*, studied *Vedas* etc.
1865 January to June	—	Went to Gwalior; denounced *Bhagwata* there.
	—	Visited Karauli; stayed at the garden of Gopal Singh; met the Maharaja several times.
November	—	Visited Gangapur.
1865 November to 1866 March	—	Visited Jaipur, discussed grammar problems with the *Pandits* of the Sanskrit College and defeated them; preached *Shaivism*.
March	—	Visited Bagru, Dudoo and finally Kishangarh; stayed for 5/6 days; denounced the *Bhagwata* and the *Vaishnavism*.
March 23 to May 30	—	Went to Pushkar; denounced idol worship and the *Vaishnava* faith; criticized the followers of Ramanuja.
May 30-June	—	Visited Amjer; disputation with Revs. Gray, Robinson, Shoolbrade and Maulvi Murad Ali (this was the first public disputation of the *Swami* with the Christians and Muslims); met Col. Brook, Agent, English Government for cow protection.
October	—	Visit to Jaipur.
November	—	Came to Agra; wrote a pamphlet condemning the *Bhagwata purana*
	—	Visited Mathura; presented two *gold Mohars* to Swami Vrijananda; had discussion with him (Vrijananda) on several problems (the last meeting with the *Guru*).
1866 December to 1867 April	—	Going via Meerut reached Hardwar to attend the *Kumbha* fair; hoisted *Pakhanda Khandan Pataka* on the hut; had 15/16 *Sanyasi* disciples with him; had discussions with famous *Visudhananda;* Swami Mahananda converted to his faith.

April-May	—	Gave up everything in the possession to become a True *Sanyasi*.
	—	Toured the U.P., preaching his new ideology (i.e., condemning *Puranas*, idol-worship, false gods *Tantra, mantra*, liquor, *Bhang*, adultery, stealing, cheating, etc.);
	—	Visited Kankhal, Landaura, Shuktal, Miranpur, Muhammadpur, Garh, Mukteshwar, Chasi, Karanghat, Ramghat.
May-November	—	Visited Sokon, Patiali, Kampil, Kayamganj, Farukhabad, Anupshehr and Karan; and had discussion with Ambadatt, Purbati, a Sanskrit scholar from Anup Shahr; *Pandita* defeated; many people became Swami's followers: visited Ahar, Chasi, Ramghat and Beloon.
1867 November		Visited Karnawas again and had
1868 February		*Shastraratha* with Harivallabh, a great scholar; defeated Harivallabh became Dayananda's follower; Thakur Hansa also became disciple.
	—	Gave *Gayatrimantra* to a woman
	—	first time people saw a woman reciting *Gayatri*. Thakur Karan Singh, *Vaishnava*, quarrelled; the Swami broke his sword into two pieces.
1868 February-September	—	Toured the countryside along the course of the Ganga.
	—	Visited places like Ramghat, Kachhila ghat, Gadiaghat Ambagarh, Soron, practised *Yoga*.
14 September	—	Swami Vrijananda died. Dayananda exclaimed: "Alas, the sun of *Vyakarna* has set".
October	—	Visited Saravol, Shahbazpur, Qadarganj, Nadauli.
November-December	—	Came back to Naduauli; Gosain Rampuri became a follower.

	—	Visited Qayamganj; had discussions with missionaries and *Panditas* over various issues; all defeated.
	—	Visited Kampil and Shakallapur (Farrukhabad); had discussions with Gopal and Haldhar at the latter place.
1869 December June	—	Stay at Farrukhabad
June	—	Visited Jalalabad, Kanauj, Sitapur and Nadarpur.
July	—	Reached Kanauj; Pt. Harishankar became his follower.
	—	Went to Bithur and Madarpur.
	—	Visit to Kanpur; had *Shastrartha* on 31 July with Pt. Haldhar Ojha on idol worship. Haldhar defeated; many persons became followers; attacked by a mob who were beaten back.
August-October	—	Visited several places, like Shivrajpur, Allahabad, Ram Nagar.
October 2 to December	—	Visited to Benaras; challenge thrown to the orthodox *Panditas* to defend idol worship.
	—	*Shastrartha* held with 21 *Panditas* on 16 November 1869 at Amadbagh in the presence of 50 thousand men on the theme of idol worship; the *Shastrartha* ended in a pandemonium created by the defeated *Panditas*.
December 5-February 1870	—	Stay at Mirzapur.
February	—	Arrived at Allahabad on the Occasion of *Kumbha* fair; met Devendranath Tagore; invited by Tagore to Calcutta; attacked by some Muslims.
February-December	—	Visit to Mirzapur; disputation with *Pandita* Govind Bhatt.

	—	Started a seminary for the Vedica studies under Yugal Kishore (June 1870).
	—	Toured the Ganga valley; stayed for sometime at Benaras; wrote a book denouncing non-duality of Shankar's *Advaita*.
	—	Visited Soron—Kasganj where a *Vedic* seminar was opened.
	—	Visiting Balram, Chakeri, Harnot, Ramghat, reached Anup Shahr; condemned idol worship, propagated cow protection; advocated formation of Panchayats.
December 1871-March	—	Stayed at Soron
March-April	—	Visited Kasganj.
May 1872-February	—	Visited Ramghat Karanwas, Anupshahr, and Farrukhabad; toured the Ganga Valley.
February-April	—	Visited Benaras; challenge thrown to the *Panditas* for *Shastrartha;* but none came forward.
April-August	—	Visited Mughal Sarai; had a discussion with a missionary named Day, stayed for 10 days.
	—	Visited Dumraon and stayed with the Maharaja of that place; discussions with the *Panditas*; gave two public lectures on the *Vedic Dharma*.
September 6-9, October 2	—	Visited Patna; threw challenge to the *pandits* for *Shastrartha*, but none came forward.
October 3-October 18	—	Visited Mongheyar.
October 15-December	—	Visited Bhagalpur; gave a public lecture on the *Vedic Dharma*. Maharaja of Burdwan called on him and discussed certain ideological aspects of his teachings.

December 16 1873- April 1	— Visited Calcutta; discussions held with Keshab Chandra Sen, Debendranath Tagore, Dvijendranath, Taranath Tarakvachaspati, etc.
	— Advised by Keshab Chandra Sen to speak in Hindi and to wear clothes, the *Swami* accepted the advice.
April 1-10	— Visited Hoogly; gave public lecturers.
April 11	— Visited Burdwan.
April 17	— Visited Bhagalpur; delivered several public lecturers.
May	— Visit to Patna; issued public notice for discussion and debates; delivered two public lectures on idol-worship etc.
May 25	— Visit Chhapra; discussion held with *Panditas* led by Jagannath; Pandemonium created by the defeated *Panditas*.
June 11	— Reached Arrah; stayed with the Maharaja of Dumraon; discussions held with Rudra Datta who was defeated.
August 8	— Visited Mirzapur; closed the old *Pathashala* and opened a new one in its place.
August	— Visited Allahabad.
October 20 to November 6	— Visited Kanpur, where several lectures were delivered.
November	— Visited Lucknow; had *shastrartha* with the *Panditas* on 18 November, delivered several lecturers.
November 21	— Reached Farrukhabad; met British officials and advocated ban on cow-slaughter.
December 10-20	— Stay at Kashganj; lecturers delivered.
December 26, 1873- January 22 1874	— Visited Aligarh on invitation from Raja Jaikrishan Dass, C.S.I., Collector of Aligarh; gave lectures; met sir Sayyad Ahmed Khan.
	— Raja Jaikishan Dass requested the *Swami* to publish his teachings in a book form; the result was *Satyaratha Prakash*.

January-February	—	Visited Hathras; condemned idol-worship.
February 26-March	—	Visited Bindraban to hold a *Shastrartha* with Rangachari who did not come; delivered ten lectures.
Maoh 14	—	Came to Mathura; delivered lectures condemning idol-worship.
Maιch-May		Went to Mursan and then to Allahabad.
May-June	—	Visited Benaras; delivered his first lecture in Hindi, gave a lecture at the residence of Sir Sayyad Ahmed Khan.
June	—	Dictation of *Satyaratha Prakash* began.
July	—	Allahabad; gave several lectures.
October	—	Went to Jabbalpur; gave learned exposition of his ideologies, photographed.
	—	Visited Nasik; stayed for four days; delivered public lecturers; had *Shastrartha* with the *Panditas*.
October 26, 1874	—	Visited Bombay; denounced the *Vaishnava* sect and the *Vallabhacharis*.
November	—	Pt. Vishnu Purushram and Dr. R.G. Bhandarkar called upon the *Swami*.
November 25	—	First lecture delivered on idol-worship at Bombay.
November 28	—	Second lecture on the history of the Aryas; wrote *Vedanta Dhavanta Nirwana*; denounced the *Advaita* philosophy; and published a commentary of the first *shukta* of the *Rigveda* as a sample; wrote *Vallabhacharya Mata Khanadana*; several attempts made on his life.
December	—	Visited Surat, Baroda, Ahmedabad, Nadia and Rajkot and gave lectures.
January 1875	—	Visited ahmedabad; vain attempt to convert the Prarathana Samaj into Arya Samaj.
	—	Surat visited.
January 29	—	Visited Bombay again.
April 10	—	Founded Arya Samaj.
June	—	*Satyaratha Prakash* published at Benaras.

June-September	—	Visited Poona on the invitation of Mahadev Govind Ranade; delivered 15 lectures.
September	—	Visited Satara; had discussions with learned men.
October 16	—	Visited Bombay again.
	—	Went to Baroda; delivered lectures.
1876	—	Went to Ahmedabad, Baroch, Surat; met Dr. Von Bulter, a great scholar of Sanskrit Institute.
	—	Visited Bulsan; gave lectures.
	—	Visited Basdlu Road; gave two lectures.
	—	Visited Bombay; gave lectures. Sir Monier Williams of Oxford attended lectures.
May 1876	—	Visit to Farrukhabad; delivered 4 lectures.
May 27	—	Visited Benaras.
August-September	—	Visited Jaunpur, Ayodhya, Lucknow; started writing the *Rigvedadi Bhashay Bhumika.*
November	—	Visited Shahjahanpur, Bareilly, decision to learn English taken.
November-December	—	Visited Moradabad, Karanawa, Chhalesar, Rajghat, Aligarh.
January 1877	—	Visited Delhi at the time of Imperial Darbar held by Lord Lytton; converted a meeting of the leaders of the different faiths to work in unity; failed.
January	—	Visit to Meerut, Saharanpur, Shahjehanpur.
February	—	Visited Saharanpur; delivered lectures.
March	—	Visited Chandpur fair of all religions; had *shastrartha* with the men of different religions.
March 31-April 19	—	Visited Ludhiana (Punjab); delivered lectures.
April 19	—	Visited Lahore; delivered lectures
June 24	—	Arya Samaj Lahore founded; Sanskrit School opened.

July 5	—	Visited Amritsar, delivered lectures; Arya Samaj established.
August 11	—	Published *Aryaratnamala* at Amritsar.
August 17-August 24	—	Visited Gurdaspur; gave several lectures; Arya Samaj established.
September 13	—	Reached Jullundur; gave 35 lectures.
October 17	—	Visited Lahore again.
October 26	—	Visited Ferozepur; gave 38 lectures.
November 5	—	Visited Lahore again; byelaws of Arya Samaj Lahore framed.
November 7-December 26	—	Visited Rawalpindi; Arya Samaj established, published *Vedanga Prakasha*.
December 27	—	Visited Jhelum; gave lectures; Arya Samaj established.
January 1878	—	Visited Gujarat; delivered lectures; *Shastrartha* with Kashmiri *Panditas*.
February 2	—	Went to Wazirabad.
February to March 3	—	Went to Gujarat; gave lectures; *Shastrartha* with Christians; Arya Samaj established.
March 4	—	Came to Lahore; criticised Islam.
March 12-April 4	—	Visited Multan; 35 lectures delivered; Arya Samaj established.
April 17 to May 15	—	Visited Lahore.
May 15-July 11	—	Visited Amritsar; Criticised Christianity; several Christians embraced Hinduism.
July	—	Visited Jullundur; then Ludhiana.
July-August	—	Visited Roorki; delivered lectures; Arya Samaj established.
August 22	—	Visited Aligarh, gave lectures.
August 26	—	Visited Meerut; gave 9 lectures.
October 30	—	Reached Delhi; gave lectures.
November 1	—	Arya Samaj established at Delhi.

November 7	—	Reached Ajmer; visited Pushkar; delivered lectures; discussions with missionaries; discovered some fragments of *Dhanurveda*.
December 2	—	Visited Masuda on its Istamarar's invitation.
December 10	—	Visited Nasinabad.
December 14- December 23	—	Visited Jaipur, gave 3 lectures; Maharaja annoyed and ordered exit; order disobeyed and stayed for 9 days more.
December 24- January 5, 1879	—	Visited Rewari on the invitation of Rao Yudhistra Singh; gave lectures; founded the first *Gaushala*.
January 9	—	Visited Delhi; gave 3 lectures.
January 16	—	Went to Mathura, via Saharanpur, Rewari, Javalapur.
February 27- April 14	—	Attended Kumbha fair at Hard- war; discourses given: Taken ill of diarrhoea; left Hardwar.
April 14	—	Visited Dehradun; gave lectures.
May 1-3	—	Visit to Saharanpur; met Col. Alcott and Madam Balavatsky, the Theosophists from America; both joined Arya Samaj.
May 3-23	—	Visit to Meerut, with the Theosophists.
May 23	—	Went to Aligarh; taken ill—suffered from sprue.
May 28-July 3	—	Visit to Chalesar; treatment; some relief.
July 3	—	Visited Moradabad; gave 3 lectures only, owing to poor health, Civil Surgeon, Dr. Deane treated; Arya Samaj established (20 July 1879).
July 31-August 14	—	Visited Badaur; had *Shastrartha* with *Panditas*, gave lectures.
August	—	Visited Bareilly, delivered several discourses; *Shastrartha* with Rev. T.G. Scott.
September	—	Munshi Ram (Swami Shradhananda) met Dayananda for the first time (at Bareilly); sent the first instalment of his autobiography to be published in the *Theosophist* (Adyar, Madras).

September 4-17	—	Visit to Shahjehanpur; gave discourses.
September 18	—	Visited Lucknow; stayed for 6 days.
September 24-October 8	—	Visited Kanpur; Farrukhabad; gave discourses; Permanent Fund opened.
October 16	—	Visited Kanpur; doing *Veda Bhashya* only; Arya Samaj established.
October 17	—	Visited Allahabad; gave 2 lectures.
October 23	—	Visited Mirzapur; taken ill: delivered 3 lectures.
October 30 to November 19	—	Visited Danapur gave discourses
November 19, 1980	—	Visit to Benaras; challenge to the *Panditas* to prove their points; gave several discourses.
February 12, 1980	—	*Vedic Yantralya* set up at Benaras; 14 lectures delivered.
May 5	—	Still suffering from sprue of the Sanohar variety.
May 5	—	Visit to Lucknow; gave several lectures.
May 20-June 30	—	Visit to Farukhabad; gave 5 lectures.
July 1-6	—	Visited Manipur.
July	—	Visit to Meerut; famous Ramabai *Pandita* called upon the *Swami*.
August 16	—	Made his will; established *Propakari Sabha*.
September 15	—	Visited Muzaffarnagar, gave 10 lectures.
September-October	—	Visited Meerut; gave 2 lectures.
October-7 Nov. 20	—	Visited Dehradun.
November-December	—	Visited Meerut; stayed for five days; gave 25 lectures; Arya Samaj established.
March 19	—	Visited Bharatpur; stayed for 10 days; no lectures.
March 20	—	Visited Jaipur; gave one lecture, and some discourses.

May 5	— Visited Ajmer, gave 26 lectures; Pt. Lekh Ram met Dayananda for the first time (5 May 1882).
July 23-August 1	— Thakur of Masuda Bahadur Singh became his disciple; several lectures delivered.
August 18-September 8	— Went to Raipur; gave lectures.
September 8-21	— Visited Rewari again; gave lectures.
September 21-October 6	— Went to Masuda and stayed there for 25 days.
October 26	— Reached Banera (Mewar).
October 27-December 14	— Visit to Udaipur, Maharaja H.H. Sajjan Singh called on him.
	— Visit to Indore; stayed for a few days; went to Bombay.
December 3	— Reached Bombay; gave lectures.
March 28, 1882	— Severed all connection with the Theosophists;
	— Decided to present a memorial to Queen Empress and the Viceroy, signed by two crore people to prohibit cow slaughter.
June 25	— Reached Khandwa; gave lectures.
July 3	— Visited Indore; stayed for two days.
July 25	— Visited Chitor; then Nimbahra and finally Udaipur.
August 11	— Visit to Udaipur; Maharana Sajjan Singh called on the Swami.
February 27, 1883	— Revised will again registered at Udaipur.
March 1	— Visited Nimalura, Chittor.
March 9	— Visited Shahpura; gave several lectures: Raja Nahar Singh called on the Swami.
March 31	— Visited Jodhpur; gave lectures, Maharana Jaswant Singh called on him thrice during his stay.

September 29- October 16	—	The Swami poisoned; treated by Alimardan Khan until 16 October; deterioration in the condition. Left for Abu for a change.
October 21	—	Reached Abu; condition further deteriorated.
October 26	—	Came to Ajmer; developed Pneumonia.
October 30	—	Breathed his last (6 P.M.)
October 31	—	Cremated at Malusar Cremation Grounds, Ajmer.

Bibliography

Ahluwali, M.M. *Freedom Struggle in India* (1858-1909), Delhi, 1958.

Amar Singh. *Three-quarter Century of Arya Samaj*, Lahore, 1943.

Arjan Singh, Bawa. *Dayananda Saraswati: Founder of the Arya Samaj*, Lahore, 1901.

Andrew, C.F. *The Indian Renaissance*, London, 1912.

Annanda Swami, *Bhagwan Shankra aur Dayananda*, Lahore, n.d.

Argov, Daniel. *Moderates and Extremists in the Indian Nationalist Movement*, London, 1967.

Arvind Ghose. *Bankim, Tilak Dayananda*, Calcutta, 1947.

Arya Directory, Sarvadeshik Arya Pratinidhi Sabha, Delhi, 1940.

Arya Samaj at a Glance, Delhi, 1969.

Atmananda, Swami. *Adarsh Brahmachari*, Delhi, n.d.

Atma Ram. See under Lekh Ram Pandita.

Babadurmal. *Dayananda: A Study in Hinduism,* Hoshiapur, 1962.

Balavatsky, Madam H. *From the Caves and Jungles of Hindustan*, Adyar, Madras.

Barrier, N.G. *Punjab Politics and the Panjab Disturbances,* 1907 (unpublished Thesis), Duke University, 1966.

Besant, Annie, *The Birth of New India*, Madras, 1917.

—. *Builders of New India*, Madras, 1942.

Bevan, Edwyn. *India a Nation*, Madras, 1930.

—. *Indian Nationalism*, London, 1913.

Bhalla, K.C. *Arya Samaj: A Political Body*. Allahabad, 1917.

Bhattacharya, E. (ed), *Cultural Heritage of India*, Vol. IV, Calcutta.

Bhawainlal, Bhartiye. *Arya Samaj Ki Samskrit Sahitya Ko Den*, Bahalgarh, 1970.

—. *Maharishi Dayananda aur Raja Ram Mohan Roy*, Agra, n.d.

—. *Maharishi Dayananda aur Annya Bhartiye Dharmacharya*, Jodhpur, n.d.

—. *Rishi Dayananda Ka Rastravada*, Jaipur, 1962.

—. *Maharishi Dayanand Ke Shastrartha* Ajmer, 1956.

Bhimsen, Shastri. *Vrijnanda-Prakash*, Delhi 1959.

Bose A.C. *Ten Principles of the Arya Samaj*, Kohlapur, n.d.

Bose N.S. *Indian National Movement: An Outline*, Calcutta, 1945.

Bose, P.N. *Hindu Civilization during British Rule*, Calcutta, n.d.

Buch, M.A. *Rise and Growth of Indian Militant Nationalism*, 1940.

Census Reports, Government of India, Punjab, U.P., 1891, 1901, 1911, 1921.

Chhaju Singh, Bawa. *The Life and Teaching of Dayananda Saraswati*, Lahore, 1903.

—. *Teachings of the Arya Samaj*, Lahore, 1903.

—. *What is the Arya Samaj*? Lahore, n.d.

Chamupati. *The Ten Principles of the Arya Samaj*, Madras, n.d.

—. *Glimpses of Dayananda*, Delhi, 1937.

—. *Ten Commandments of the Arya Samaj*, Lahore n.d.

—. *Hamare Swami*, Lahore, n.d.

—. *Rishi Ka Chamatkar*, Lahore, n.d.

Chandra, S. *The Case of Satyaratha Prakash in Sindh*, Delhi, 1947.

Chatopadhyay, Becharam. *The Danger in Arya Samaj*, Sukku, 1893.

Chatopadhya, Nagendra Nath. *Mahatma Dayananda Saraswati Ki Sankshipta Jiwani*, Calcutta, 1886.

Chaube, S.P. *Some Great Indian Educators*, Agra, 1957.

Chiman Lal, Munshi. *Jiwancharita,* Tilhar, n.d.

Chintamani, C.Y. *Social Reform*, Madras, 1901.

—. *Swami Dayananda Saraswati*, Allahabad, 1917.

—. *Indian Politics since the Mutiny*, London, 1940.

Chirol, Valentile, *Indian Unrest,* London, 1910.

—. *Indian Old and New*, London, 1921.

—. *The Occident and the Orient*, Chicago, 1924.

Cotton, Henry. *New India*, London.

Coupland, R. *The Indian Problems* (1883-1935), London, 1935.

Dayananda Saraswati. *Sandhya*, Agra, V.S. 1920.

—. *Bhagwat Khandana,* Agra, V.S. 1923.

—. *Advaitamata Khandana*, Benaras, V.S. 1927.

—. *Gardabhatapani Upanishad*, Unpublished.

—. *Satyaratha Prakasha,* Benaras, 1875 and 1884.

—. *Sandyhaopashnadi Panchamahayagyavidhi*, Bombay, V.S. 1931 and Benaras, V.S. 1934.

—. *Vedantidhwanta-nivarana*, Bombay, V.S. 1931.

—. *Shikshapatridhwanta nivarana*, Benaras, V.S. 1931.

—. *Vedavirudhmata-Khandana*, Bombay, V.S., 1939.

—. *Aryabhivinaya*, Bombay, 1876.

—. *Rigvedadi Bhashyebhumika*, Bombay, 1878.

—. *Specimens of Rigveda Bhashya*, Bombay 1872 and V.S. 1933.

—. *Rigvedabhashya (9 parts)*, Vedic Yantralaya, Ajmer, different dates.

—. *Yajurvedabhashya* (4 parts), Vedic Yatralya, Ajmer, different dates.

—. *Yajurvedabhasha-Bhashya,* Vedic Yantralya, Ajmer.

—. *Aryodesharatnamala*, Amritsar, V.S. 1934.

—. *Bharantinivarana,* Shahjahanpur, V.S. 1934.

—. *Ashthadhyayi-Bhashya,* Saharanpur, V.S. 1935-36.

—. *Atmacharita* (V.S. 1936-37), incomplete.

—. *Vedanga-Prakasha*, 14 Vols., different dates.

—. *Sanskrita Vakyaprabodha*, Bombay, V.S. 1936.

—. *Vyehwarabhanu*, Bombay, V.S. 1936.

—. *Gautma-Ahalya-Ki Katha*, Bombay, V.S. 1937.

—. *Bharamochhedana*, Bombay, 1937.

Dayananda Saraswati. *Anubhramachhedana*, Bombay, V.S. 1937.

—. *Gokarunanidhi*, Bombay, V.S. 1937.

—. *Prashnauttra-Hadhar*, Bombay, V.S, 1926.

—. *Kashi-Shashtrartha*, Bombay, 1880.

—. *Hugali-Shastrartha aur Pratima- Pujanavichara*, Benaras, 1873.

—. *Satyadharma-Vichara*, Bombay, 1937.

—. *Jalaushara-Shashtrartha*, Lahore, 1877.

—. *Satyasatyaviveka*, Shahjahanpur, 1930.

—. *Udeypura-Shashtrartha*, unpublished.

—. *Chaturveda Vishaya-Suchi*, unpublished.

—. *Rigveda Mantra-Suchi*, unpublished.

—.*Yajur-Atharva Mantra-Suchi*, unpublished.

—. *Atharva Mantra-Suchi*, Unpublished.

—. *Veda Brahmaana-Suchi*, unpublished.

—. *Nirukta Vishya-Suchi*, unpublished.

—. *Aitriya Brahmana-Suchi*, unpublished.

—. *Satapatha Brahmana Sishya-Suchi*, unpublished.

—. *Taitiriyopanishadi Mishrita Suchi*, unpublished.

—. *Rigveda Vishya Smaranartha-Suchi*, unpublished.

—. *Nirukta-Satapathamula Suchi*, unpublished.

—. *Satapatha Brahmana Suchi*, unpublished.

—. *Dhatupatha Suchi*, unpublished.

—. *Karitika Sanketa-Suchi*, unpublished.

—. *Nighantu Suchi*, unpublished.

—. *Kurana Suchi*, unpublished.

—. *Bible Suchi*, unpublished.

—. *Jainadharma Suchi*, unpublished.

—. *Vartikapatha Shabhashya*, unpublished.

—. *Manusmriti: Selected, Shlokas*, unpublished.

—. *Vidurapraja: Selected Shlokas*, unpublished.

—. *Ashtadhyayi Yadipatra*, unpublished.

—. *Qurana* (Hindi), unpublished.

—. *Prakriti-Sanskrit Anuvada*, unpublished.

—. *Ram Shehi Mata ka Gutka*, unpublished.

—. *Jaina Shlokas: A Selection*, unpublished.

—. *Aitria Upanishad Suchi*, unpublished.

—. *Chandogyopanishad Suchi*, unpublished.

—. *Rigvada Sukta Suchi*, unpublished.

Dayananda Saraswati. *Satapatha Shilash* [illegible] *chi*, unpublished.

—. *Mahabhashya: Sankshepa*, unpublished.

Dayananda Ke Patra aur Vigyapana, ed. Bhagavatdatta, Amritsar, 1955.

Dayananda Commemoration Volume, ed. Harbilas Sharda, Ajmer, 1933.

Dayananda Saraswati and Satyaratha Prakash, Propkarini Sabha, Ajmer, 1944.

Dayaram, Tehsildar: *Jiwan Charita*, Lahore, n.d.

Dayashankar Pathak, *Maharishi Dayananda Ka Jiwan Ghanta Parichya*, Jaipur, n.d.

Desai A.R. *Social Background of Indian Nationalism*, Bombay, 1954.

Dua, R.P. *Social Factors in the Birth and Growth of the Indian National Congress Movement*, Delhi, 1968.

Devendra Nath Mukhopadhaya. *Dayananda Charita*, Calcutta, 1896.

—. *Adarsha Sudharka Dayananda*, Hindi Tr. by Anubhavananda, n.d.

—. *Maharishi Dayananda Saraswati Ka Jiwan Charita*, 2 Vols., Hindi tr. Ghasi Ram, Ajmer, V.S. 1990.

—. *Vrijananda Charita*, Hindi tr. Ghasi Ram, Meerut, 1924.

Devi Chand. *Educational Work by the Arya Samaj in India, A Report of:* Amritsar, 1952.

Dhawan, Thakur Datt. *Public Spirit,* Lahore, 1897.

Dharma Deva. *Christianity and Vedic Dharma,* Mangalore, 1924.

—.*Tributes to Rishi Dayananda and Satyartha Prakash*, Delhi, 1945.

—. *Arya Samaj and World Problems,* Delhi, 1950.

Diwan Chand. *The Arya Samaj,* Lahore, 1942.

—. *Modern Thought and the Arya Samaj*, Lahore, 1906.

Diwan chand Sharma. *Swami Dayananda Saraswati,* London.

Drashnananda, Swami, *Dayananda Ka Uddesha,* Delhi, n.d.

—. *Dayananda Ka Lakshye*, Delhi, n.d.

Durga Prasad. *Maharishi Swami Dayananda Saraswati's Exposition of Vedic Religion,* Lahore, 1903.

—. *Maharishi Swami Dayananda Saraswati on Indian Religion*, Lahore, 1900.

—. *Maharishi Swami Dayananda,* Lahore, 1892.

Durrani, F.K. Khan. *Swami Dayananda,* Lahore, 1929.

Farquhar, J.N. *Modern Religious Movements in India,* Delhi, 1967.

Forman, Henry. *The Arya Samaj,* Allahabad, 1887.

Fuller, J.P.C. *India in Revolt*, London, 1950.

Gandhi, M.K. *Hindu Dharma,* Ahmedabad, 1950.

Ganga Prasad Upadhaya. *Origin, Scope and Mission of Arya Samaj,* Allahabad, 1940.

—. *Swami Dayanand's Contribution to Hindu Solidarity,* Allahabad, 1935.

—. *Caste: Its Social Evils and their Remedies,* Agra, 1900.

—. *Christianity in India*, Allahabad, 1941.

—. *Philosophy of Dayananda,* Allahabad, 1955.

—. *Superstitions.* Allahabad, 1941.

—. *The Claims of the Arya Samaj,* Allahabad, 1929.

—. *The Light of Truth:* English Translation of the *Satyaratha Prakasha* of Dayananda, Allahabad, n.d.

—. *Vedic Woman-hood,* Allahabad, 1940.

—. *Daily Home,* Allahabad, 1942.

—. *Suddhi,* Allahabad, 1940.

—. *The Arya Samaj,* Allahabad, 1939.

—. *The Arya Samaj and the Depressed Classes,* Allahabad, 1940.

—. *The Arya Samaj and Hinduism*, 1941.

—. *The Arya Samaj: A World Movement,* Allahabad, n.d.

—. *The Evils in our Customs*, Allahabad, 1940.

—. *The Five Great Sacrifices of the Aryas,* Allahabad, 1929.

—. *The Vedic Conception of God,* Allahabad, 1929.

—. *The Vedic View of Life,* Allahabad, 1940.

—. *We are our Critics,* Delhi, n.d.

—. *Worship,* Allahabad, 1940.

Govind Ram. *Dayananda Matmardan naquish nibandha*, Lahore, 1887.

Graham, R. *Arya Samaj as a Reformation in Hinduism,* (unpublished thesis), 2 Vols., Yale University, 1942.

Griswold, H.D.W. *Insight into Modern Hinduism*, New York, 1934.

—. *The Problems of the Arya Samaj*, Lahore, 1901.

—. *The Arya Samaj*, Lahore, 1903.

Gurudatta, Vidyarathi. *The Terminology of the Vedas*, 2 parts, Lahore, n.d.

—. *Vedic Philosophy*, Lahore, 1900.

Hans Raj, Lala. *Vedas: As Interpreted by Swami Davananda*. Allahabad. 1917.

Hansrai [illegible] *[illegible] Samaj in Kerala and the Neighbouring Territ[illegible],* [illegible]andrum, 1950.

Harbilas Sharda. *Works of Maharishi Dayananda Saraswati and Paropakarni Sabha,* Ajmer, 1942.

—. *Life of Swami Dayananda Saraswati,* Amjer, 1946.

—. *Shankra and Dayananda,* Ajmer, 1944.

Harishchandra. *Arya Samaj Ka Itihasa*, Lahore, 1946.

Hemisath, C.H. *Indian Nationalism and Hindu Social Reforms*, Princeton, 1964.

Indra Vidyavachaspati. *Arya Samaj Ka Itihasa*, 2 Vols., Delhi, 1957.

Jawahar Singh. *Amal-e-Arya*, Lahore, 1889.

Jiwan Dass. *Papers for the Thoughtful* (Essays) Lahore, 1902.

—. (Ed) *Works of Late Pandita Gurudatta Vidyarathi*, 2 parts, Lahore, 1897-1902.

Jnani, K. *Saying of Swami Dayananda*, Madras, 1936.

—. *An Outline of Arya Samaj*, Madras, 1936.

—. *Hinduism Vs. Christianity*, Madras, 1936.

—. *Hinduism Vs. Islam*, Madras, n.d.

—. *The Vedic Caste System*, Madras, n.d.

Karunakaran, K.P. *Religion and Political Awakening in India*, Meerut, 1965.

Kedarnath Gupta, *Swami Dayananda*, Prayaga, n.d.

Kishori Lal, Prof. *Jiwancharita* (Dayananda), Aligarh, n.d.

Kohn Hans. *History of Nationalism in the East*, New York, 1929.

—. *Orient and Occident*, New York, 1934.

Krishna Chandra Virmani. *Dayananda Sidhanta Bhashkara*, Delhi, n.d.

Kulyar, S.P. *Swami Dayananda Saraswati*, Patna, 1938.

Lajpat, Rai, Lala. *History of the Arya Samaj*, Bombay, 1952.

—. *The Political Future of India*, New York, 1919.

—. *Swami Dayananda aur Unka Kam*, Lahore, 1887.

—. *India's Will to Freedom*, Madras, 1921.

—. *Swami Dayananda Ka Jiwan Charita*, Lahore.

Lekh Ram, Pandita, *Maharishi Swami Dayananda Saraswati Ji Maharaja Ka Jawan Charita*, Jt. Author: Atma Ram, Lahore, 1897.

Lillington, F. *Brahmo Samaj and the Arya Samaj*, Calcutta, 1901.

Lovett, V. *History of the Indian Nationalist Movement*, London, 1921.

MacDonald, J. Ramsay. *The Awakening of India*, London, 1910.

Madan Mohan. *Arya Samaj: A Political Body*, Kangri, n.d.

Madan Mohan Seth. *Sayings and Precepts of Swami Dayananda*, Allahabad, 1917.

—. *Thoughts and Precepts of Swami Dayananda*, Delhi, 1944.

—. *High Government Official on Arya Samaj and its Work*, Allahabad, 1917.

Mahesh Praśad, Maulvi *Maharishi Ka Apurva Bhramana*, Kashi, n.d.

—. *Maharishi Dayananda*, Kashi, n.d.

—. *Maharishi Dayananda, Kab Aur Kahan*? Kashi, n.d.

Mangal Deva. Shastri *Bharitya Sanskriti Ka Vikasa*, Benaras, 1956.

Majumdar, B. *History of Political Thought from Raja Ram Mohun Roy to Dayananda*, Calcutta.

—. *History of Indian Political and Social Idea*, Calcutta, 1961.

Majumdar, J.K. *Raja Ram Mohun Ray and Progressive Movements of India*, Calcutta, 1947.

Majumdar, R.C. *History of Freedom Movement in India*, Vol. I, Calcutta, 1962.

—. *On Raja Ram Mohan Roy*, Calcutta, 1912.

Max Mueller, F. *Biographical Essays*, London, 1884.

—. *Ram Mohun Roy to Rama Krishna*, Calcutta.

Mehra, L.C. *Arya Samaj as an Educational Movement*, Dissertation, California, 1925.

Morison, John. *New Idea in India during the 9th Century*, London, 1907.

Mulraj. *The Arya Samaj*, Lahore, 1894.

Munshi Ram, See Under Ramdeva.

—. *The Arya Samaj and Politics*, Lahore, 1908.

—. *The Future of the Arya Samaj*, Lahore, 1893.

—. *Future of the Arya Samaj*, Lahore, 1893.

Murdoch, J. *Vedic Hinduism and the Arya Samaj*, London, 1902.

Nand Kishore, *General Survey of the Life and Teachings of Swami Dayananda*, Delhi, n.d.

Narang, G.C. *Real Hinduism*, Lahore, 1947.

Natrajan, S: *A Century of Social Reform in India*, London, 1959.

Navinson, H.W. *New Spirit in India*, London.

Nigam, Zorawar Singh. *The Vedic Religion and its Expounder Swami Dayananda*, Allahabad, 1914.

O'Dwyer, Sir Michael. *India, as I Knew it*, London, 1925.

O'Malley. *Modern India and the West,* London 1910.

Oman, J.C. *Cults, Customs, and Superstitions in India,* London, 1908.

Pandey, D. *The Arya Samaj and the National Movement in India*, 1875-1919, Delhi, 1972.

Parmeshwaran, C. *Dayananda and the Indian Problems*, Lahore, 1944.

Parvate, T.V. *Makers of Modern India*, Jullunder, 1964.

Phadke, Dr. Sadashiv Krishna. *Nav Vedic Dharama Arya Athava Samajacha, Vivechaka Itihasa*, Vol. I, Poona, 1928.

Radha Krishan, Mehta. *Tarikh-i-Arya Samaj*, Lahore, 1903.

Rajendra. *Rishi Dayananda Ke Punye Sansmarana*, Atroli, n.d.

Raj Kanwar. *Beauties of the Vedic Dharma*, Lahore, 1905.

Ralla Ram. *Is Theism Insufficient without Christianity*, Lahore, 1889.

—. *The Arya Samaj: What is it?* 2 Parts Lahore, n.d.

Rahul Sankrityayana. *Himalaya Parichay,* Delhi, n.d.

Ramdeva. See Under Munshi Ram.

—*The Inner Man and Other Lectures on the Arya Samaj*, Madras, 1934.

Ram Gopal, *Dayananda Chittravali,* Calcutta, n.d.

Ramvilas Sharda. *Arya Dharmendra Jiwana*, Ajmer, n.d.

Ranade, M.G. *Religious and Social Reform: A Collection of Essays and Speeches*, Bombay, 1902.

—. *Writings and Speeches*, Bombay, 1915.

Ray, B.G. *Contemporary Indian Philosophy,* Allahabad, 1947.

Risley Herbert. *Peoples of India,* London.

Romian Rolland, *Prophets of the New India*, London, 1930.

Roshan Lal. *Stray Thought on the Arya Samaj,* Lahore, n.d.

Sahni, Ruchi Ram. *The Nivoga Lecture of the Arya Samaj,* Lahore 1897.

—. *Aubobiography of an Octogenarian*, MS. Nehru Museum and Library, Delhi.

Sarbadayal. *Swanihi-umri Shri Swami Vrijananda Saraswati,* Lahore, 1902.

—. *Maharishi Swami Vrijananda Ka Jiwancharita,* Delhi, 1924.

Sarda, Harbilas. See Harbilas Sharda.

Sarvadeshika Arya Pratinidhi Sabha Ka Tis-Varshiya Itihas, Delhi, 1939.

Sarvadeshika Arya Pratinidhi Sabha Ka Sankshipta, Delhi, 1961.

Satyananda, Swami, *Shrimadyananda Prakasha,* Delhi, 1950.

Satya Prakash. *A Critical Study of the Philosophy of Dayananda*, Ajmer, 1938.

—. *Agnihotra, Delhi,* 1937.

Scott, R.W. *Social Ethics in Modern Hinduism,* Calcutta, 1953.

Scott, T.J. *Missionary Life Among the Villages of India,* London, 1868.

Sharma, B.M. *Swami Dayananda*, Lucknow, 1933.

Sharma, D.C. *Makers of the Arya Samaj*, London, 1935.

Sharma, D.S. *Hinduism through the Ages,* Bombay 1956.

Sharma, S.R. *Mahatma Hansraj,* Jullundur, 1965.

Sharma, Vishnu Lal. *Handbook of the Arya Samaj,* Lucknow, 1912.

Shradhananda Swami. (Autobiography) ed. M.R. Jambunathan, Bombay, 1961.

—. *Tatvaveta Dayananda,* Delhi, n.d.

—. *Inside Congress,* Bombay, 1946.

Shivnarain Agnihotri, *Dayananda Ka Kaljugi Mazhab,* Lahore, 1887.

—. *Vedic Mahapope,* Lahore, 1889.

—. *Mahapope Ki Samaj,* Lahore, 1890.

Sitaram Singh. *Nationalism and Social Reform in India,* 1885-1920, Delhi, 1968.

Suraj Bhan. *Dayananda, His Life and Work,* Jullundur, 1956.

Tagore, R.N. *Nationalism,* London, 1917.

Tara Chand, Prof. *Penance and Victory,* Shikarpur, 1932.

—. *Swami Dayananda on Bhakti,* Shikarpur, 1932.

Tikam Das. *Dayananda and Other Essays, Interpretation of,* Shikarpur, 1932.

Tikekar, P.P. *Aj Kalacha Maharashtra*, Bombay, 1935.

Tungar, Hari Sakharam. *Arya Samaj Mehnje Kaye*? Kolhapur, 1924.

—. *Maharashtra wa Arya Samaj*, Kohlapur, n.d.

—. *Prathma Devopuja Kin Ishvaropasana*, Kohlapur, 1924.

—. *Arya Dharmendra Dayananda Saraswati Yanchi Puneyathye Vyakhane*, Kolhapur, 1847, Saka.

—. *Maharishi Dayananda Saraswati Yanchi Charitra Wa Kamgiri*, Kolhapur, 1920.

Varma, V.P. *Modern Indian Political Thought, Agra*, 1961.

Vaswani, T.L. *Torch Bearer: Some Reflections on Rishi Dayananda and the Aryan Ideal*, Karachi, 1925.

—. *Voice of the Aryavarta*, Karachi, 1925.

—. *Swami Dayananda Saraswati*, Allahabad, 1917.

Vedananda, Tirtha. *Wisdom of the Rishis or Complete Works of Pt. Gurudatta Vidyarathi*, Lahore, n.d.

Vishwa Prakash. *Life and Teachings of Swami Dayananda*, Allahabad, 1935.

—. *Life of Swami Dayananda*, Allahabad, 1936.

Vyas, K.C. *Social Renaissance in India*, Bombay, 1957.

Walker, B. *Hindu World*, 2 Vols., London, 1968.

William, T. *Exposure of Dayananda Saraswati*, Delhi, 1889.

Yadhishtra Mimanska. *Rishi Dayananda Ke Granthon Ka Itihasa*, Delhi, 1949.

—. *Rishi Dayananda Ka Pitrivansha aur Swasrivansha*, Delhi, 1959.

Zacharias, H.C.E. *Renascent India: From Ram Mohun Roy to Mohun Das Gandhi*, London, 1933.

Journals and Newspapers

Arya Gazette, Jullundur.

Arya Jagat, Jullunder.

Arya Martanda, Ajmer.

Arya Mitra, Lucknow.

Arya Premi, Ajmer.

Aray Samaj, Calcutta.

Aryodya, Jullundur.

Aryavarta, Gwalior.

Arya Vira, Jullundur.

Behar-Bandhu, Patna.

Biradra-i-Hind, Lahore.

Bombay Gazette, Bombay.

Bombay Samachar, Bombay.

Christian Intelligencer, The Benaras.

Dharamaratna, Calcutta.

Friend of India, The Calcutta.

Index

R

S

T